Applied Computing

T0212423

Springer
London
Berlin
Heidelberg
New York
Barcelona
Hong Kong
Milan
Paris
Santa Clara
Singapore
Tokyo

The Springer-Verlag Series on Applied Computing is an advanced series of innovative textbooks that span the full range of topics in applied computing technology.

Books in the series provide a grounding in theoretical concepts in computer science alongside real-world examples of how those concepts can be applied in the development of effective computer systems.

The series should be essential reading for advanced undergraduate and postgraduate students in computing and information systems.

Books in this series are contributed by international specialist researchers and educators in applied computing who draw together the full range of issues in their specialist area into one concise authoritative textbook.

Titles already available:

Deryn Graham and Anthony Barrett
Knowledge-Based Image Processing Systems
3-540-76027-X

Linda Macaulay
Requirements Engineering
3-540-76006-7

Derrick Morris, Gareth Evans, Peter Green, Colin Theaker
Object Orientated Computer Systems Engineering
3-430-76020-2

John Hunt
Java and Object Orientation: An Introduction
3-540-76148-9

David Gray
Introduction to the Formal Design of Real-Time Systems
3-540-76140-3

Mike Holcombe and Florentin Ipate
Correct Systems: Building A Business Process Solution
3-540-76246-9

Jan Noyes and Chris Baber
User-Centred Design of Systems
3-540-76007-5

Arturo Trujillo
Translation Engines: Techniques for Machine Translation
1-85233-057-0

Ulrich Nehmzow
Mobile Robotics: A Practical Introduction
1-85233-173-9

Available in the Advanced Perspectives in Applied Computing series:

Sarah Douglas and Anant Mithal
The Ergonomics of Computer Pointing Devices
3-540-19986-1

Fabio Paternò

Model-Based Design and Evaluation of Interactive Applications

Springer

Fabio Paternò PhD
CNUCE - CNR, 56126 Pisa, Italy

Series Editors
Professor Ray J. Paul, BSc MSc PhD
Department of Information Systems and Computing, Brunel University,
Uxbridge, Middlesex UB8 3PH, UK

Professor Peter J. Thomas, MIEE MBCS CEng FRSA
Centre for Personal Information Management, University of the West of England,
Frenchay Campus, Bristol BS16 1QY, UK

Dr Jasna Kuljis, PhD MS Dipl Ing
Department of Mathematical and Computing Sciences, Goldsmiths College,
University of London, New Cross, London SE14 6NW, UK

ISBN 1-85233-155-0 Springer-Verlag London Berlin Heidelberg

British Library Cataloguing in Publication Data
A catalogue record for this book is available from the British Library

Library of Congress Cataloging-in-Publication Data
Paternò, Fabio, 1960-
    Model-based design and evaluation of interactive applications /
Fabio Paternò.
        p.   cm. – (Applied computing)
    Includes bibliographical references.
    ISBN 1-85233-155-0 (alk. paper)
    1. User interfaces (Computer systems)   2. Human-computer
interaction.   3. Software engineering.   I. Title.   II. Series.
    QA76.9.U83P38   1999   99-12334
    005.4'28—dc21   CIP

Typesetting: Camera ready by author
Printed and bound at the Athenæum Press Ltd., Gateshead, Tyne & Wear
34/3830-543210 Printed on acid-free paper SPIN 10713419

Background of author

Fabio Paternò received his Laurea Degree in Computer Science from the University of Pisa (Italy) and a Ph.D. in Computer Science from the University of York (UK).

Since 1986 he has been a researcher at CNUCE-C.N.R., Pisa, where he is head of the HCI group. He has worked in various national and international projects on user interfaces-related topics. He has been the coordinator of the MEFISTO (Modelling Evaluating and Formalising Interactive Systems Using Tasks and Interaction Objects) Long Term Esprit European Project.

He has developed the ConcurTaskTrees notation for specifying task models, which has been used in various industries and universities, and related methods for supporting the design and evaluation of interactive applications. His current research interests include Methods and Tools for User Interface Design and Usability Evaluation, Formal Methods for Interactive Systems, and Design of User Interfaces for Safety Critical Interactive Systems. He has published more than sixty papers in refereed international conferences or journals.

He was the chair of the first International Workshop on Design, Specification, Verification of Interactive Systems. He is co-editor of a book on Formal Methods in Human-Computer Interaction. He has been a member of the Programme Committee of the main international HCI conferences. He is a member of the IFIP Technical Committee 13 on Human Computer Interaction. He has been Papers Co-Chair of the ACM CHI 2000 conference.

Preface

This book aims to be a bridge. A bridge between science and practice, creativity and engineering, human-computer interaction and software engineering, with possible links to artificial intelligence and formal methods.

Bridges are important because they allow communication between worlds which were previously separated, thus enabling new results to be obtained.

Ponte di Mezzo, Pisa.

The increasing diffusion of interactive software-based applications in an increasing number of contexts, possible purposes and types of users, requires new methods for improving the design cycle of interactive applications and obtaining more usable artefacts. This stimulated the need to bring together aspects such as task modelling, dialogue design, reuse patterns, and usability evaluation with the purpose of explaining the basic ideas and concepts and discussing the possible results. The logical structure of the book focuses on reporting recent thinking in this area showing the connections between the various parts. It makes accessible work which has previously mainly appeared only in research-oriented publications.

I hope it will prove useful to help the reader understand issues concerning the use of models in design and evaluation of interactive applications, to indicate possible solutions, and to foster new work able to improve previous solutions. A lot of work needs still to be done to improve current methods and tools to design and develop usable interactive applications.

Fabio Paternò
August 1999,
Pisa, Italy

ACKNOWLEDGEMENTS

Over the years I have discussed the topics considered in this book with many people. It is difficult to mention all of them. In particular, I wish to thank for their help: Cristiano Mancini, Carmen Santoro, Giulio Ballardin, Simone Bellani, Andreas Lecerof, Ilse Breedvelt-Schouten, Nicole de Koning, Silvia Meniconi, my students, and the researchers who discussed with me some of the issues addressed in this book in the MEFISTO (http://giove.cnuce.cnr.it/mefisto.html) and GUITARE (http://giove.cnuce.cnr.it/guitare.html) projects. I also want to acknowledge the support received from the European Commission through these projects. Last, but not least, I would like to thank Claudia, Linda and PierPaolo for their continuos support.

Contents

1 Introduction

1.1 WHY MODEL-BASED DESIGN AND EVALUATION OF INTERACTIVE APPLICATIONS ?

Interest in design and development of interactive software applications has increased considerably over the last few years. The underlying reason for this interest is the need to allow the greatest number of people access to software applications for the largest number of purposes and in the widest number of contexts. However, making systems easier to use implies taking into account many factors in the design of an interactive application, such as tasks to support, context of use, user preferences, media and interaction techniques available, need for multiple dialogues between the user and the application active at the same time. It is thus important to have structured methods for allowing designers to manage such complexity.

Fortunately, nowadays, the means to access software applications has changed from the days when people interacted with computers using rather rudimentary tools (see Figure 1.1 for an example of how operators interacted with computers in the 1960s to control their functions).

However, despite the many direct manipulations tools currently available to designers to enable rapid building of user interfaces with graphical icons and multimedia effects, the design of interactive applications is still difficult. End users often find interfaces difficult to understand and use in order to attain their desired ends. One of the main reasons for this is that in many cases users have trouble understanding what tasks are supported or how to associate the desired logical actions with physical actions of the user interface. Such problems could be largely solved if designers had methods and tools to provide indications about the most effective interaction and presentation techniques to support the possible user activities.

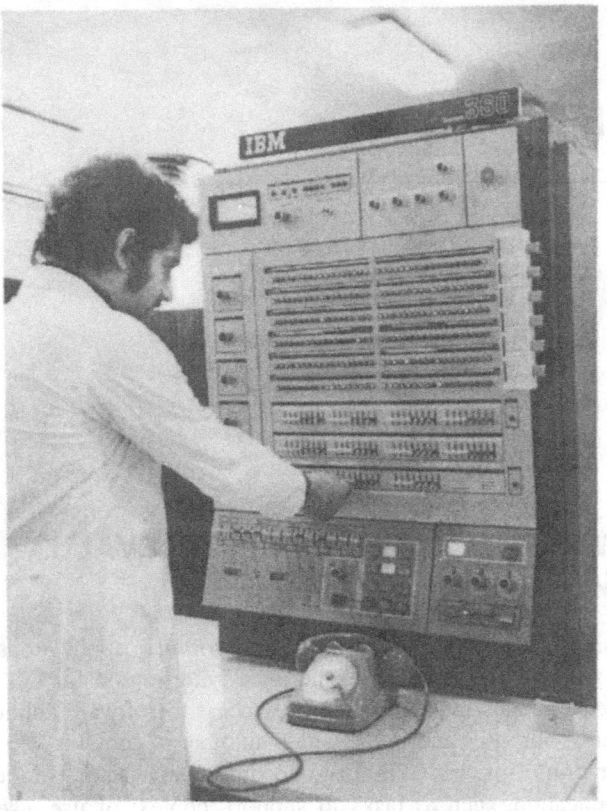

Figure 1.1: How operators interacted with computers in the 60s.

Models can help in the design and evaluation of interactive applications even if when people hear the word "model" they sometimes have a negative reaction because they assume that there is an interest towards something that is rather theoretical, far from the reality. However, if we think of what we do in practice we can discover that we often use models. As soon as there is some complex entity to manage, people try to identify what the main aspects to take into account are. So, we build models to understand reality and to lead our way to interact with it.

There are many types of models, depending on the kind of information that they contain, the level of formality that we use, how we represent them, and the level of abstraction. One important design choice is to select the most appropriate model for the current goal.

Different models imply different representations as they have different users and purposes. For example, the users of task models can be designers, developers, end users, managers and other actors involved in the task modelling phase. The purpose is to describe ways to perform the tasks identified in the task analysis phase.

Whereas in the case of an architectural model what we need is a representation which is useful for the software designers and developers. The purpose is to give an implementation-independent description of the basic components and their possible communication.

More precisely, task models describe how activities can be performed to reach the users' goals when interacting with the application considered. They should incorporate the requirements raised by the people who should be taken into consideration when designing an interactive application (designers, software developers, application domain experts, end users, and managers). They are the meeting point, where the viewpoints that should be considered when designing a new application or analysing an existing one, integrate.

Wide agreement on the importance of task models has been achieved because they capture what the possible intentions of the users are and describe logically the activities they should perform to reach their goals. These models also allow designers to develop an integrated description of both functional and interactive aspects thus improving traditional software engineering approaches which mainly focused on functional aspects. Task analysis is not new. For example, hierarchical task analysis was proposed in [AD67]. However there is still a lack of systematic methods that support the development and the use of task models for the design and usability evaluation of interactive software applications.

More precisely, task models can be useful for different purposes:

- *Understanding an application domain*: as they require a precise identification of the main activities and their relationships, they help to clarify many issues that at the beginning may not be immediately recognised;
- *Recording the results of interdisciplinary discussions*: many people can be involved in the design of an interactive application: user interface designers, software developers, managers, end users, experts of the application domain. It is thus important to have a representation of the activities that can integrate all the requirements raised and supports focusing on a logical level that can be understood by all of them;
- *Designing new applications consistent with the user conceptual model*: because of the lack of structured methods supporting task-driven design it happened in various projects that first people developed task models for a new application and then they did not use them for driving the design. This made the task modelling an exercise with limited advantages whereas if the application was designed following a task-based approach it would have been more usable because it would have incorporated the user requirements captured in the task model;
- *Analysing and evaluating usability of an interactive systems*: task models can be useful in various ways to support the usability evaluation of an interactive application. They have been used to predict the users' performance in reaching their goals (especially in GOMS-like approaches) or to support analysis of user

behaviour to identify usability problems. Possible examples are described in chapter 8.

- *Supporting the user during a session*: creating a correspondence between tasks and the interaction objects composing the user interface can be useful also at run-time, for example to provide context-sensitive, task-oriented help systems.

Thus, task models can be useful both to analyse and evaluate an existing system or as a starting point to design new applications from scratch. There are two main classes of people who receive the greatest benefits from task models, they are:

- *Designers*, because task models provide high-level, structured approaches which allow an integrated framework to both functional and interactional aspects right from the first stages of the design cycle and to focus on relevant logical aspects without being immersed in implementation details. As confirmation of the complexity of the interactive part of an application, we can mention a study [MR92] that analysed a set of applications and it found that there was an average of 48% of the code, 45% of development time, 50% of implementation time, and 37% of maintenance time dedicated to user interface aspects.
- *End users*, because task models support the development of more usable systems, where it is easy to understand how the user interface aids the user activities because the physical actions supported by the user interface can be easily mapped onto logical actions and the representations provided can effectively support the possible tasks.

This means that task models can be useful to both improve the process of design and development and to obtain more usable interactive software applications. More generally, task modelling is an area which has received many contributions from both computer and cognitive science because it is located at the intersection between these two disciplines that are both concerned with designing interactive applications. Such an intersection is mainly the Human-Computer Interaction (HCI) field.

However, there is a lack of engineering approaches to task models. An engineering approach should address at least four main issues:

- availability of *flexible and expressive notations* able to describe clearly the possible activities; it is important that these notations are sufficiently powerful to describe interactive and dynamic behaviours; such notations should be readable so that they can be interpreted also by people with low formal background;
- need for *systematic methods* to support the specification, analysis, and use of task models, to facilitate their development and support designers in using the knowledge that they incorporate to address the design of the user interface and its evaluation; we note that often even designers who developed some task analysis and modelling did not use them for the detailed design of the user interface because of this lack of structured methods which should give rules and

suggestions about how to use information in the task model for the concrete design.

- support for the *reuse* of good design solutions to problems which occur across many applications (using for example task patterns [PM97a]); this is relevant especially in an industrial context where developers often have to design applications which address similar problems, thus it would be useful to have design solutions structured and documented in such a way as to support easy reuse and tailoring in different applications.

- availability of *automatic tools* to support the various phases of the design cycle, including usability evaluation; for example, once structured methods for the design have been identified it is possible to incorporate their rules in automatic tools which can support designers giving easy to interpret representations of useful information and suggestions of possible solutions, still leaving to the designer the possibility to tailor them and to choose the solution more suitable to the specific case study considered.

The goal of the book is to give an introduction to these problems and to discuss their possible solutions, thus giving the reader useful information to better understand such problems and how to address them.

1.2 BASIC CONCEPTS

Tasks are activities that have to be performed to reach a goal. They can be either logical activities such as *Retrieving information about the movies projected tonight* or physical activities such as *Selecting the button in the top left corner*.

A goal is either a desired modification of the state of an application or an attempt to retrieve some information from an application. For example, *Accessing a flight's database to know what flights are available* is a goal which does not require the modification of the state of the application, whereas *Accessing a flight's database to add a new reservation* requires a modification of the state of the application.

As you can see tasks and goals are closely connected. Each task can be associated with one goal, that is the goal achieved by performing the task. One goal can be achieved by performing one or multiple tasks. In some cases it is possible to choose among different tasks to achieve a certain goal.

We can distinguish between the task analysis and the task modelling phases. *The purpose of task analysis is to identify what the relevant tasks are.* This understanding not only requires a strong end user involvement but must also take into account how activities are performed currently. It can be obtained using different techniques:

- interviews or workshops;
- questionnaires;

- observing users in their work place;
- considering how activities are performed in the current environment;
- considering existing documentation and training methods.

This analysis can be used to identify various types of abstractions (scenarios, domain models, task models, properties, user and system models) that will be discussed in the next chapters.

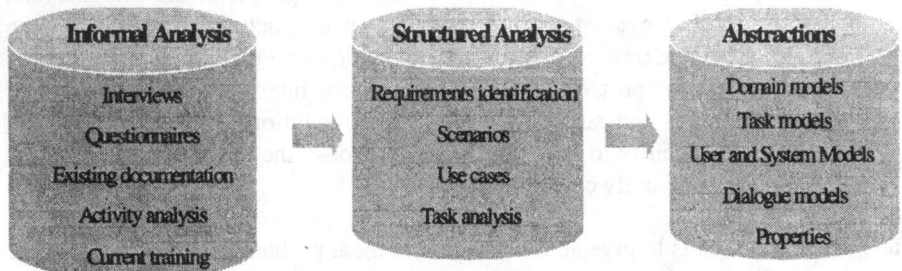

Figure 1.2: Moving from informal to structured representations.

The general objective with task analysis is the identification of the possible tasks. This analysis may have very different scopes, depending on the focus of interest. It can range from activity of a single user at work in a given environment, involving computer-supported activities as well as other types of activities, to the processes occurring in the whole environment, potentially involving several co-workers.

The result of task analysis is an informal list of tasks relevant for the application domain considered which can be supplemented with indications of possible problems, task attributes, and user preferences. The activities effectively performed by a user are sometimes complex processes which are difficult to understand fully or predict: an activity often results from a compromise between conflicting goals; goal-directed processes may be modified by opportunistic processes, the occurrence of particular conditions, exceptions, etc. It is thus important in the task analysis and modelling phases to be able to capture the main elements of such flexibility.

Various classifications have been proposed for task-based approaches. In Chapter 2 there is an example of a possible classification. The task modelling phase occurs after the task analysis phase. *The purpose of task modelling is to build a model which describes precisely the relationships among the various tasks identified.* These relationships can be of various types, such as temporal and semantic relationships. The task model is usually structured in such a way as to address various logical levels. When we reach tasks which cannot be further decomposed we have basic tasks. In some cases basic tasks require one single physical action to be performed. The level of decomposition to reach in task modelling depends on its purpose. For example, in Chapter 8 there is a discussion of a usability evaluation method which requires that basic interaction tasks are associated with single user actions. It is important that task models are rich in information and flexible so as to capture all the main activities that should be performed to reach the desired goals and the different ways to accomplish them.

In terms of software engineering phases, task analysis can be useful to support the requirements phase whereas task models can be useful for the design phase.

1.3 STRUCTURE OF THE BOOK AND INTENDED AUDIENCE

The book is divided into eight chapters. In Chapter 2 there is an introduction to the motivations for model-based approaches, to basic concepts and state-of-the-art of task-based approaches for the design and development of interactive applications. Some relevant works developed are introduced and discussed. Next, there is a description of techniques that help designers in an initial informal phase to gather information useful for building their models. The fourth chapter gives a complete description of ConcurTaskTrees, a notation for specifying task models, along with the description of how it can be used for capturing cooperative aspects. The support which can be obtained from automatic tools will also be discussed. Small modelling exercises are proposed to improve the interactivity and effectiveness of the book.

Then, there are chapters dedicated to describing how task models can be used to support the design of interactive applications. This is based on the use of the task model as an abstract specification which can support the work of designers and software developers. Various relevant aspects of the design will be considered: the presentation of the user interface, the software architecture, possible task patterns, interactive applications.

Finally, how task models can be used for supporting usability evaluation will be discussed. After an introduction to usability evaluation and possible approaches, there is a discussion of examples of methods for usability evaluation and possible tool support, including that for remote evaluation.

This book has a potentially diverse audience. The reader should have knowledge of elementary concepts of design and development of user interfaces. More generally, the book is intended for anyone interested in understanding the possibilities given by the systematic use of task models in the design, development, and usability evaluation of interactive software applications. It also provides a discussion of related issues that are relevant in designing user interfaces. Readers will learn the state-of-the-art in this field, methods recently developed, current results, problems and trends. Details of the notation and analysis discussed, including case studies that can have industrial interest, are available if the reader wants to apply them for applied projects and in industrial contexts.

Its structure supports its use as a text book for a range of academic and industrial courses on task models and methods for user interface design and evaluation. It can be a useful supplementary reading for any course on human-computer interaction and software engineering. It can also be useful for software engineers in their development projects.

The book has been developed so as to allow a modular use depending on the interests and background of the readers. They do not have to read sequentially all the chapters. After the first chapter the main dependence is that all the remaining chapters, except Chapters 2 and 3, can be better understood by reading Chapter 4. Besides, Chapter 7 should be read after Chapter 4 and 6. So, for example, one possible reading path can be Chapter 1, 4, and 5 if the reader is mainly interested in reading about design aspects, another is Chapter 1, 4, 8 if the main interest is in usability evaluation whereas if the interest is in analysis of interactive applications then the suggested reading path is Chapter 1, 3 and 4. Some chapters (such as Chapter 6) require more effort when being read because they provide more detailed case studies and they address topics mainly interesting for software engineers or application developers, including details of the methods described. Thus, for example, human factors experts can skip Chapter 6 unless they are interested in understanding the principles of design of the architectures underlying the user interface.

1.4 OTHER SOURCES OF INFORMATION

This section indicates some additional information sources on the topics considered in this book and related topics. The growing interest in this area has also generated an increasing number of sources of information so only some of the more relevant are indicated here. There are also many web sites where it is possible to find information on the topics considered in this book. However, their content is not always accurate or updated. Only in a few cases it is possible to recommend some particularly interesting sites, a good example is the HCI Bibliography: Human-Computer Interaction Publications and Resources at http://www.hcibib.org/.

1.4.1 Conferences

There is a growing number of conferences that address the topics considered in this book or related topics. The Association for Computing Machinery (ACM) organises the CHI conference that usually has about 2400 participants. It is the biggest conference on HCI at world-wide level. It is technologically oriented even though it is possible to learn new advances at a methodological level as well. There is always a good presence of works showing results obtained by empirical studies. Another important HCI conference at international level is INTERACT organised by the International Federation for Information Processing (IFIP). It is bi-annual and more oriented toward presenting methodological advances thus complementing CHI.

ACM also organises the Intelligent User Interfaces (IUI) conference that has model-based user interface design as one of the main topics whereas tools and interaction techniques are more considered at UIST (User Interface and Software Technology) conference, and design issues at DIS (Designing Interactive Systems). More formal approaches are usually presented in the Design, Specification, Verification of Interactive Systems, series of international conferences. In 1994 I organised the first edition in Bocca di Magra (Italy) [P95]. The use of formal techniques and model-based approaches in the user interface domain is also sometimes considered in software engineering conferences, such as the International Conference on Software Engineering (ICSE).

1.4.2 Journals

ACM publishes *ACM Transactions on Computer-Human Interaction* (http://www.acm.org/tochi) which is considered the archival journal for new contributions in HCI. There are other journals that are relevant in this area such as *Human-Computer Interaction* (http://www.parc.xerox.com/HCI/) published by Lawrence Erlbaum Associates, the *Journal of Human-Computer Studies* (http://www.academic.press.com/ijhcs) published by Academic Press, *Interacting with* Computers (http://www.elsevier.com/locate/intcom), journal promoted by the BCS-HCI group, published by Elsevier.

The topics considered in this book are sometimes addressed by papers published in the software engineering area, such as the *IEEE Transactions on Software Engineering* (http://www.computer.org/tse) or *Empirical Software Engineering* (http://www-wkap.nl/journalhome.htm/1382-3256) journals.

There is also the *Journal of Visual Languages and Computing* (http://www.academicpress.com/JVLC) published by Academic Press which is more focused on visual aspects whereas multimedia aspects are better considered in journals such as *Multimedia Systems*, jointly published by ACM and Springer Verlag (http://link.springer.de/link/service/journals/00530/index.htm).

1.4.3 Books

There are at least three books that provide an overview of basic concepts in the human-computer interaction field. Two of them share the same title, *Human-Computer Interaction*, one by Dix, Finlay, Abowd, Beale, [DFAB98] the other by Preece, Rogers, Sharp, Benyon, Holland and Carey [PRSBHC94]. The third is entitled *Designing the User Interface* by Ben Shneiderman, different editions have been published, the last one is [S98].

Another book that addresses similar topics to this book is *Developing User Interfaces* by D. Hix and R. Hartson [HH93] where the authors' focus is mainly on the User Action Notation (UAN). Readers more interested in formal aspects will find the book *Formal Methods in Human-Computer Interaction* (edited by Palanque and Paternò) [PP97b] useful.

1.4.4 Associations

The main associations in the HCI domain are SIGCHI, a very large ACM group of interest on human-computer interaction (http://www.ac.org/sigchi/), and the Technical Committee N.13 (http://www.csd.uu.se/ifip_tc13/) of IFIP that is an association of associations (http://www.ifip.or.at/). Then in many countries there are national associations. One with a particular high number of participants is BCS-HCI, the HCI section (http://www.bcs.org.uk/hci/) of the British Computer Society.

2 Model-Based Approaches

The purpose of model-based design is to identify high-level models which allow designers to specify and analyse interactive software applications from a more semantic-oriented level rather than starting immediately to address the implementation level. This allows them to concentrate on more important aspects without being immediately confused by many implementation details and then to have tools which update the implementation in order to be consistent with high-level choices. Thus, by using models which capture semantically meaningful aspects, designers can more easily manage the increasing complexity of interactive applications and analyse them both during their development and when they have to be modified.

Various approaches have considered, for example, dialogue models. *A dialogue model is an abstract description of the actions, and their possible temporal relationships, that users and systems can perform at the user interface level during an interactive session.*

One of the first works in this area was the User Interface Development Environment (UIDE) [FS94] developed by Jim Foley's group at the GVU Center of Georgia Tech. In this environment it was possible to specify the pre- and post-conditions related to each interaction object of the user interface. Pre-conditions have to be satisfied in order to make the interaction object reactive whereas post-conditions indicate modifications of the state of the user interface which have to be performed after a user interaction with the related object. How to control user interface objects through pre- and post-conditions is discussed in [GF92]. A simple example is a button to stop a compact disk (CD). Its pre-condition is that the CD is not already stopped. When it is verified then this button is enabled. Once the user has selected the button then its post-condition is that the CD has stopped.

The work developed on the basis of the UIDE environment has given suggestions for various topics such as: automatic help generation [SMSG94], adaptive user interfaces [SF93], automatic generation of user interfaces [KF93], and applying design transformations that map a dialogue model to another one that changes the user interface while preserving the application functionality [FKKM91].

In the last decade various model-based approaches have been proposed. Humanoid [SLN92, SLN93] provided a declarative modelling language consisting of five independent parts: the application semantics, the presentation, the behaviour, the dialogue sequencing, and the action side effects. One of its purposes was to overcome one limitation of traditional tools for user interface development: lack of support for exploration of new design that requires undoing portions of the existing design and adding new code. The reason for this limitation was that such tools do not have a notion of what is specific to a design as this information is embedded in the code. Trident [BHLV95] used an Activity Chaining Graph to specify the task model (it is a graph describing the information flow between the application domain functions which are necessary to perform the task goal) and an entity-relationship diagram for the information modelling part of the functional requirements.

Now there is a general agreement that task models are fundamental models in user interface design and all model-based proposals include some sort of task models. A task-driven approach can be found in Adept [WJKCM93], developed by Wilson, Johnson et al.. In their proposal they address the design of a task model, an abstract architectural model, and a related implementation. The task modeller provided a graphic environment to construct and edit task models described in terms of Task Knowledge Structures. The output of this component was used to feed the Abstract Interface Model to generate a high level specification of the interaction, expressed in terms of the dialogue structure and abstract interaction objects. A generator tool created a default Concrete Interface Model (CIM) that can be edited by the designer. The CIM can be translated into a platform dependent implementation based on a standard set of widgets. This was one of the first research prototypes aiming to give support to the use of task models to support user interface development. However, the set of temporal operators among tasks considered and the rules for creating relationships within the levels considered have then been discussed and expanded in other methods and tools.

MAD, Methode Analytique de Description des taches [SP89], is another example of such approaches. It is provided with software tools which allow computer-supported task modelling; it addresses the representation of goal hierarchies through a graphics-based notation, and the description of task objects as a class hierarchy (in an "object-oriented" fashion). The notation used in MAD does not have a formal semantics. The representation of goal hierarchies and task objects along with some graphics-based representation are features which constitute the common basis for various recently reported task modelling approaches.

The MOBI-D (Model Based Interface Designer) [P97b] approach developed by Angel Puerta and his group at Stanford University is a model-based interface development environment for single-user interfaces that enables designers and developers to interactively create user interfaces by designing interface models. The environment integrates model-editing tools [PM97b], task elicitation tools [TMP98], an intelligent design assistant [PE99] and interface building tools [PCTM99].

In the field of formal methods for human-computer interaction there are approaches which consider the specification of task level aspects, examples can be found in [PP97b]; in these cases often the focus is oriented to analyse the dialogue of existing systems rather than supporting the design of new envisioned systems.

Other approaches to task-driven design are in [SF94] [S95a], where authors mainly consider more presentation-related aspects rather than analysing the dialogue and the corresponding software architecture. In particular, in [SF94] Sutcliffe and Faraday, have developed a method for the design of multimedia presentations based on the analysis of tasks and resources. The task analysis is performed by creating trees of subgoals, and by attaching to them the type of information needed for their accomplishment. The resource analysis provides a description of the resources available for the designer to present data, and the type of logical information that it contains is attached to any media. The selection of which resource to use to support a given task is based on the dialogue acts and the type of information related to the task. Finally, the authors use guidelines derived from psychological literature to validate the presentation built beforehand.

There are other types of models that can provide support for the design of an interactive application even if they have different main goals.

On the one hand, in the computer science area, we can find more traditional object-oriented modelling techniques. The most successful has been the Unified Modelling Language (UML) [BRJ99]. They share similar purposes with task-oriented approaches. In both cases there is a description of both activities and objects. The main difference is in the focus. Task-based approaches first identify activities and then the objects that they have to manipulate. Object-oriented methods follow an inverse process as they mainly focus on modelling the objects composing the system. Consequently, task-based approaches are more suitable to design user-oriented interactive applications because in this way the main focus is on effectively and efficiently supporting users' activities whereas object-oriented techniques have been more successful at engineering the software implementation level.

On the other hand, in the cognitive science field, various types of cognitive models have been proposed in the literature. In cognitive architectures [GYK97] there is an integrated description of how human-cognitive mechanisms interact with each other. This makes their simulation by automatic tools possible. Examples of cognitive architectures are ICS (Interacting Cognitive Subsystems) [BM95] or EPIC [KSM97]. A different approach, with different aims, is distributed cognition [H95] which incorporates contributions from cognitive, anthropological and social sciences. In this case the basic goal is to understand how people use the resources in their environment to improve their cognitive possibilities.

2.1 TASK-ORIENTED APPROACHES

Task modelling is a research area which has received contributions from computer, and cognitive sciences and HCI. In cognitive sciences there has been more attention on how to characterise and identify tasks thus contributing more to the task analysis phase, examples are Task Knowledge Structures (TKS), Groupware Task Analysis (GTA) and MAD, or on how to use task models for predicting user performance, an example is the Keystroke-Level Model (KLM) approach.

In computer science the focus has been more on finding notations suitable to represent tasks and their relationships more precisely (examples are UAN and ConcurTaskTrees, which will be described in chapter 4) and using them to support interactive software development, examples are: MOBI-D and Tasks Interactor Modelling (TIM) [PMM97].

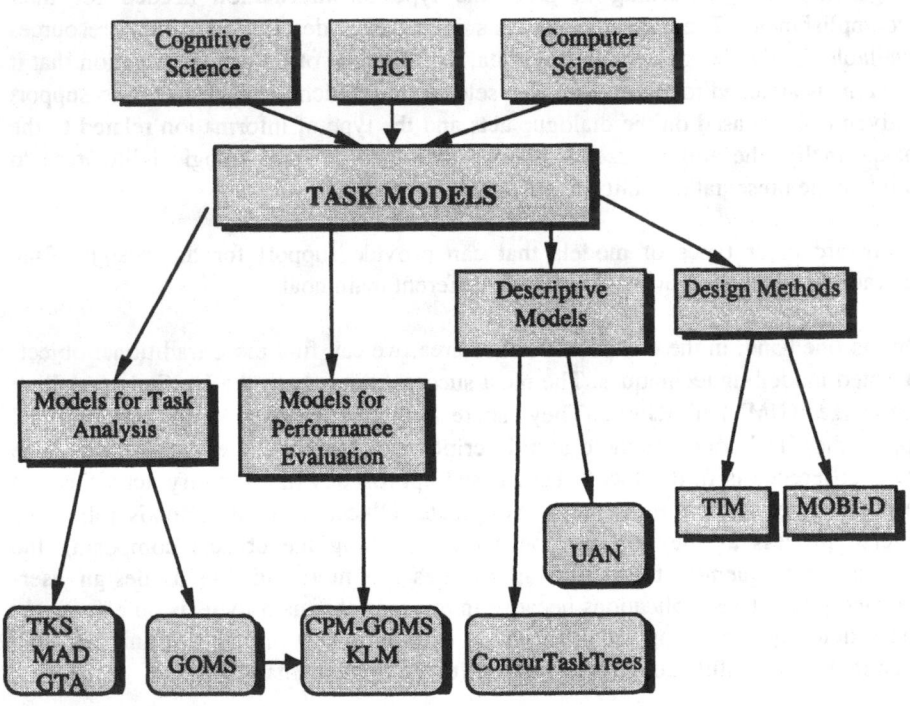

Figure 2.1: Approaches to task models.

Task-oriented approaches can be classified in many ways, a broad classification can be done considering three different dimensions:

- *The type of formalism they use to represent the model.* Various formalisms have been proposed: for example, formal grammars (Backus Naur Form (BNF)

[R81], extended attribute grammars, etc.), TAG (task-actions grammars) [PG86], extended task-action grammars [T90], production systems (production rules), knowledge models (declarative as well as procedural knowledge), transition networks and Petri nets [PB90].

- *The type of information they contain.* There are approaches which are oriented to only identify the activities and their logical decomposition, others also include indications of temporal relationships, others add information related to the artefacts manipulated by the tasks identified and other properties of such tasks.

- *The type of support they provide.* Methods can differ for how they support the design and development of interactive systems, in some cases they support the evaluation phase. The type of support given depends also on the modelling notation used. Thus methods can be classified depending on if they aim to support user interface design (TAG, GOMS, for example) or user interface software development or both (TIM and MOBI-D, for example). Another example of approaches of the first category is in [LL94] where the authors propose the development of a structured human factors method within which task analysis stages are instantiated. Other methods have been oriented to use models to support usability evaluation (an example is RemUSINE described in Chapter 8).

Many notations have been developed in this area and we will see examples of some of them in the next Sections. Some of them are based on task decomposition and association of tasks with the user actions which are necessary to support them. Generally these notations can differ for many aspects, for example:

- *the type of syntax:* textual versus graphical (for example UAN is a textual notation whereas ConcurTaskTrees graphically represents the logical structure of the task model),
- *the level of formality:* in some cases the semantic (i.e. the meaning of the operators and their possible compositions) is precisely provided whereas in other cases little attention has been paid to this aspect.
- *the richness of operators that they offer to designers:* for example the traditional GOMS considers only sequential tasks whereas UAN and ConcurTaskTrees also provide concurrent operators.

One of the first attempts to formalise the relationships between user tasks and dynamic behaviour was made by Reisner [R81]. She used traditional Backus Naur Form grammars to describe the actions needed to support user's tasks. She identified three important aspects to evaluate the usability of user interfaces: *the number of different terminal symbols*, which are the set of different actions available to users; *string simplicity*, which is the number of actions needed to support a given task - here the assumption is the fewer the actions the more usable the user interfaces will be because this means that users have less to learn and remember; and *structural consistency*, which is the number of rules which define the user interface language - once again the most usable user interfaces have the least number of rules because this means that the user interface is consistent as the same rule can be applied in similar situations. The order of importance proposed is: structural consistency, string simplicity and number of different terminal symbols. Another proposal was the task-actions grammar [PG86]. This consists of a set of rules for task decomposition to arrive at basic tasks which are associated with user actions. The rules in the grammar describe the semantic features, objects and commands which we want the user to be able to manipulate. One goal of these grammars is to model the tasks as the user sees them instead of how the designer implements them. Once again the number of schemes indicates the consistency of the interface language: in similar situations it is possible to have the same effects with the same actions.

A proposal for a taxonomy of formalisms for the specification of formalisms for interactive systems can be found in [BB95]. The taxonomy is based on three dimensions and twelve criteria: expressive power (ability to describe users task and actions, interface state and system feedback, sequencing of actions, parallelism of actions, presentation of the user interface, and management of user errors), generative capabilities (code generation, predictive analysis, prove properties, derive user interface functions such as contextual help), extensibility and usability.

2.2 GOMS

GOMS (Goals, Operators, Methods, Selection rules) was the first systematic approach to the design of user interfaces. It is a method, originally introduced by Stuard Card, Thomas Moran, and Allen Newell, that has a long history and considerable influence. It is based on a cognitive model (the Human Processor Model) which is described by a set of memories and processors and a set of principles underlying their behaviour. More precisely, it is decomposed into three subsystems interacting with each other (perceptive, motorial and cognitive subsystems).

```
GOAL: EDIT-MANUSCRIPT
       GOAL: EDIT-UNIT-Task repeat until no more unit tasks
           GOAL: ACQUIRE-UNIT-TASK
               GET-NEXT-PAGE if at end of manuscript
               GET-NEXT-TASK
           GOAL: EXECUTE-UNIT-TASK
               GOAL:LOCATE-LINE
                   [select: USE-QS-METHOD
                            USE-LF-METHOD]
               GOAL: MODIFY-TEXT
                   [select: USE-S-METHOD
                            USE-M-METHOD]
               VERIFY-EDIT
```

Table 2.1: Example of a GOMS specification from [CMN83].

GOMS provides a hierarchical description to reach goals in terms of operators. Operators are elementary perceptual, motorial and cognitive acts. Actions at one level can be goals at a lower level. Methods are sequences of subgoals and operators used to structure the description of how to reach a given goal. The selection rules indicate when to use a method instead of another one. An example is when moving the cursor in a specific location of a document. If the desired position is close to the current one then it is sufficient to move the cursor by the arrow strokes, otherwise it would be better to select the new position with the mouse support.

This notation is especially valid to describe the performance of tasks and it is scaleable as it has been demonstrated by some industrial applications.

In Table 2.1 there is an example of a GOMS specification taken from [CMN83]. It describes how a user segments the larger task of editing a manuscript into a sequence of small, discrete modifications, such as to delete a word or to insert a character. The term unit task is used to denote user-defined subtasks, which are used to describe how the user segments tasks into subtasks. As you can see the user can select from two methods for selecting a line: in the *LF-method* the linefeed key is pressed repeatedly, causing the editor to advance one line each time. To use the other method, mouse selection is used to identify the line. Usually the former method is selected when the text for the unit-task is within a few lines of the text for the current unit task and the other method is selected when the new unit task is farther away. Similarly, there are two ways to modify the text. In either case, a verify-edit operation is evoked to check that what actually happened matched the user's intentions.

More generally, there are several different versions of GOMS in use today. In the first proposal [CMN83] there was both a description of how to express a goal and subgoals in a hierarchy, methods and operators, and how to formulate selection rules and a simplified version called Keystroke-Level Model (KLM). KLM uses only keystrokes-level operators, no goals, methods or selection rules. The analysis simply lists the keystrokes, mouse-movements, and mouse-button presses that a user must perform to accomplish a task then uses a few simple heuristics to place a single type of coarse "mental operator" which approximates many kinds of unobservable events. KLM models are easier to construct, but classic GOMS models provide more information for the qualitative design. NGOMSL includes a more rigorous set of rules for identifying the GOMS components and information such as the number of steps in a method, how goals are set and terminated, what information needs to be remembered while performing the task [K96].

One limitation of GOMS approaches is that it considers error-free behaviour and only sequential tasks. The latter limitation is partially overcome by one of the extensions [JK96] of the GOMS approach that has been developed, CPM-GOMS [GJA92].

CPM-GOMS uses cognitive, perceptual, and motor operators in a critical path method (PERT chart), a common tool used in project management, to show the activities that can be performed in parallel. The parallelism of a task is represented in a schedule chart (Figure 2.2). Each operator in a task is represented as a box with a name centred in it with an associated duration above the top right corner in milliseconds. Dependencies between activities are represented as lines connecting the boxes. For example, telephone operators helping customers cannot press the collect-call key until they hear the customer request a collect call. Therefore, there would be a dependency line drawn between a box representing the perception of the word *collect* and boxes representing cognitive operators that verify the word *collect* and initiate pressing the collect-call key. The boxes and their dependency lines are drawn according to a detailed understanding of the task, goal decomposition, and operator-placement heuristics. An important concept in analysing the total task time for complex parallel tasks is the critical path. The critical path is the sequence of activities that takes the longest time and determines the total time for the entire task. However, in CPM-GOMS operators for representing explicitly dynamic enabling and disabling of activities are not provided.

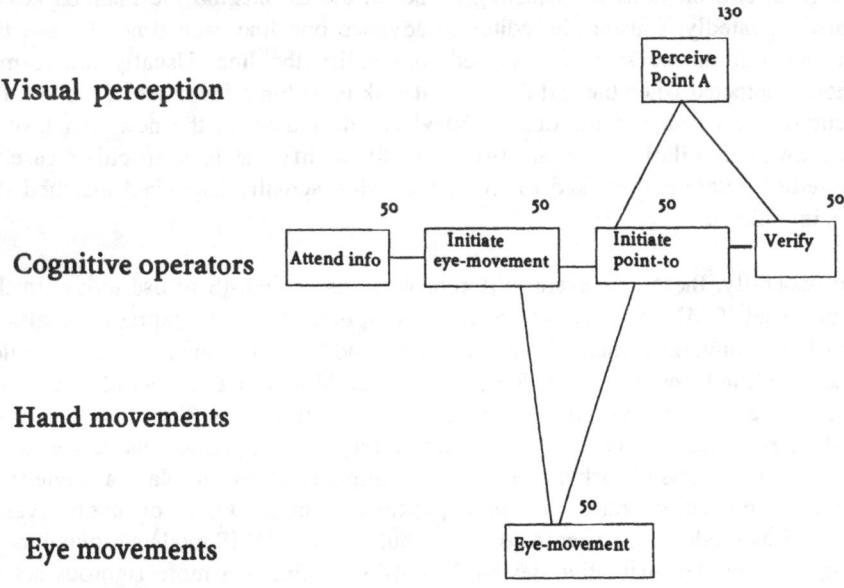

Figure 2.2: An example of CPM-GOMS analysis.

A problem in predicting time performance with GOMS-based approaches is that when distributed applications are considered (such as Web-based applications) the time requested by the application to respond to the user interactions is difficult to predict because it can depend on unpredictable external factors (such as networks delays). Detailed discussion of the respective strengths and weakness of the various versions in the GOMS family can be found in [JK96].

The GOMS approach has raised interest particularly in the USA whereas in Europe other techniques for task modelling have mainly been developed and mainly used.

2.3 NORMAN'S CYCLE

Norman [N88] provided a model identifying the main phases in a user interaction thus giving a useful and structured indication of main aspects to consider when designing a user interface. This model provides a sound, even if simplified, framework for design and evaluation.

He offers seven stages of action as a model of human-computer interaction:

1   Forming the goal
2   Forming the intention
3   Identifying the action
4   Executing the action
5   Perceiving the system state
6   Interpreting the system state
7   Evaluating the outcome

For example, a goal can be a certain modification of the content of a letter. This general goal can be decomposed into some more specific intentions such as modifying the conclusions. This requires specific actions, such as modifications of some words by selecting them and typing the new words. Once these actions are performed, users can look at the result of the interactions they performed and realise, for example, that they accidentally modified some words that were okay. In so doing, they have not completely achieved their goal and therefore need to perform an additional modification.

Norman locates his stages in the context of cycles of action and evaluation and identifies the gulf of execution (the difference between the user's intentions in terms of actions to reach and the allowable actions) and the gulf of evaluation (the difference between the system's representation and the users' expectation).

In user interfaces with low usability, where the possible tasks are badly supported, the two gulfs can be useful to identify the mismatches between user's actions and expectations (execution gulf) and system's actions and presentations (evaluation gulf) as it is possible to see in Figure 2.3. In both cases we can identify a cognitive distance indicated by the amount and quality of information processing needed to fill the gap in the gulf considered.

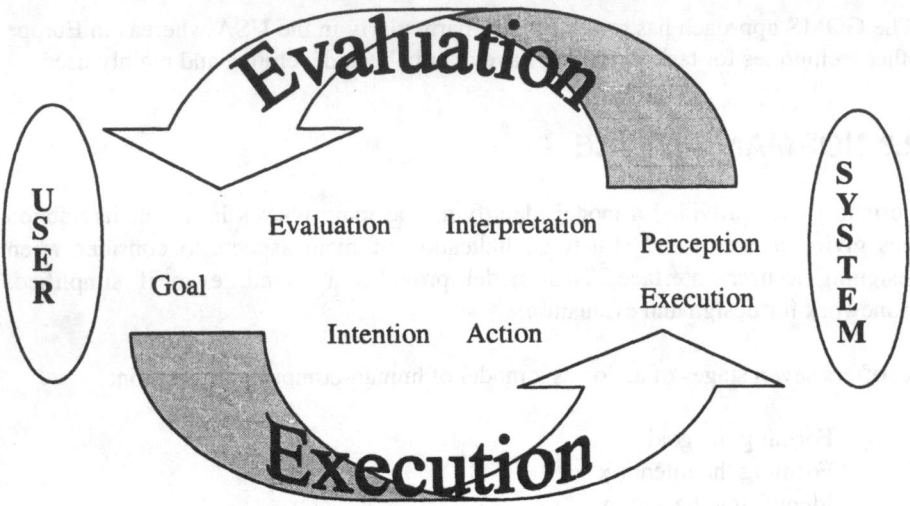

Figure 2.3: Norman's cycle of interaction.

2.4 TASK ANALYSIS METHODS

Some task analysis methodologies are devoted to the acquisition and modelling of specific knowledge used by the human operators when performing an activity. TAKD and TKS are examples of this class of methods.

2.4.1 Task analysis

Task Analysis for Knowledge Description (TAKD) [D89] is one of the first approaches, developed by Dan Diaper, for gathering and analysing information on the knowledge people have when carrying out tasks. TAKD uses observations of the user activities as well as interview data as input data. TAKD consists of a data analysis and a task description; it focuses on the analysis and categorising of the semantic aspects of the actions and objects used in tasks. The resulting model of activity represents the knowledge used for performing the tasks in terms of objects and actions, with knowledge representation grammars. Tasks are described as an informal *activity list*, i.e. sequences of steps identified through observation or interview. The analysis of *activity list* provides lists of specific individual actions and specific conceptual objects. Actions and objects are then classified into a *Task Descriptive Hierarchy* (TDH), emphasising the similarities between actions or objects through an abstraction process. A TDH takes the form of a tree where nodes correspond to generic objects and generic actions, and leaves are the specific objects or actions. The TDH may also be used to organise potential suggestions from the observed users (e.g. new objects and new actions needed by the users).

The aim of the Task Knowledge Structure (TKS) approach is to provide a theoretical base with an associated method that can be used early in the design process. It was developed by Peter Johnson and Hilary Johnson [JJWS88], and it assumes that task knowledge is represented in a person's memory and can be described by a TKS which is assumed to be activated during the task execution. Thus, a TKS is a summary representation of the different types of knowledge that have been acquired through learning and performing a given (and an associated) task; these TKSs are dynamically represented in the long-term memory, are recruited in order to perform the task and are further processed when the task is performed. From TKS theory a method has been developed for analysing task knowledge, called Knowledge Analysis of Tasks (KAT) [JJ91]. This process of analysis produces a description of the knowledge of a person or a group concerning the performance of the tasks.

The main assumption of the TKS theory is that within TKSs are represented different types of knowledge on the task: goal-oriented substructures, task procedures and taxonomic substructures. *Goal-oriented substructures* represent a person's knowledge about goals and their enabling states, as subgoals and procedures; *task procedures* differ from *goal structures* because they are directly executable; consequently, associated to each *procedure* there is a conditional and contextual knowledge that allows use of the procedure in the appropriate conditions; finally, *taxionomics substructures* represent knowledge about the properties of task objects (both physical and informational) and their associated actions. Another basic assumption of the theory is that the knowledge contained in a TKS can differ in terms of its *representativeness* and *centrality* with respect to the task. *Representativeness* is concerned with the instances (the different knowledge used in performing a given task) and their relations to the class (the task) and is a matter of degree rather than an all-or-no property of the knowledge. *Centrality* is concerned with the critical points in the task performance which determine its success or failure. Moreover, it is assumed that knowledge which is deemed to be central to the task is more likely recruited and transferred to similar tasks in differing context (i.e. when the task is carried out using different technologies), since this knowledge is "tightly bound" to the specific task goal.

A TKS, as a representation of a task's knowledge, is related to other TKSs by a number of different relations. The main forms of relation between TKSs are within- and between- role relations, where the role is the collection of tasks that a person occupying that role performs: within a role each task to be performed will have a correspondent TKS, thus a person is supposed to have the knowledge of the tasks that together define a particular role (the within-role relations); the between-role relation is defined in terms of similarity of task across different roles; in such cases it is possible that a common TKS can be assumed to exist comprising the task knowledge common to each role-task instance. It is important to point out that there are further possible relations between TKSs; in particular the temporal and experiential relations allow designers to take into account the fact that the representation of the tasks are restructured and modified over time because of the learning and the knowledge acquisition mechanisms.

2.4.2 Groupware Task Analysis

Groupware Task Analysis (GTA), developed by Gerrit van der Veer [VLB96], is one of the first attempts to model the complexity of the results of task analysis in groupware applications. This approach considers three different activities: analysis of the *current task situation* (task model 1); specification of a task situation for which the future system is being designed (*future task situation*, task model 2); specification of the semantics of the future system, that is the conceptual model (the user's virtual machine (UVM)).

Design starts with the description of task model 1. In this phase, the method provides a conceptual framework which aims at considering the organisation as composed of: *People*: A concept of organisation of people is needed as well as a distinction between actors (individual person) and roles (classes of actors). The organisation refers to the relation between actors and roles with respect to task allocation and it describes the human structure in the community of practice. *Work*: It can be split into different tasks, whereas a task structure describes the various levels of complexity of tasks. A unit task is a task on the lowest level of decomposition and it consists of different actions that have to be performed. *Situation*: It describes the environment and the objects. The object description includes an analysis of the object structure. The environment includes actors with roles, conditions for task performance, relevant objects, and artefacts like information technology, that are available for subtask delegation.

The model of the future task (task model 2) is directed to a future work practice that may not yet be in use. This model might result in novel task organisation. So, this model might reflect a rather different organisation of the work processes, which might be dissimilar to the current business at hand. Further on, additional work duties, technical and organisational constraints, as well as the specific wishes of the clients have to be taken into consideration. So for task model 2 design decision related to problems and conflicts that are represented in task model 1, in combination with important parameters as formulated in interaction with the client, have to be taken.

The design of the user's virtual machine (UVM) produces an abstract description of the system as far as it is of direct relevance to the user interface. It is important to notice that the UVM model describes the solution in terms of technology, whereas task model 2 focuses on the task structure and work organisation. Design iteration is needed between the specification of these two models.

New developments in GTA include an ontology [WVE98] for the concepts considered in task modelling and a tool, Euterpe, to support it.

2.5 UAN

The main purpose of UAN, a notation developed by Rex Hartson and others [HG92], is to communicate design. It allows designers to describe the dynamic behaviour of graphical user interface. It combines concepts from task models, process-based notations and user actions descriptions. It is a textual notation where the interface is represented as a quasi-hierarchical structure of asynchronous tasks, the sequencing within each task being independent of that in the others. A rich set of operators to describe temporal relationships among tasks is available.

A UAN specification is usually structured into two parts:

- one part describes task decomposition and the temporal relationships among asynchronous tasks,
- the other part associates each basic task with one table. These tables have three columns indicating the user actions, the system feedback and the state modifications requested to perform it. Some specific symbols are used in these specifications, for example to indicate button pressing or releasing.

An example of specification of a task in terms of its subtasks and their temporal relationships is:

> *Task: BuildRequest:*
> *((SelR | ClearR | IconifyR)**
> *--> SpecField+)*

This expression describes the task of building a request for a database (*BuildRequest* task). This task is performed by one or more occurrences (+ operator) of the task for specifying single values of the fields of the request (*SpecField*). This task can be interrupted, as indicated by the one-way interleaving operator (-->), by the tasks described with the expression *((SelR | ClearR | IconifyR)**. This expression describes the possibility to perform zero, one or more times (* operator) the choice (| is the choice operator) of one of the tasks indicated: selecting another request (*SelR*), clearing the request (*ClearR*), iconifying the request (*IconifyR*). Once the interrupting task is terminated then the interrupted task can continue from the state that it had reached.

In Table 2.2 we have an example of a description of a basic task. The user has to move the cursor (~ symbol) on a specific icon (indicated by the [x,y in AppICON] expression). Then s/he has to double click the button of the mouse within a certain amount of time indicated by $t_{doubleClick}$ ($\vee\wedge$ ($t<t_{doubleClick}$) $\vee\wedge$). After that if some window was highlighted (indicated by the ! operator) because previously selected then it becomes dehighlighted (dehighlighted presentation elements are indicated by the -! operator). Overall this behaviour is indicated by the expression: w'! : w'-!. Then the application unmaps the menu bar associated with the previous application, and it maps the menu bar associated with the selected application and

finally unmaps the icon of the selected application. As a consequence the state of the application is modified because the selected application becomes the current application and likewise the menu of the selected application becomes the current menu. As you can see in UAN the specifications should be read sequentially left-to-right and then vertically (top to bottom from line to line) when there are the tables associated with basic tasks.

Task: SelApplication

User Action	Interface Feedback	Interface State
~[x,y in AppICON] ∨∧(t<t$_{doubleClick}$) ∨∧)	w'!: w'-! UnMap(PrevAppliMenu) Map(AppMenu) UnMap(AppICON)	CurAppli=App CurMenu=AppMenu

Table 2.2: An example of a UAN specification.

If we consider the UAN notation we can find that it is valid to specify tasks, which are the components of the specification, given its rich set of operators for their composition. It provides good support to specify low level actions sequencing as well. One of the possible limitations is that it stimulates large specifications sometimes with many details not always useful for the designer (for example, often it is not important to specify all the elementary feedback provided by the user interface, for instance when the cursor is on a button then its colour changes slightly). Another limitation is that the order which has to be followed to interpret the tables of the basic tasks (left-to-right) can be rigid and inadequate especially when the modification of the state of the application triggers the performance of the basic task considered. This means that it is an item on the far right column that triggers events described by the other columns.

2.6 PETRI NETS

Petri Nets is a formalism dedicated to the modelling and the analysis of discrete event systems. When modelling with Petri Nets a system is described in terms of an oriented graph with state variables (called *places*, depicted as ellipses) and by state-changing operators (called *transitions*, depicted as rectangles), connected by annotated *arcs*. The state of the system is given by the *marking* of the net, which is a distribution of *tokens* in the net's places. In coloured Petri nets, the tokens assume values from predefined types, or *colours*.

State changes result from the *firing* of transitions, yielding a new distribution of tokens. Transition firing involves two steps: (1) tokens are removed from *input* places and their values *bound* to variables specified on the input arcs, and (2) new tokens are deposited in the *output* places with values determined by *emission rules* attached to output arcs. A transition is *enabled* to fire when all of its input places contain tokens, and the value of those tokens satisfy the (optional) Boolean constraints attached to the input arcs.

Petri Nets allow designers to describe basic constructs in concurrent programming (such as sequence, condition, iteration, parallelism and synchronisation). For example, in the left side of Figure 2.4 we can see an example of sequential and iterative behaviour (the user can first fill the field 1, followed by field 2, before sending the request and then starting the sequence of these three actions again), whereas in the right side there is an example of parallelism and synchronisation (the user can first activate the form, then fill field 1 and 2 in any order and, finally, when both fields are filled, send the request).

Due to the limitation of the early model (lack of structuring construct, no data modelling, etc.) more powerful and generic ones have been proposed in order to overcome these limitations. An example is called Petri Nets with Objects (PNO) in which objects are used both for structuring and data modelling. PNO is a Petri net model where tokens can hold values and more precisely references (in object-oriented environments they can be object identifiers).

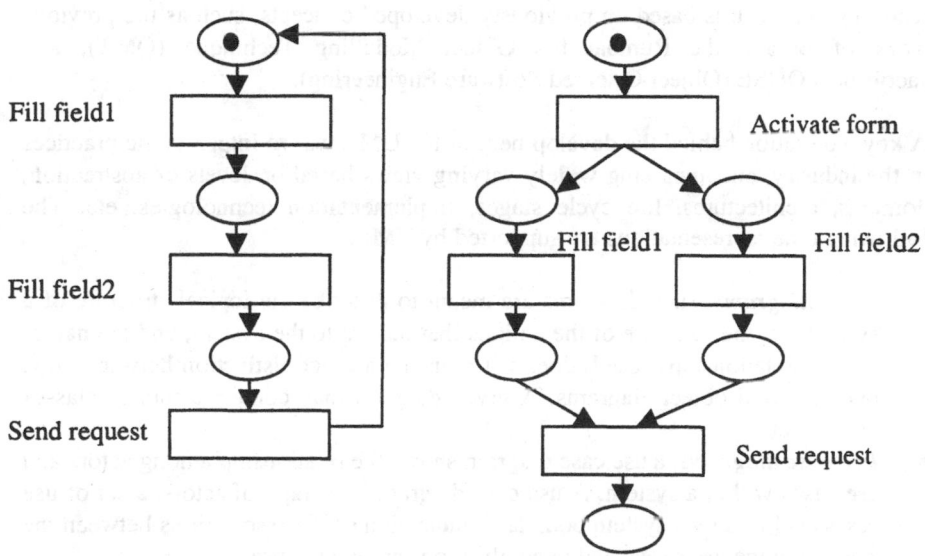

Figure 2.4: Examples of Petri Nets expressions.

ICO [PB94], developed by Palanque and Bastide, is a formalism for describing concurrent objects classes with a behaviour (if needed) and a user interface part (if needed). In these classes there are four components: attributes and methods (as in classical object-oriented approaches), a behaviour (described using a PNO) and information in order to take into account the user interface. ICO has the notion of user service which is an operation of the system that can be interactively triggered by the user through some user interface device. In addition, there is also the notion of rendering function which describes how the state of the system is made perceivable by the user. Another work where Petri Nets have been used to support design of user interfaces is described in [DDS98]. Whereas TADEUS [SE96] is a task-oriented method to develop user interfaces using specifications in Dialogue Graph, a graphical notation that aims to extend the possibilities of Petri Nets.

Petri Nets have been shown to be effective and easy to understand for small specifications because with them it is easy to follow how the dynamic behaviour can evolve. Problems can arise when the specification is large because it can be difficult to interpret the meaning of a large number of interconnecting arcs and it can be difficult to modify them.

2.7 UML

The Unified Modelling Language (UML) [BRJ99] is a modelling environment that has become a de facto industrial standard. It provides a set of representations useful for specifying, constructing, visualising, and documenting software systems. The resulting approach is based on previously developed concepts, such as the previous work of Booch, the Rumbaugh's Object Modelling Technique (OMT), and Jacobson's OOSE (Object-Oriented Software Engineering).

A key motivation behind the development of the UML was to integrate the practices in the industry, encompassing widely varying views based on levels of abstraction, domains, architectures, life cycle stages, implementation technologies, etc. The following nine representations are supported by UML:

- *Class diagrams*: such diagrams are meant to describe the logical structure of a system, i.e. the structure of the entities that belong to the system, and the nature of their relationships. UML does not mandate a strict distinction between class diagrams and object diagrams. A given diagram may contain a mix of classes and objects.
- *Use case diagrams*: a use case diagram shows the relationship among actors and use cases within a system. A use case diagram is a graph of actors, a set of use cases enclosed by a system boundary, indication of the associations between the actors and the use cases, and generalisations among the use cases.
- *Interaction diagrams*: a pattern of interaction among objects is shown on an interaction diagram. Interaction diagrams come in two forms based on the same underlying information but each emphasising a particular aspect of it: *sequence diagrams* and *collaboration diagrams*. Sequence diagrams and collaboration diagrams express similar information but show it in different ways. Sequence diagrams show an interaction arranged in time sequence. In particular, they show a table with the objects participating in the interaction along one and the messages that they exchanged arranged in time sequence along the other axis. They do not show the associations among the objects. Collaboration diagrams

show the relationships among objects that are represented by arcs and are better for understanding the effects on a given object and for procedural design.

- *State diagrams*: a state diagram shows the sequences of states that an object or an interaction goes through during its life in response to received stimuli, together with its responses and actions. The semantics and notation are substantially those of David Harel's statecharts [H87] with some minor modifications. His work was a major advance on the traditional flat state machines.
- *Object diagrams*: they give a static view of a set of objects and their relationships that can be found in class diagrams.
- *Activity diagrams* represent the dynamic behaviour of a system showing the flow of control among a set of activities. They can be used for representing different types of activities: workflow activities, operations of an object and so on.
- A *component diagram* aims at representing the structure of components that are composed of classes, interfaces, or collaborations.
- A *deployment diagram* represents an architecture composed of run-time processing nodes and the related components.

UML has mainly been used to design software systems paying little attention to the user interface aspects. It is more oriented to support a structured design of functionally correct and engineered systems. Two questions are raised when comparing task-based approaches and UML:

- How can task-based approaches be positioned in the set of representations provided by UML?
- How is it possible to integrate task-based approaches with UML?

Regarding the first issue, generally speaking we can note that task models give a more user-oriented view of an application behaviour whereas UML is more oriented to provide a representation of the internal, system-oriented behaviour of an application. Concerning the specific techniques used within UML we can note that use cases are quite similar to the output of task analysis because they both mainly address the requirement analysis phase. Activity diagrams have similar purposes as notations for task models however they do not seem particularly flexible, for example to show multiple abstraction levels and their relationships, whereas sequence diagrams indicate the activities that are performed including the actors and the messages that are exchanged, thus producing descriptions that address aspects similar to those considered in task models but more limited to the software implementation and to specific interactions.

Regarding the second issue various solutions are possible. In [LPL98] a method is proposed that supports the transformation from a sequence diagram into a task model by removing the internal system-oriented information that is not needed in the task model. The rationale for such an approach is that UML is widely used so in this way it is possible to take advantage of pre-existing knowledge sources by reusing the information that they contain in order to reduce the effort required to develop task models that can be used to better support documentation once they are obtained. An alternative solution is to develop task models using the information contained in use cases and activity diagrams, then the information in the task models can be used to develop the system design in terms of interaction and object diagrams capturing better the user-oriented aspects.

2.8 FORMAL METHODS FOR HCI

Formal methods for HCI is an area that has stimulated a good deal of effort over the last fifteen years: an example is the work of Cardelli on *Squeak* [CP85], while other early attempts were introduced in the book edited by Harrison and Thimblebly [HT90]. The work of Dix [D91] was useful to provide precise definitions of the fundamental concepts of interactive systems. A more updated description of many approaches in this area can be found in the book on formal methods in human-computer interaction [PP97b].

Sometimes it is not easy to determine when a method can be considered formal. The answers offered to this question differ slightly depending on the authors' background (software engineering, human-computer interaction, artificial intelligence, etc.). For example, in cognitive sciences a formal method aims to model user behaviour. Such models can be used to make predictions and attempt to verify these predictions through empirical studies. Whatever background we consider, there is a broad consensus that in a formal approach the aspects of interest are rigorously and precisely described, and this can be best achieved using a notation whose semantics is likewise precisely defined.

The formal methods community in software engineering has encountered some significant difficulties in tackling human-computer interactions. This is because of its structural complexity, stemming from the fact that functional aspects are only part of the concerns in interactive systems design: the other, interactive component, involves user issues, their tasks and the context of use, which are difficult to represent in a formal model.

Using notations with a precise semantics to describe relevant aspects in the design of user interfaces has some advantages:

- They allow designers to identify and remove ambiguities from the specifications performed thus improving communication among those who develop them and those who read and use them (often they are the same people but not always).
- They allow rigorous reasoning about the properties of the specification; a property summarises a relevant feature of the specification and it can be rigorously demonstrated by use of tools such as model checking tools [P97a] [AWM95], [ASDR98]), or theorem provers.

The main challenge in formal approaches is to show that they are able to support systematic methods considering multiple aspects and to address medium-large specifications. Various formal notations from the computer science area have been used to describe user interfaces. We can find many examples of these types of works. The list below, grouped by formal notations, is not exhaustive. However it is noticeable that people usually address limited aspects, they do not take into account previous work and there is a lack of methodology to indicate how the model underlying the formal notation used is mapped in the models describing the semantics of interactive systems. Examples of works concerning the application of formal methods in this area are:

- *CSP* which was used, for example, to describe hierarchical graphical input devices [DHL90];
- *Temporal logics* are a set of notations. Some of them have been used in this area: *Action-Based Temporal Logic* was considered to investigate properties of user interfaces [P97a]; Johnson used temporal logics to support the specification and prototyping of concurrent multi-users interfaces [J91] and, with Harrison, to support the specification and prototyping of interactive control systems [JH92]. Wang and Abowd developed some work using *CTL* [AWM95]. Duke and Harrison have used *modal action logic*, see for example [DH95]. Lamport's *TLA* (Temporal Logic of Actions) is a linear time temporal logic which has been applied to express properties of behavioural specification [S95b].
- Z has received various applications in this area: for example, to specify some functionalities of the X Window System [B92], or a model for User Interface Systems [KD90];
- *VDM* has been used, for example, at Praxis to specify the CERD user interface [AH92] for an air traffic controller;
- *OBJ* for the revision of GKS [DD92]: David Duce's group has investigated many possible approaches in the formal specification of graphics standards;
- *LARCH* to specify visual languages [WZ91];
- *Petri Nets* [BP90] [DDS98] [JWZ93] for the design, validation and prototyping of user interfaces. They are a powerful notation able to describe true concurrency and time with graphical representations but in large specifications they may be difficult to interpret and it may be difficult to compose Petri-nets specifications.
- *Esterel* is a notation used to specify concurrent systems and thus it can be used to specify the behaviour of graphical objects [CI89].
- RAISE was developed on the basis of the VDM language and has the support of some automatic tools. It has also been used to specify user interfaces [L95].
- B has been used to check properties and to develop specifications incrementally [AGJ98].

2.9 EXERCISES

1. Develop a GOMS specification of a simplified word processing application.
2. Develop a UAN specification of the same application as above exploiting the possibility to specify more flexible temporal relationships.
3. Develop a Petri-Net specification of the application considered in the previous example.
4. Analyse possible user interactions with the Norman cycle for the application designed above. Try to identify whether there are possible mismatches in the gulf of evaluation and execution.

3 Analysis of Interactive Applications

Before building a model it is necessary to understand clearly what has to be included in such a model. In this chapter we discuss some techniques useful to identify information that is important in modelling interactive applications. For this purpose we consider various techniques (scenarios, use cases, task analysis) that are usually applied in the requirement elicitation and specification phases. They usually provide information that is informally structured. As we will see the three approaches that we consider in this chapter (scenarios, use cases, and task analysis) differ mainly in terms of generality: scenarios are very specific descriptions of an example of use; use cases group sets of uses; task analysis is more general and aims at identifying possible general tasks and their features.

3.1 SCENARIOS

Scenarios are an important technique that is often used along with task analysis and task modelling. They provide informal descriptions of a specific use in a specific context of an application. A careful identification of a meaningful scenario can include most of the activities that should be considered in a task model. Usually they are selected to highlight specific issues. The main difference between a task model and a scenario is that while the task model should indicate all the main activities and their possible temporal relationships, a scenario indicates only one specific sequence of occurrences of such activities.

In Table 3.1 there is an example of a scenario. As you can see there is a clear indication of a specific user and a specific sequence of actions that s/he can perform.

An example of a scenario

Silvia is looking for interesting papers on patterns. She makes a request to the on-line library by giving the name of the topic as parameters of her request, and indicating that she is interested in papers written in English. The order of providing these two parameters is not important. She receives a long list of references. As she is interested in recent contributions she adds a further constraint in the request so that she receives information only on papers published in the last five years. The new list of publications is more manageable. She understands that the works by Gamma are very relevant. She would like to have them grouped so that they are presented together. Thus she makes a new request adding the constraint that the author has to be Gamma. The result is the information that she was looking for. Now she can move to another request for another topic.

Table 3.1: An example of a scenario.

Scenarios can be used for various purposes:

- *understanding an application domain*: in this case scenarios can be used to highlight its main aspects;
- *eliciting requirements*: for example, in interactive safety-critical applications scenarios can be used to highlight safety-critical aspects in the current interactive applications that should be avoided in new applications;
- *supporting task analysis and modelling*: one or a group of scenarios can provide useful information to identify relevant tasks, their attributes and relationships;
- *evaluation purposes*: for example, it is possible to provide scenarios to check whether an application satisfies some usability problems or to compare different design options.

There have been several proposals to structure the description of a scenario. For example, in the Techniques for Human Error Assessment (THEA) method [FHW98] they are described in terms of agents, rationale, situation and environment, task context, system context, action and exceptional circumstances. A discussion on various ways to use scenarios in design can be found in [C95]. User's stories are different from scenarios because they are still less structured. They can include personal considerations and emotional aspects that, in some cases, can be useful to consider in the design of an interactive application.

3.2 USE CASES

Another approach which addresses similar problems is the Use Case Model [J92c]. This model is used in the requirements analysis phase. It aims to define what exists outside the system (actors) and what should be performed by the system (use cases). When a user interacts with the system s/he performs a behaviourally related sequence of transactions in a dialogue with the system. This special sequence is called a use case. Each use case describes and organises external interactions with the system. Each actor will perform a number of use cases in the system. Like actors, use cases can be instantiated and this is done every time a user performs a use case in the system.

The Use Cases approach has some points in common with task-based approaches; for example it captures system requirements from the user's perspective and users are involved. However, there are some disadvantages, too [AM95]. For example, it is very difficult to identify use cases for a large complex project and it is difficult to identify the correct granularity of use cases for a given application. They are often described in natural language. UML provides diagrams allowing designers to represent some aspects of a use case. This lack of formality in the definitions of the terms *use case*, *actor* and so on may cause miscommunication and misunderstandings. For example, Cockburn [C97b] found 18 definitions of use cases mainly depending on four issues: Purpose, Contents, Plurality and Structure. He agrees with the usual definition by Jacobson (then incorporated in UML) where Purpose = requirements, Contents = consistent prose, Plurality = multiple scenarios for use cases, Structure = semi-formal.

3.3 TASK ANALYSIS

Task analysis is usually performed in the requirements elicitation phase. Its main purpose is to identify the tasks that should be performed and their main properties. The result of task analysis is the input for the task modelling phase.

Example: Task analysis of tourists visiting a virtual museum application

Tourists are characterised by a low average knowledge of the topics considered. Usually they prefer to have guided tours through the rooms of the museum and the town with pictures and information about the works of art. However linear predefined tours alone would be too restrictive so some degree of navigational freedom is important. Access to the information is provided with the support of spatial representations: the museum and town maps. This allows users to have immediate information about the locations of the works.

Tourists want general information on the artistic works, and this information has to be presented clearly and in a limited amount because it has to be interpreted easily. Thus a work will be presented by an image, the title, a short description, the name of the author, the material and technique used for its creation, and when it was made. Additional information about the museum and the town can be provided on request, such as the path to get to the museum from the closest railway station or airport, information (title, data, location) on further exhibitions, and historical information on the town and the museum.

Table 3.2: An example of the result of task analysis.

The identification of the tasks to support is usually performed using information gathered by interviewing end users, observing them in their work place, considering how in current applications the desired goals are reached and so on. We have seen in previous paragraphs some techniques supporting task analysis.

3.4 SUPPORT FOR TASK IDENTIFICATION IN INFORMAL SCENARIOS

The difficulties that designers and developers often have during the development of task models has limited their use. Usually the main problem is identifying what is useful for the development of such task models from a lot of informal information.

Some notations to specify task models have been proposed (examples are UAN, ConcurTaskTrees, the GOMS family). We have seen that they can differ according to various aspects, for example: the type of syntax, the level of formality and the richness of operators that they offer to designers. However, they all share a common problem: designers often find them difficult to apply, especially designers working in industries that often do not have a strong background in structured methods and have tight time deadlines in their projects. The reason for this problem is that it is not easy when analysing an existing application or envisioning a new one to know immediately the structure and the elements of the task model.

To overcome such limitations we have to consider that when approaching the design of a new application or the re-design of an existing application, designers often have a lot of informal information available: documentation concerning existing applications, notes from meetings with users, requirements provided by customers, scenarios, use cases and so on. They have to refine this material to identify the task structure underlying the existing application to analyse, or the structure corresponding to the new application to design.

Scenarios are a well-known technique in the HCI field often used during the initial informal analysis phase. As we have seen in previous sections they provide informal descriptions of a specific use in a specific context of an application. A careful identification of a meaningful scenario allows designers to obtain a description of most of the activities that should be considered in a task model.

The use of some tool support in the task elicitation phase was proposed in [CMP98]. A different solution oriented to support the development of task models specified in ConcurTaskTrees, was introduced in [PM99c]. In this case designers can start with an informal description of a scenario or a use case. These descriptions should be selected so as to include performance of most of the main activities involved by the application considered. It can be either the description of a specific use of an existing system or an envisioned use of a new application to design depending on what the designer's goal is. Next the designer can load such a description (left part of Figure 3.1) and identify the roles involved in the task model (see 2 in Figure 3.1) from the agents involved in the scenario (see 1 in Figure 3.1), and then select the words related to activities (such as detection of conflict, paper strip's update, sends clearance, guide the departing aircraft, see 3 in Figure 3.1) and add them to the list of tasks (see 4 in Figure 3.1). The names of such tasks can be edited in order to make them more general.

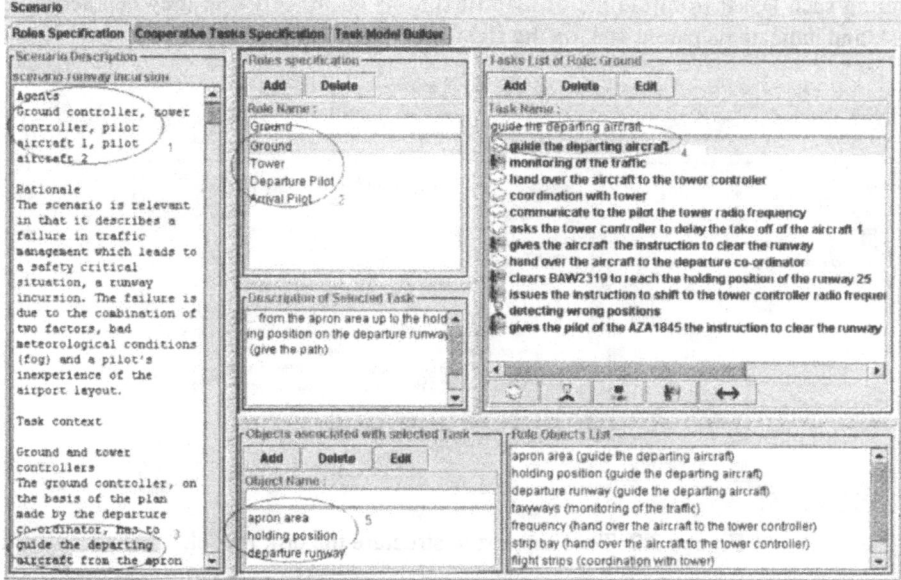

Figure 3.1: The environment supporting task identification.

The designer can also interactively indicate how to allocate the performance of the task: to the user (if only internal cognitive actions are required), to the application, to a user interaction (if the performance consists in user interactions with some device). This is specified by selecting the icon associated with the task allocation chosen. In the scenario's description it is also possible to select the objects and indicate to what tasks they are associated. One task can manipulate multiple objects during its performance and one object can be manipulated by multiple tasks. In this way designers have an environment allowing them to rapidly identify tasks, objects and their relationships. At any time, the designer can select a role and receive the list of tasks identified for that role and the related objects.

The next step is to identify the structure of the task model. It is possible to split this activity into two steps: identify the hierarchical structure among tasks and define their temporal relationships. The input for this phase is the list of tasks identified with the scenario support. This list is not definitive. It can be further modified, for example to add new tasks whose purpose is to logically group a set of identified tasks that are semantically connected and share some temporal relationship. For instance, in the example considered (Figure 3.1) we can group the tasks considered in the scenario in two main logical activities (handling change of air traffic sector and handling traffic in a sector).

In this tool designers can activate an environment (see Figure 3.2) which has the list of tasks identified as input and allows designers to indicate a logical hierarchy among such tasks: from the list of identified tasks on the left side they can select a task and indicate its parent task on the right side.

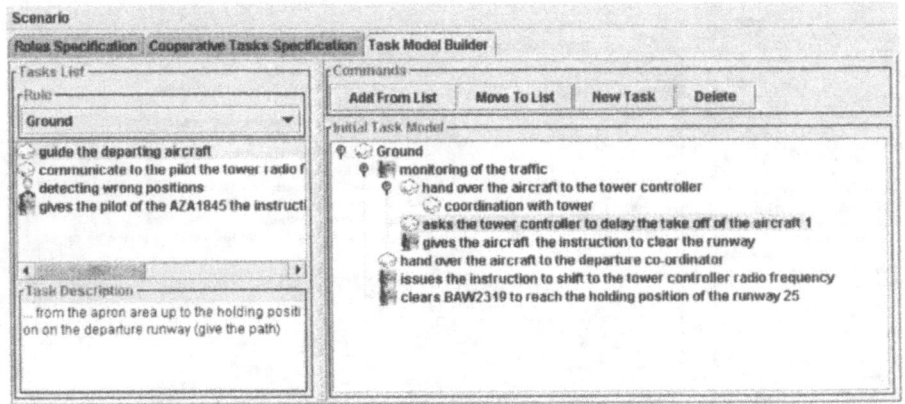

Figure 3.2: Tool support to structure the task model.

We thus obtain a hierarchical structure of a task model that can be further edited to complete it. The difference is that now designers do not have to start from scratch but they have available the hierarchy of tasks and most of the objects manipulated by such tasks have already been identified. Thus, in addition to some refinement to the task model structure, the temporal relationships among the tasks have to be specified with the support of this editor. In the next chapter a detailed description of the possible temporal relationships will be given.

Another interesting issue is the inverse process, *how to derive scenarios from task models*. If we consider in a task model the performance of one specific sequence of tasks then we identify the structure of a scenario. Then the problem is to provide all the detailed information characterising a scenario that often is not contained in a task model. However, this abstract description of a scenario can be useful for various purposes. For example, to compare two task models (they could be the task model of the current system and an envisioned task model or two different solutions to the design of a new application) to check whether both are able to support the sequence of activities identifying such a scenario.

3.5 TASK AND ERRORS

An error is an action not useful to perform the current task. There are different types of errors and they can be classified in different ways. One classical distinction is in [R90] where the author introduced the difference between slips, when an action is incorrectly performed, often because little attention has been paid in its execution, and mistakes, that are knowledge-based errors, often associated with problem solving. Another classification of errors can be provided depending on their impact:

- minimal errors, where a single action allows reaching a correct state,
- recoverable errors, where a sequence of actions is required to reach a correct state,
- unrecoverable errors, which not allow reaching a correct state anymore in the current session.

In the chapter on evaluation (Chapter 8), methods supporting the identification of errors along with how to use such information to improve the design will be discussed. Especially in interactive safety-critical applications it is important to design applications supporting safe user interactions because a user error can threaten human life. In this case an important aspect is to obtain a design that does not decrease its usability in order to guarantee a safe environment. For example, an environment supporting flexibility where users cooperating can exchange their roles depending on a particular situation is flexible and usable but it has to be designed so that this flexibility does not decrease the safety of the environment.

One technique to improve the design is described in [PSF99] where the possible user deviations are identified using a new method based on HAZOP-like techniques. HAZOP [K92] was originally developed in the petro-chemical industry to analyse possible deviations in the data flow in industrial or power implants. The basic idea is to use systematically some guidewords that are associated with the main types of possible deviations. Guidewords are single words identifying a class of deviations. Table 3 illustrates a small set of guidewords associated with possible deviations in performing tasks.

None	The task has not been performed or it has been performed but it has not produced any result.
Other than	The task has been performed using the wrong data or producing wrong data
Ill-timed	The task has been performed at the wrong time.

Table 3.3: Guidewords for analysing interaction failures.

Thus, if we consider the task of *Sending a clearance* in an air traffic control application, the *None* deviation means that either the controller does not send the clearance or sends it but it has no effect, for example because of hardware failure.

The *Other than* deviation means that the task is performed with wrong data, for example that a wrong new flight level is sent to the flight. Whereas an *Ill-timed* performance of the task means that, for example, the new command is transmitted too early or too late with respect to the problem to solve. These guidewords can be further refined. For example *Other than* can be split into *More, Less, Different* depending on whether more or less, or information different from that expected is used to perform the task. Similarly, *Ill-timed* can be refined to *Late* or *Early* depending on whether the task is performed too late or too early.

The advantage of this type of approach is to stimulate designers to think about possible deviations, to identify their possible causes and consequences, and to provide possible protections or recommendations to obtain an improved design. For example, in user interfaces for air traffic control it is important to highlight when an aircraft is going to change sector in order to capture the attention of controllers and remind controllers to provide the information useful for the pilot to access the next sector. This issue can be detected by the use of the *None* guideword because it stimulates the designer to think about what could happen when the controller does not realise that a flight is going to change sector. Thus the designer has a precise indication of the need for solutions that make this event unlikely. This type of analysis is also useful to introduce in the user interface warning messages to the user. The intensity of the warning depends on the impact that the task performance deviation has on the overall safety of the environment controlled by the application.

The analysis of the possible deviations should be done taking into account the various phases of the cycle of an interaction because deviations can occur in each of them: in forming the intention, in performing the related actions, in perceiving the system feedback, and in interpreting the system output. Thus, it is different that a controller does not send a command because s/he did not realise the need for it and when the command is not sent because the controller has selected the wrong button. The different cognitive causes for the same deviation require different improvements of the user interface design in order to avoid again such a deviation.

3.6 EXERCISES

1. Develop two scenarios for the use of a tourist kiosk.
2. Use the scenarios developed in the previous exercise to identify a list of tasks that the application should support.
3. Develop a task analysis for an application supporting registration to university.
4. Analyse possible deviations in interactions performed in an interactive safety-critical context.

4 The ConcurTaskTrees Notation

4.1 INTRODUCTION TO CONCURTASKTREES

Two research streams have affected the design and development of ConcurTaskTrees: model-based user interface design and formal methods for human-computer interaction. The main purpose of this notation is to support the specification of flexible and expressive task models that can be easily interpreted even by people without formal background. Such representations can be useful for designers in the various phases of the design cycle and can be used for both prescriptive and descriptive purposes.

As introduced in Chapter 2, in model-based design the basic idea is to identify high-level models that allow designers to describe and analyse interactive software applications from a more semantic-oriented point of view rather than starting immediately to address the implementation level. Such models can be represented by using formal or semi-formal notations. There is a general agreement that task models are fundamental models in user interface design and most model-based proposals include some sort of task models. The use of a formal approach is innovative in the practice of task modelling where often people use available operators without paying sufficient attention to their exact meaning, especially when they are composed to obtain more complex expressions.

4.1.1 Motivations for ConcurTaskTrees

ConcurTaskTrees was developed after first studies [PF92] developed to specify graphical user interfaces by using the LOTOS notation [ISO88]. LOTOS is a concurrent formal notation which seemed a good choice to specify user interfaces because it allows designers to describe both event-driven behaviours and state modifications. However, it showed some limitations. It was soon realised that there was a need for new operators to express a richer set of dynamic behaviours in human-computer interactions and additional information that is useful in analysing task models. Moreover, LOTOS has a textual syntax that can easily generate complex expressions even when the behaviour to describe is quite simple. Thus, a new notation was developed, ConcurTaskTrees. It is a notation for task model specifications. Its main aim is to be an easy-to-use notation that can support the design of real industrial applications, which usually means applications with medium-large dimensions. This is the problem of many notations, such as Interface Object Graph [C94] which, while effective for simple limited examples, shows low scalability for specifications of real case studies, thus quickly becoming difficult to interpret.

ConcurTaskTrees allows designers to describe concurrent tasks differently from the GOMS proposal which uses hierarchical task decomposition but it is only able to analyse sequential tasks. As it was indicated in Chapter 2 some more recent proposals such as CPM-GOMS [GJA92] have overcome this limitation but they still are unable to describe interactive behaviours such as dynamic disabling of tasks. UAN has been another important contribution in notations for specifying task models because it provides a rich set of operators for describing temporal relationships. However, it still has some limitations, for example, it entails specifying a lot of details (such as highlighting buttons when the cursor is over them). Such details expressed in its textual syntax and the lack of tool support make UAN specifications difficult to interpret especially in real, large size, case studies. Thus, ConcurTaskTrees was developed to propose a solution to the limitations of previous approaches and taking into account that modern multimedia user interfaces are highly interactive, this affects the modalities of performance of the tasks thus requiring notations with the possibility to describe interactive, dynamic, and concurrent behaviours. Besides, as task models for industrial applications can be complex, it is thus important to have notations that allow designers to manage such a complexity.

4.1.2 Main features of ConcurTaskTrees

The main features of ConcurTaskTrees that aim to solve the above problems are:

- *Focus on activities:* thus it allows designers to concentrate on the most relevant aspects when designing interactive applications that encompass both user and system-related aspects avoiding low-level implementation details that at the design stage would only obscure the decisions to take.
- *Hierarchical structure*: a hierarchical structure is something very intuitive, in fact often when people have to solve a problem they tend to decompose it into smaller problems still maintaining the relationships among the various parts of the solution; the hierarchical structure of this specification has two advantages: it provides a wide range of granularity allowing large and small task structures to be reused, it enables reusable task structures to be defined at both low and high semantic level.

- *Graphical syntax*: a graphical syntax often (though not always) is more easy to interpret, in this case it should reflect the logical structure so it should have a tree-like form.
- *Concurrent notation*: a rich set of possible temporal relationships between the tasks can be defined. This sort of aspect is usually implicit, expressed informally in the output of task analysis. Making the analyst use these operators is a substantial change to normal practice. The reason for this innovation is that after an informal task analysis we want designers to express clearly the logical temporal relationships. This is because such ordering should be taken into account in the user interface implementation to allow the user to perform at any time the tasks that should be active from a semantic point of view. Unlike UAN, in ConcurTaskTrees two tasks can synchronise. This happens when they have to exchange information because the output information of one task is the input information for the other task.
- *Task allocation:* how the performance of the task is allocated is explicitly indicated by using icons.
- *Objects:* once the activities are identified it is important to indicate the objects that have to be manipulated to support their performance.

This notation has been applied by people with different backgrounds in different application domain showing two positive results:

- *An expressive and flexible notation* able to represent concurrent and interactive activities where a goal may be achieved performing different tasks, also with the possibility to support cooperations among multiple users and possible interruptions.
- *Compact, understandable representation*, the key aspect in the success of a notation is the ability to provide a lot of information in an intuitive way without requiring excessive efforts from the users of the notation. ConcurTaskTrees is able to support this as it has been demonstrated by its use also by people working in industries without a background in Computer Science. Many notations have mainly been used only by the people who developed them, as they are too complicated, requiring complex expressions to describe simple behaviours. This made them substantially useless.

4.2 TASK ALLOCATION

One point that is often overlooked in notations for software design is the possibility of representing explicitly the choices made for allocating the task performance. Since there is an increasing number of activities that can be performed by automatic systems it becomes important to be able to represent such choices. In ConcurTaskTrees this can be done by using different icons thus stimulating designers to think about these options.

This type of choice can occur in many applications. For example, consider an application for flight reservations. We can design it following two approaches: in one case the application gives a list of flights that satisfy the parameters of the user request (departure town, arrival town, date, etc.) and then gives the users the choice of the flight that best fits their needs. Another option is to design an application that, based on parameters such as cost, duration, number of intermediate stops, automatically suggests the flight that should better satisfy the user needs. In the former case the task of selecting the flight is allocated to the user, in the latter to the application. In the ConcurTaskTrees notation there are four categories of tasks (the icons representing them are also indicated):

User tasks	Tasks performed by the user: usually they are important cognitive activities, for example, thinking about and deciding what the best strategy to solve a problem is.
Application tasks	Tasks completely executed by the application: application tasks can supply information to the user, for example, presenting results given by a database.
Interaction tasks	Tasks performed by the user interacting with the system by some interaction techniques, for example, pushing a button, editing a picture.
Abstract tasks	Tasks which require complex activities whose performance cannot be univocally allocated, for example, a user session with a system.

Table 4.1: Possible task allocations.

In the hierarchical structure of a task model the category of a task depends also on the category of its children tasks. If the children are of the same category then the parent too is associated with that category whereas if the children have different categories then the parent task is an abstract task because it means that its allocation cannot be uniquely allocated. In Table 4.1 examples of icons to represent different categories of tasks are indicated. However, if the modelling exercise is performed by pen and paper it is possible to use different geometric shapes (see, for example, Table 4.2) to represent them with the name of the related task inside it or below them.

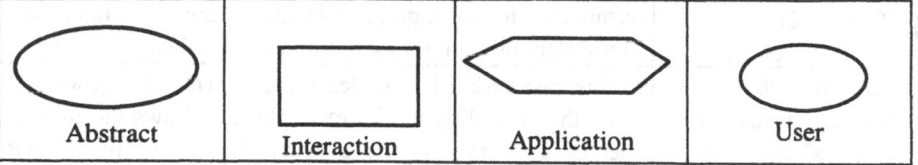

| Abstract | Interaction | Application | User |

Table 4.2: Shapes to represent different categories.

4.3 TEMPORAL RELATIONSHIPS

This section describes the operators used to indicate the temporal relationships among tasks. Two generic tasks, T1 and T2, are considered independently from their category (there is no limitation from this point of view). They are:

Independent Concurrency (T1 ⫴ T2)	Actions belonging to two tasks can be performed in any order without any specific constraints, for example monitoring a screen and speaking in a microphone;
Choice (T1 [] T2)	It is possible to choose from a set of tasks and, once the choice has been made the task chosen can be performed and other tasks are not available at least until it has been terminated. This operator is useful in the design of user interfaces because it is often important to enable the user to choose from various tasks. An example is, at the beginning of a word processor session when it is possible to choose whether to open an existing file or a new one. Also the system can choose to perform one task from a set of application tasks depending on its current state.
Concurrency with information exchange (T1|[]| T2)	Two tasks can be executed concurrently but they have to synchronise in order to exchange information. For example, a word processor application where editing a file and scrolling its contents can be performed in any order and they exchange information when they are performed because it is possible to edit only the information that the scrolling has made visible.
Deactivation (T1 [> T2)	The first task is definitively deactivated once the first action of the second task has been performed. This concept is often used in many user interface implementations when the user can deactivate the option of performing a set of tasks and enable a new set of possible task accomplishments by a specific action (for example by selecting a button).
Enabling	In this case one task enables a second one when it

(T1 >> T2)	terminates, for example, a database where users have first to register and then they can interact with the data.
Enabling with information passing (T1 []>>T2),	In this case task T1 provides some information to task T2 other than enabling it. For example, T1 allows the user to specify a query and T2 provides the query result that obviously depends on the information generated by T1.
Suspend-resume (T1 |> T2),	This operator gives T2 the possibility of interrupting T1 and then when T2 is terminated, T1 can be reactivated from the state reached before the interruption. For example, the editing text task which, in some applications can be suspended by a modal printing task, and once the printing task is accomplished then editing can be carried on from the state reached beforehand. For example, this operator can be used to model a type of interruption.
Iteration T*	In the tasks specification we can have some tasks with the * symbol next to their name. This means that the tasks are performed repetitively: when they terminate, the performance of their actions automatically starts to be executed again from the beginning. This continues until the task is deactivated by another task.
Finite Iteration (T1(n))	It is used when designers know in advance how many times a task will be performed.
Optional tasks ([T])	They give the possibility of indicating that the performance of a task is optional. Optional tasks are indicated in square brackets. For example, we have optional tasks when we fill a form in and there are some fields that are mandatory and others optional.
Recursion	This means that in the subtree originated by the task considered there is another occurrence of it. This possibility is used, for example, with tasks that, for each recursion, allows performance of the recursive tasks with the additional possibility of performing some new tasks, until a task interrupting the recursion is performed.

4.4 TASK TYPES

In addition to the category of a task indicating how its performance is allocated, it is useful to identify a set of task types for each category. They are useful to distinguish tasks that raise different requirements in terms of presentation and interaction techniques supporting them.

Examples of task types of user category are:
Planning: a cognitive activity to organise a sequence of actions to perform;

Comparing: when the user has to evaluate some information, such as comparing some quantities or identifying the maximum value from a list of values;

Problem solving: when the user has to find a solution for a problem, for example there is a conflict between the route of two flights and the controller has to find ways to avoid a collision.

We can classify Interaction tasks into various types, for example:

A *Selection* task is very common in many applications. The user can select one or more items from a set or range of items. We can further classify this type of task depending on whether single or multiple selections are supported, whether the selectable items are of the same class.

Edit tasks are tasks that allow users to specify input data and this information can be modified before being definitively sent to the application.

In *Control* tasks the user triggers actions explicitly. This means that this type of interaction task needs to be presented very clearly in the user interface, since triggers have important effects on the overall activity of the user. There is no data type involved in a control task, since its purpose is to generate an event indicating when something should happen.

Application tasks are used to indicate that the application performs an activity. In combination with the purpose of the presentation and the data types, some presentation rules can be defined. There are application tasks that perform some internal processing and then present its results on the user interface, for example:

Overview: the application shows a summary of a set of data that does not provide all the elementary data.

Comparison: the purpose of the presentation generated is to assist the user in comparing the values of some quantities of the same type.

Locate: the application gives detailed information on a set of data so as to allow the user to rapidly find the desired information, giving the option to provide multiple ordering according to multiple criteria.

Grouping: there is a one-to-many relationship among two data attributes which have to be presented at the same time and this relation has to be highlighted in the presentation.

Processing feedback: the application gives information on some processing without requiring a specific request from the user, such as generating feedback on the time left before a certain event.

4.5 ADDITIONAL INFORMATION ASSOCIATED WITH TASKS

4.5.1 Objects

Objects are entities that are manipulated to perform tasks.

They can be classified into two types:

Perceivable objects are either output objects for presenting information (such as windows, tables, graphs) or items which users can interact with using their senses, for example menus, icons, windows, voice, sounds, and so on.

Application objects are entities which belong to the application domain. Information concerning such objects needs to be mapped onto perceivable objects to be presented to the user. Examples of application objects are an order in a business application or a flight in an air traffic control application.

Each object can be manipulated by one or more tasks. In order to identify them during task modelling the designer should answer the following questions:

- Does the task need the user to provide information to the application?
- Does the task need the application to provide information to the user?
- Does the task need to access or manipulate information belonging to the state of the application?

4.5.2 Further task-related information

It is possible to add further information to enrich the description of a task:

- *Informal description.* This is useful to the designer in order to annotate elements that characterise the task considered.
- *Information on time requested for its performance.* In case the designer is interested in gathering information on possible time performance it can be useful to give the option of specifying information about possible time requested to perform the task (for example, minimum requested time, maximum time detected, average time required by the users considered).
- *Frequency.* This is important information especially in designing the interaction techniques supporting the task and their location because more frequent tasks should be better supported and highlighted to guarantee a good user performance.
- *State-related precondition.* Apart from the preconditions derived from the temporal relationships among tasks it is possible to find other preconditions which depend on the values received as input or the current state of the objects of the task. For example, if we consider an application task whose purpose is to present the results of a query to a database it will actually have two options (two subtasks) depending on whether the query requires information which is in the database, if not an error message will be generated, otherwise the query result will be presented.

4.6 STRUCTURING THE TASK MODEL

The hierarchical structure of the task model is represented in a tree-like structure even though the same task can appear in different parts of the model structure. This structure provides a description of possible tasks at different levels of abstraction, ranging from top (more abstract levels) to bottom (more detailed levels). At each level the temporal evolution should be followed reading from left to right. As we will see in the sequel it is possible to go back at some point in a level of the structure by using iterative parent tasks.

4.6.1 The ambiguity problem

A problem when building task models using these operators is the possibility of ambiguity of expressions. For example, in Figure 4.1, we can interpret the specification in two ways: (T1 [] T2) ||| T3 or T1 [] (T2 ||| T3).

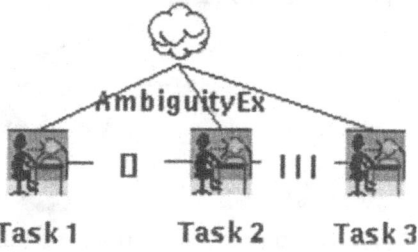

Figure 4.1: An example of ambiguity.

To solve the ambiguity problem we have two options. The first option is to use the priority order among operators:

choice > parallel composition > disabling > enabling

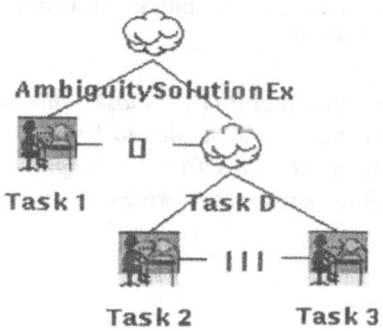

Figure 4.2: A solution to solve ambiguity.

If the designer does not want to use this priority another option is to introduce a task (Task D) which disambiguates the expression, see Figure 4.2. This solution can be adopted only if the new abstract task introduced represents a meaningful logical grouping of the sub tasks.

4.6.2 Inheritance of temporal relationships

If a specific temporal relationship is indicated between two tasks, this relationship holds also for their subtasks. For example, if two tasks are sequential the related subtasks will also share this relationship. In Figure 4.3 we can see an example: since *SelectRoomType* and *MakeReservation* are sequential the choice between *SelectSingleRoom* and *SelectDoubleRoom* can be done only before the performance of the sequence of tasks: *ShowAvailability* and *SelectRoom*.

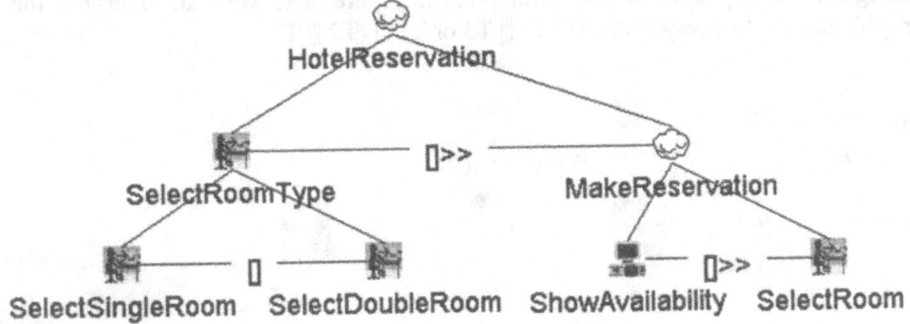

Figure 4.3: An example of inheritance of temporal relationships.

4.6.3 Relationships between parent task and its subtasks

One contribution of ConcurTaskTrees with respect to other notations for building task models is that it provides the semantics associated with the relationships between parent task and its subtasks.

For example, *if a task is iterative and it has subtasks, this means that when the last child is terminated then the first one is enabled to be performed again*. Thus in the example in Figure 4.4, after *CloseCurrentNavigation* is performed then *SelectMuseum* (its first child) can be performed again because the root task is iterative.

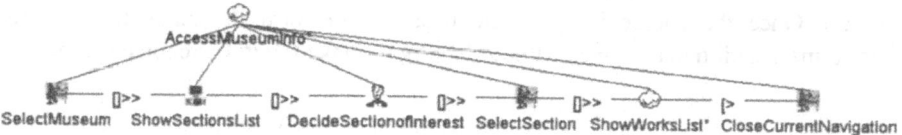

Figure 4.4: Example of parent/children relationships.

The movement of an iterative operator from the parent task to the children or vice versa can have effects on the meaning of the expression. For example, in the next diagram there are two possibilities: two tasks are performed in interleaving in both cases but if the iteration is at the parent level then we mean *order independence performance*: tasks can be executed in any order but before executing them again both tasks have to be terminated. In the second case, with iteration introduced at the subtask level, we have a *continuous interleaving among tasks* which means that once one task is terminated it can be executed again without waiting for the termination of the other task.

An example of order independence is when specifying a request for a flights database then users have to specify both departure and arrival towns but the order is not meaningful (Figure 4.5, left). Once the request is transmitted then a new one can be composed in the same way. An example of continuous interleaving is between the editing of a document task and the printing of the content of the current document task: they can both be executed many times without any limitation on their order (Figure 4.5, right).

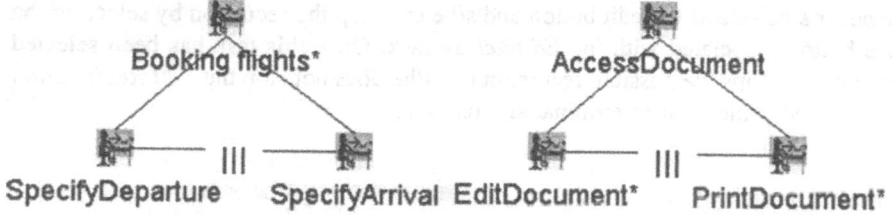

Figure 4.5: An example of order independence and continuous interleaving.

Similarly, if we have the choice operator, instead of the interleaving operator, between the two subtasks, the location of the iterative operator has different effects depending on if it is at the parent or child level. In fact, if it is at the parent level it means an iterative choice of the task to perform, whereas if it is at the child level it means that once the first choice is performed then we can iterate only the performance of the subtask chosen (Figure 4.6). For example, an electronic conference registration allows users to choose whether they want to register as a member of the organising society or not. This choice is repeated every time a user accesses the application. Whereas, we can have an application which allows the user at the beginning to choose whether to navigate on information about a city or its museum. Once the choice is made the user can perform the navigation in the selected information many times without having to make the initial choice again.

Figure 4.6: Examples of iterative choice and iterative performance of task chosen.

4.6.4 Recursion

In ConcurTaskTrees recursion means that we have a task that originates a subtree of tasks that include another occurrence of that task. We can use recursion when, depending on some condition, we want to allow the performance of a task without knowing in advance the number of times it will be performed and, at each new recursion, the performance of a new additional task is allowed. In the task tree it is sufficient to specify the possible recursion (the subtree started by the recursive task considered includes that task again) at only one level to indicate that it may happen more than once.

In the example in Figure 4.7 the user can enable a new hotel registration form whenever s/he selects the edit button and s/he can stop the recursion by selecting the close button associated with the *Edit&close* task. Once this task has been selected then the user stops the possible recursion but s/he does not stop the *Edit Registration* tasks created, which can be terminated separately.

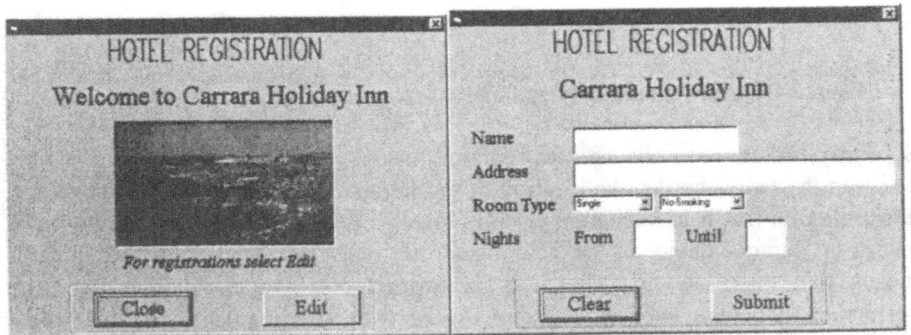

Figure 4.7: An example of recursive interaction.

In ConcurTaskTrees this behaviour can be described in the following way. We have to introduce the *HandleRegistration* task to manage correctly the priorities among operators.

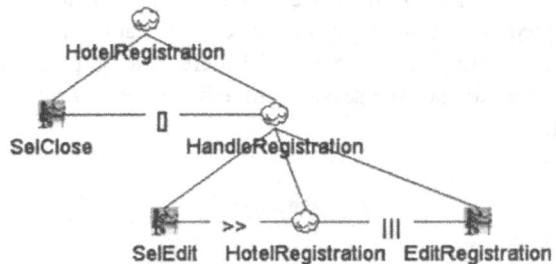

Figure 4.8: The task specification for the example considered.

4.6.5 Optional tasks

The need for an explicit operator indicating optional tasks has been raised by the consideration that there are various applications where some tasks can be enabled at the same time but the fulfilment of all of them is not mandatory for reaching the overall goal. For example, we can have a user interface for booking air flights where we must indicate the airports for departure and arrival and we can optionally give some additional information such as the type of seat (aisle or window) or whether it has to be no-smoking. Whenever we find an optional task it is implicitly indicated a choice between moving immediately to the performance of the next task (if any) or performing the optional task and then moving to the next one.

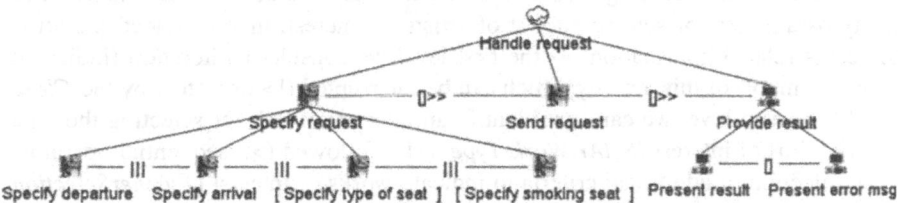

Figure 4.9: An example of an optional tasks in concurrent activities.

The above specification gives a precise indication about which tasks are mandatory and which are optional (those with their names indicated between squared brackets). The semantics of optional tasks allows, in the example shown in Figure 4.9, the performance of both the *Specifying departure, Specifying arrival, Send request* sequence of tasks and the *Specifying departure, Specifying arrival, Specifying type of seat, Send request* sequence of tasks. This means that after having performed the mandatory tasks which are indicated before the enabling operator we can either perform the task at the right of the enabling operator or the optional tasks that are not yet performed, indicated at the left of the enabling operator. However, once the first task at the right of this operator has been performed then the previous optional tasks can no longer be performed.

Optional tasks can also be used to indicate that there are tasks that may precede the performance of another task. If they are started they have to be terminated and cannot be interrupted during their performance as it happens when the disabling operator is used. For example, in Figure 4.10 there is an expression which means that it is possible either to start the session immediately or to first define parameters and then to start it.

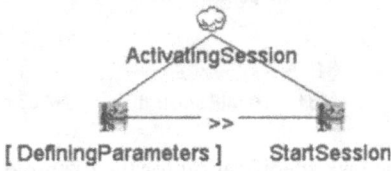

Figure 4.10: An example of a optional task in sequential activities.

4.7 EXAMPLE OF CONCURTASKTREES SPECIFICATION

In this section an example of specification of a task model using ConcurTaskTrees is shown along with an indication of the tasks that are enabled during the evolution of a session.

4.7.1 The first levels of the example

An application for accessing museum information is considered. It allows users to specify parameters for selecting a list of artists of interest, then to select one artist and access related information. At the first level we consider an iteration (indicated by the * symbol) of this activity which can be interrupted ([> operator) by the *Close* task. At the next level we can first identify an interaction task for selecting the type of work of art of interest (*SelArtWorksType* task), followed (>> sequential operator) by the selection of additional criteria to indicate works of interest (*FurtherSelection* task), then ([]>>, sequential operator with information passing) we have an iterative access to the information related to the artists selected (*AccessArtistsInfo* task) which can be closed for going back to the initial selection in order to select a different list of artists (*CloseHandleArtists* task).

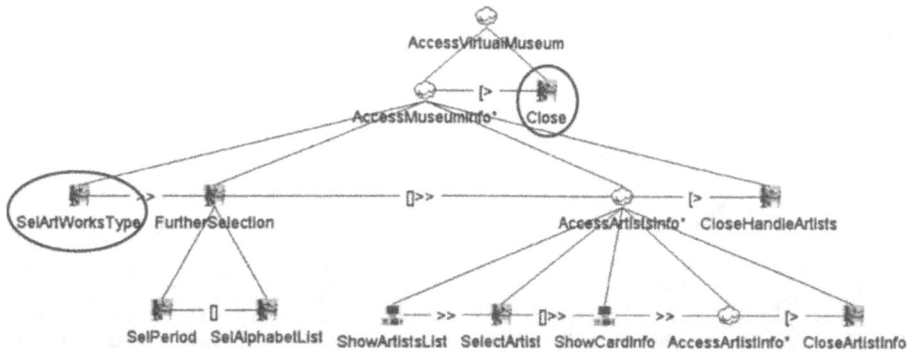

Figure 4.11: The example application at the beginning of the session.

Once we have finished considering the levels in the task tree described in the previous section, we have to decide which tasks can be decomposed into further levels. *SelArtWorksType* can be considered a basic task so it will not be decomposed anymore. The *FurtherSelection* task can be decomposed into two tasks allowing the user to search for an artist both in a global alphabetical list (*SelAlphabetList*) and in a list referring only to a specific period *(SelPeriod* task). The *AccessArtistsInfo* task can be decomposed into: *ShowArtistsList*; *SelectArtist* which allows the user to select one artist from one of the two possible lists; *ShowCardInfo* which shows some brief personal information; *AccessArtistInfo* which allows the user to manipulate all the other possible information concerning the artist selected (it may be useful to look at the current data more times, thus it is an iterative task); *CloseArtistInfo* which allows the user to close the previous task and go back to the option of selecting a new artist. In Figure 4.11 we can see the task model with the two tasks enabled at the beginning of the session highlighted by circles.

In the next figure circles highlight the tasks that are enabled once the artists of interest have been selected. As you can see the enabled tasks are: showing the list of artists selected and the controls required either to close the session or to go back to the main menu.

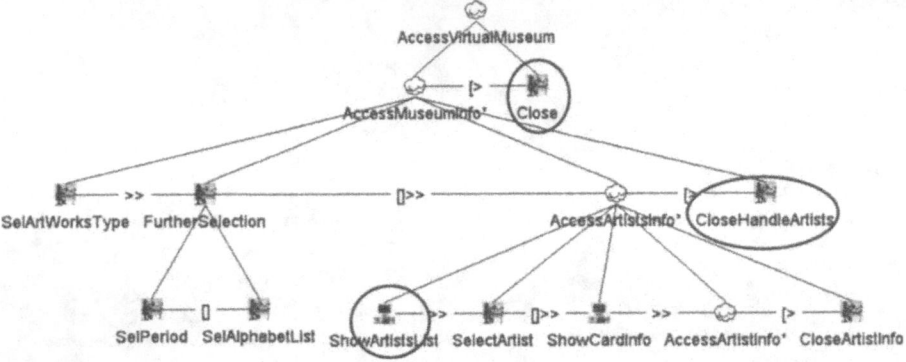

Figure 4.12: The navigation in the example application.

Finally, we can see (Figure 4.13) the tasks enabled (highlighted again by circles) when the user has selected one specific artist. As it was introduced before, one task (*AccessArtistInfo*, describing details on how to browse information on the artist selected) is not further decomposed for sake of brevity and we note that there are three control tasks (*Close, CloseHandleArtists, CloseArtistInfo*) that are enabled for the end user.

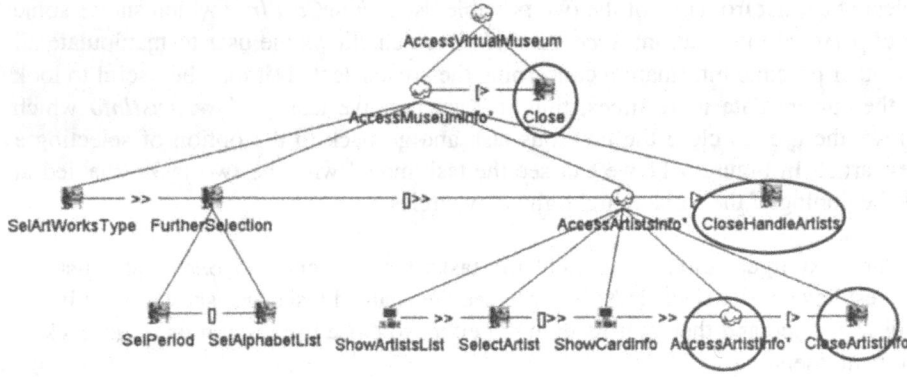

Figure 4.13: The access to the information related to an artist.

4.7.2 Refinement of the example

We can consider the last level of the task tree considered to see how to identify the objects manipulated by the tasks. The *SelPeriod* task needs an object to give the user the option of inserting a historical period for selecting the artists, and an object containing the current user request (*Req_info*). The *SelAlphabetList* task has an object which allows the user to request an alphabetical list of artists and *Req_info*.

The *SelectArtist* task manipulates the objects which visualises the list of artists which are selected by the user. The objects of the *ShowCardInfo* task are the object containing museum information and the object which visualises the first, more meaningful, data about the artist selected. This is an application task because it is completely performed by the application without any action from the user.

The objects associated with the *AccessArtistInfo* task are: the object which allows the user to handle the information related to the selected artist; the object which presents the data requested by the user; and the application object containing data about a specific artist. This object is used by the *ShowCardInfo* task too.

Further decomposing the task model we find that the *AccessArtistInfo* task is decomposed to show the information available on the selected artist (*ShowAvailableInfo* application task) and then allows the user to select the desired information (*SelectInfo* task) which can be the information available in the library (*PresLibrary* task) or a biography of the artist (*PresBiography* task) or related to video available about the artist (*PresVideoList* task) or about material which is sold containing information about the artist (*Browselling* task) or about the bibliography (*PresBibliography* task).

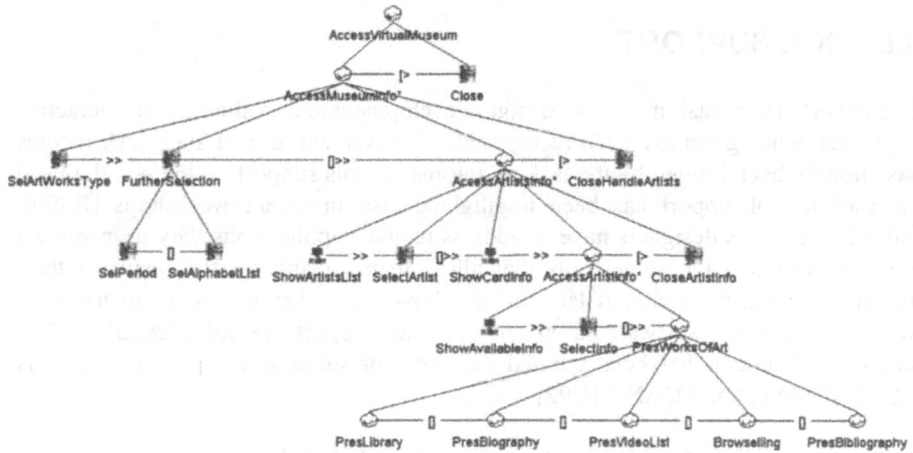

Figure 4.14: Further expansion of the task model.

Then we can carry on the task specification until we obtain the final version which is represented in Figure 4.15. It mainly describes how the user can have information about artists (biography, related videos, bibliography, etc.).

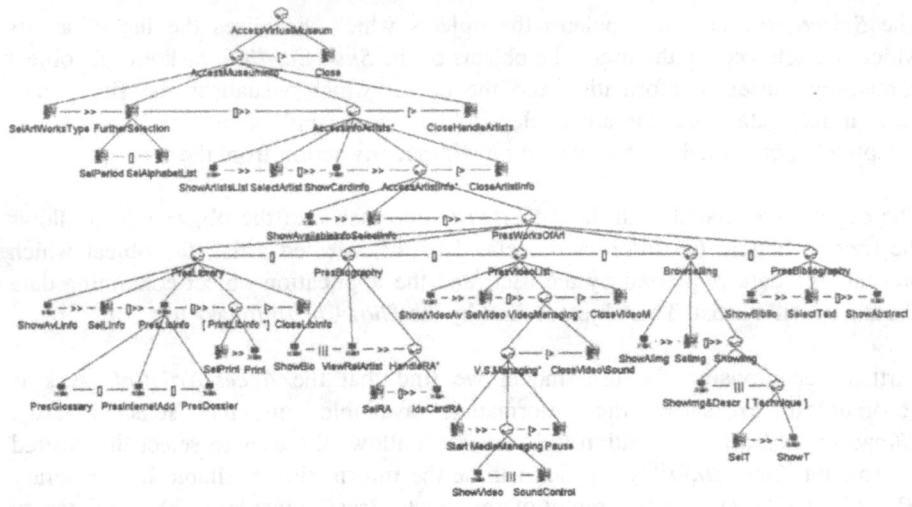

Figure 4.15: The final task model.

4.8 TOOL SUPPORT

The importance of task models in design, development and evaluation of interactive applications has generally been recognised. However, the use of such task models has strongly been limited by the lack of automatic tools supporting them and a need for such a tool-support has been highlighted also in recent workshops [BS99]. Indeed, as soon as designers have to address realistic applications they immediately feel the need to have some tools that allow them to analyse the result of their modelling work, to modify it later on, to show it to other people or to use it to implement concrete software-based artefacts that support the tasks identified. The lack of tool support has been pointed out even for successful approaches such as GOMS [CMN83] and UAN [HG92].

Different types of tools can be used in relation to task models:

- *tools that help in developing task models using information contained in informal material* (such as scenarios or textual use cases), as discussed in Chapter 3;
- *tools for editing and analysing the content of a task model, including the simulation of its dynamic behaviour;*
- *tools for supporting the design and/or the generation of user interfaces*, as discussed in Chapter 5;
- *tools for supporting usability evaluation*, as described in Chapter 8.

The tools for task-driven user interface design and development can follow two different approaches:

- *completely automatic*: where the tool according to the criteria incorporated generates the user interface;
- *semi-automatic*: where the tools give suggestions leaving the user the option to tailor them to the specific case study or to introduce new types of solution.

Which approach is preferable depends on the type of designer using it and the type of application considered. If designers are not expert and the application domain is well defined and not particularly large in terms of design issues then an automatic approach can be feasible, whereas if the designer is expert or the applications considered raise a wide variety of design issues that cannot be completely solved in advance then the semi-automatic approach is advisable.

The specification of ConcurTaskTrees is supported by an automatic tool publicly available at http://giove.cnuce.cnr.it/ctte.html, developed at the HCI group at CNUCE and implemented in Java. It provides various types of functionalities:

- *to allow designers to input and edit the information requested by the notation*: tasks and their attributes (name, category, type, related objects, ...), temporal relationships among tasks and other information;
- *to help designers in improving the layout of their specification*: supporting automatic lining up, movement of levels or subtrees of the task model, cut and paste of pieces of task model, folding and unfolding of subtrees, possibility to add tasks as sibling or as child of the current task, etc....;
- *to check completeness of the specification*: for example it is possible to automatically detect whether temporal operators among tasks at the same level are missing or whether there is a task with only one child.
- *to save the specification or parts of it in various formats:* the tool also supports functionalities such as inserting other task models in the current one or saving images containing the task model or part of it so that they can easily be included in reports or documents, saving the task model in XML format to easily export it in other environments.
- *to simulate the task model:* this is useful both in the development of the model and once the result is satisfying, as an interactive documentation of design decisions.

The tool gives also some useful statistical information on the task model: number of levels and of basic tasks, number of iterative and optional tasks, number of tasks for each category (the category of a task indicates how its performance is allocated, to the user or to the application or to their interaction), number of occurrences of each operator used to describe the temporal relationships. When there are mistakes in the specification detected by the tool it is possible to select one error and then automatically the tool highlights the related part of the specification. Figure 4.16 shows the layout of the current implementation of the tool.

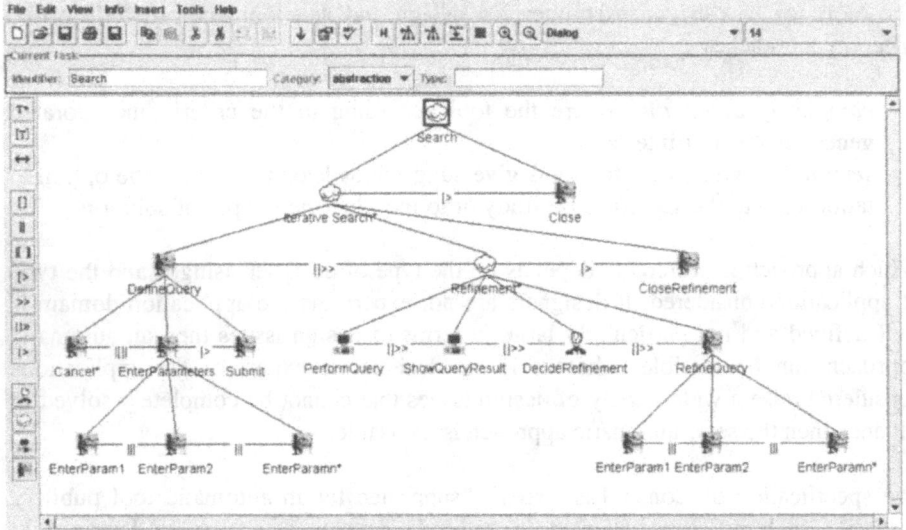

Figure 4.16: The layout of the editor of ConcurTaskTrees specifications.

Additional support can be given to check that the use of the operators is semantically correct. For example, to avoid the situation where an iterative task is followed by a sequential operator. In this case the problem is that by definition the iterative task does not terminate and so it is not possible to say when it finishes in order to allow the performance of another task. Whereas if it was followed by a disabling operator then it would be clear that the first action of the disabling task would stop the performance of the iterative task.

The information in the task model can be used to perform automatically other types of analysis: for example, reachability analysis to check whether from a certain state it is possible to reach the performance of a certain task or to count the number of interactions required to reach a goal.

4.9 TASK MODELS FOR COOPERATIVE APPLICATIONS

The increasing diffusion of Internet connections and the improvement of the speed of data transmission makes cooperation possible among various people, through computers in many types of application areas. Additionally, communication among people is getting more and more sophisticated and effectively increasing the interrelations in an organization. A significant part of our activities are spent in a group. Most applications are no longer a process where an object is passed from one hand to another until it is finished but a process where more than one person could be acting on a common object, in some cases at the same time.

However, the attention to cooperative aspects has grown in different contexts with partially overlapping concepts and goals. The design of multi-user applications has sometimes been developed under one-to-one philosophy, losing much of the great versatility that multi-user application could have. Thus, we need to develop interfaces that allow users to interact with other people who are manipulating the same object either at the same time or later.

One of the biggest advantages to working alone, and maybe the main reason why some people prefer this way of working, is that all the transformations that happen to the object with which we are working are immediately known. It is not only the immediate information that makes this work style so interesting but also because it is clear why this transformation took place, when, how and, of course, by whom. When users are working in groups the situation is quite different, but we still have to try to support all the information that working alone on an object gives by itself. This is basically what is called *awareness*. In a group it is of much interest how, when and which information is presented to the members of the group.

The purpose of this section is to highlight the more important aspects of cooperative systems and discuss how ConcurTaskTrees can be helpful for the design of a cooperative environment.

4.9.1 Possible approaches to design cooperative task models

Task models for cooperative applications need to integrate different aspects. Designers can specify models describing the tasks performed by users with different roles and then they have to indicate their relationships. A role identifies a set of tasks to perform and their relationships. One person can have different roles.

Cooperative task models should allow designers to analyse such models from different angles and to check their consistency and completeness. The viewpoints considered in ConcurTaskTrees [PST98] are essentially of two types: the first one is the viewpoint of individual users, the second refers to the relationships among the tasks of various users in reaching global objectives. For example in air traffic control (ATC) applications there are many *subjective* views (the strategic controller's view, the executive controller's view, the pilot's view), and one view which gives an overall description of the working environment including coordination and communication between users.

We can define a cooperative task as *a task that requires activities from two or more users for its performance*. After a user has performed a subtask belonging to a cooperative task, some reaction by one or more users is expected and necessary in order to complete the task. For example, the handling of the transfer of one flight to a new sector or the management of the conflict among two flights are two cooperative tasks since they require activities by more than one user. On the contrary, annotating one flight strip is not a cooperative task, according to our definition, because only one user performs it even though it might be a subtask of a cooperative task. Note that in a cooperative environment, *all* the activities performed by the users obviously aim to eventually achieve the global goals. Nevertheless, it is better to define *cooperative* as being only those tasks that strictly define the structure of cooperation, so we can highlight the roles that users play with respect to the whole cooperative activity.

As discussed in [PST98] in order to extend the ConcurTaskTrees notation to explicitly provide representations of cooperative aspects there are at least three solutions:

- *A monolithic solution*: to develop directly one global task model including cooperative and single users tasks (see Figure 4.17). Note that in this figure (as in the next two figures) the parent-child relationship describes the hierarchical decomposition of the task in its sub-tasks.

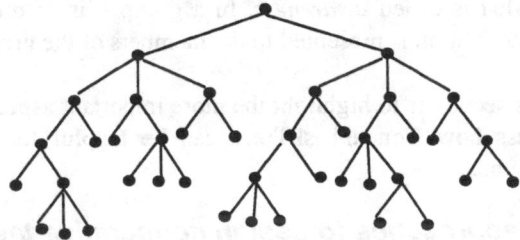

Figure 4.17: The monolithic solution for cooperative task models.

- *A graph-oriented solution*: to join together the task tree of each role involved in a single structure so that any co-related actions or sub-tasks (performed by distinct users) are connected by lines or arcs with operators showing existing temporal relationships. For example, it should be possible to represent a task of user1 activating a task of user2 by a line connecting the two tasks and the indication of the related temporal relationship associated with it (see Figure 4.18). Thus the arcs provide additional constraints to those specified in the task trees.

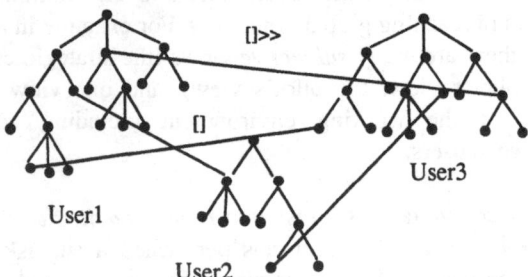

Figure 4.18: A possible representation of relationships among tasks of different users

- *A solution with an additional cooperative task solution*: to add another tree (the *Co-operative* tree) which shows the temporal relationship among cooperative tasks (see Figure 4.19). Thus, we decompose such cooperative tasks until we reach tasks performed by single users. For each basic task the user who performs it is indicated. Then, for each role, a task model indicating the related tasks is still maintained. Thus the basic tasks in the cooperative part can be further decomposed in the task specification of the related user. For example, in Figure 4.19, task t1 is decomposed in the task model of the related role (User1).

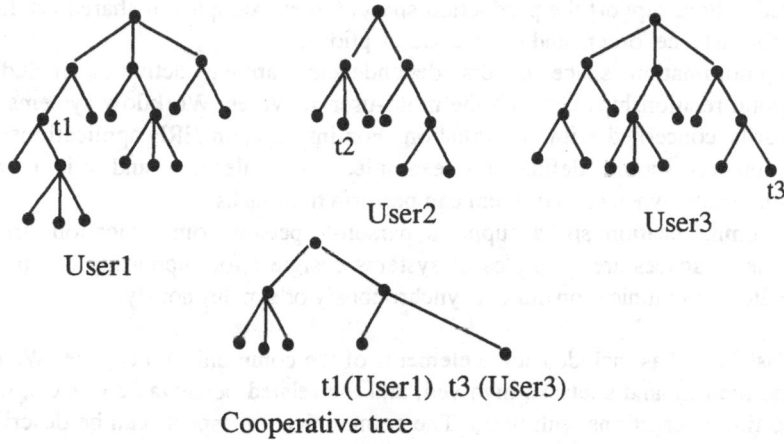

Figure 4.19: Another possible representation of cooperative tasks.

The first solution can easily generate task models that are too complex to interpret because of the high number of nodes and arcs required by a unique tree structure. Although the second solution is immediate, it does not seem to be the most effective especially when there is a high number of relations. In fact, as shown in Figure 4.18, the understanding of the overall behaviour might be difficult because the intersecting links could generate a complex graph.

The third solution (i.e. an additional cooperative task) seems to be more suitable because it enables designers to edit the cooperative part of the task model separately. It is thus possible to focus on both single user activities and their cooperation in a modular way. This solution highlights the communicative and coordination aspects in the tasks that involve cooperation between two or more users, their main features and their relationships.

4.9.2 Describing multi-user cooperation in ConcurTaskTrees

In this section we describe how ConcurTaskTrees can describe the different activities that are carried out in a cooperative task following the approach introduced in the previous section. The use of task models for designing and developing multi-user applications can overcome some limitations of current toolkits for their development that even when they address innovative solutions [RG96] they provide development environments which are still difficult to use.

As described in [CCN97] a groupware system covers three domain specific functions: production, coordination and communication:

- The production space denotes the set of domain objects that model the multi-user elaboration of common artefacts such as documents, or that motivate a common undertaking such as flying an airplane between two places. Typically, shared editors support the production space. Other examples of shared artefacts are, for instance, orders and product descriptions.
- The coordination space covers dependencies among activities including temporal relationships between the multi-user activities. Workflow systems are primarily concerned with coordination. For instance, in ERP applications the coordination should define, for example, how salesmen and clients can communicate, when each of them can perform their tasks.
- The communication space supports person-to-person communication. Email and media spaces are examples of systems designed for supporting computer-mediated communication either asynchronously or synchronously.

ConcurTaskTrees has included some elements of the communication space. We can easily find the role and subtasks involved, and the related perceivable objects, used for supporting interactions with users. The communication aspects can be described with these elements.

In the representation of ConcurTaskTrees there are operands that allow designers to describe coordination aspects of a cooperative task, indicating if they have to be performed in a certain order, simultaneously, or if no order is needed. In cooperative systems, where users are working together to get a common goal, the cooperative tasks are composed of subtasks, which end in elementary tasks that are performed by different users.

Besides tasks, it is possible to describe the domain objects in ConcurTaskTrees that compose the production space. For each task it is possible to indicate the objects that it needs to manipulate during its performance. One object can be manipulated by tasks performed by different users.

When developing a task model for cooperative applications, designers first have to identify the roles involved. A role is defined by a set of tasks and a set of relationships among such tasks. Each role has a cardinality indicating the number of users that can be active with that role during an application session. The cardinality can be one, a fixed predefined number or a variable number (in this case the number of users with the considered role will depend on the dynamic evolution of the application). In the case of variable number it is possible to indicate a maximum number of users in that role that can be active at the same time.

In the specification of the cooperative aspects we can still use a hierarchical representation with operators to describe temporal relationships among tasks at the same abstraction level. Thus we obtain an additional task tree whose main purpose is to define the relationships of the task trees associated with each type of user. In this task tree we decompose the cooperative tasks until we obtain tasks performed by a single user. If such tasks can be further decomposed into subtasks performed by that user, the description of this decomposition is given in the task tree associated with the related user.

In Figure 4.20 an example of an editor for cooperative task models is shown. It allows the designer to interactively select the part of the specification of interest. In this case an application for air traffic control is considered and it contains the description of the cooperative part and then the task model for each role considered (executive controller, strategic controller, pilot).

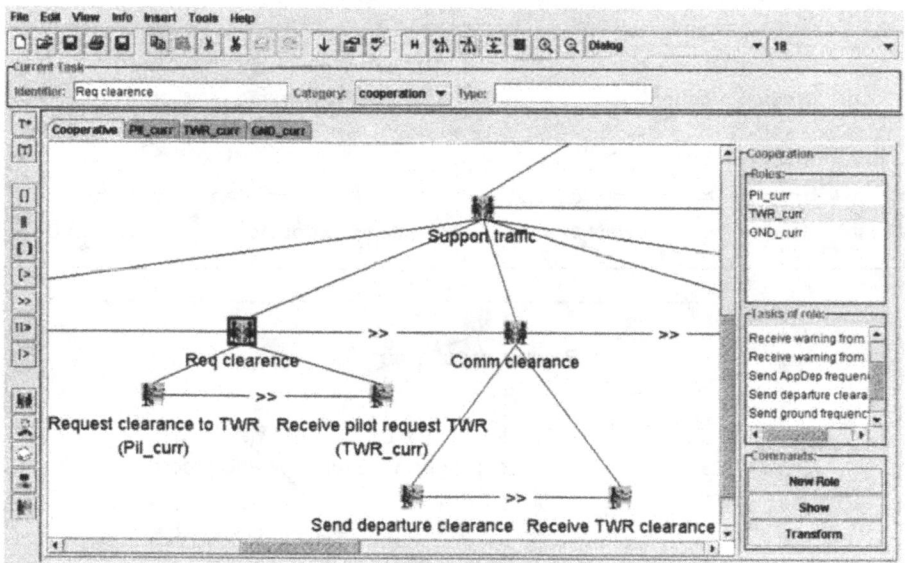

Figure 4.20: The tool supporting analysis and editing of cooperative task models.

The leaves of the cooperative task tree can be either *basic* or *high level* tasks in the tree of the related user. In the first case, leaves in the cooperative tree remain leaves in the trees of the related users, whereas in the latter case the leaves in the cooperative tree will be further decomposed in the tree of the related user. In the tool that supports the editing of cooperative task models, when the user selects a basic task in the model of the cooperative part this triggers another window. The new window shows the decomposition of the selected task in the task tree of the corresponding user, thus highlighting their relationships. The purpose of the cooperative part of the overall task model is not only to identify cooperative tasks but also to indicate their temporal relationships, these have the effect of defining additional constraints for the tasks relative to each role.

In Figure 4.21 there is a simplified example to introduce this approach (>> is the sequential operator). Below there is the cooperative part and above the two simplified set of tasks associated with the two user roles. For the sake of brevity we will only consider a small subset of the tasks that should be included if we were to describe a cooperative application supporting negotiation between a customer and a salesman.

In the example, if we considered the two roles without the cooperative part we would have at the beginning the *Ask information* and *Provide list products* tasks enabled to be performed. However, the cooperative part adds the additional constraint that *Provide list products* can be performed only after *Ask information*, thus at the beginning only *Ask information* is enabled.

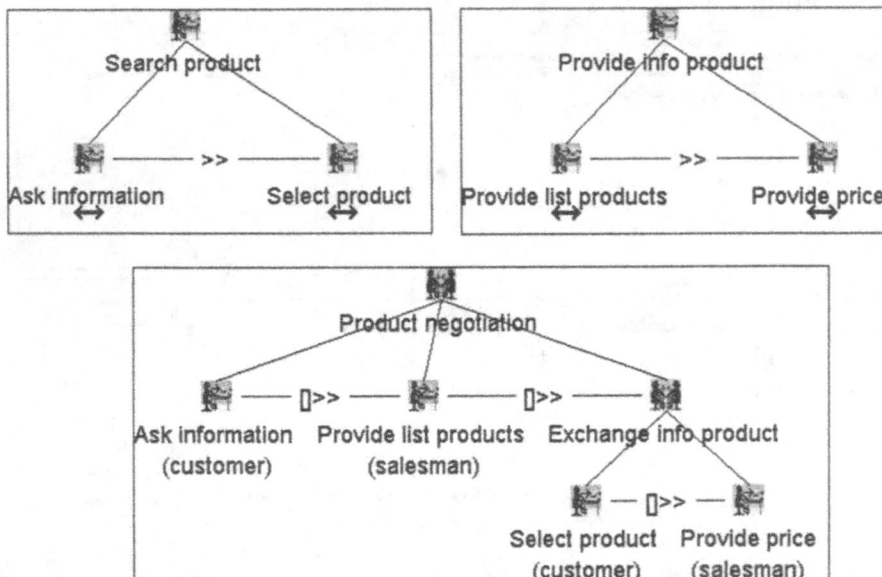

Figure 4.21: A simplified example of the parts composing a task model for a cooperative application.

As it is easy to understand the cooperative part allows designers to provide a declarative specification of session managers that control when enabling and disabling the interaction techniques available for each user depending on the state of the cooperations among them.

In order to develop and analyse a cooperative task model we can follow two main approaches:

- a *top-down* approach, in which — starting from the overall activity related to the interactive application considered — we should derive the activities of the single roles and to what extent every role contributes to carry out the general activity;
- a *bottom-up* approach, where the first analysis of every role's activity with the consequent initial task allocation helps to achieve a more modular comprehension of the overall behaviour in the cooperative application.

It is worth pointing out that the development of the specification is not a one-step process. It is an iterative process because once designers have defined the specification of all the task trees (one tree for every role, and the cooperative tree) they have to check and modify them until the complete and correct specification is achieved. For example, if designers, while analysing whether all the activities have been described in the cooperative tree discover that some are missing, they must add them in the cooperative tree and then analyse how each role takes part in them and probably perform some refinement also on the related parts.

Designers can specify the following information for each basic cooperative task (a cooperative task which is no longer decomposed into other cooperative tasks):

- roles of users involved and their cardinality;
- names of the sub-tasks which have to be performed by each role involved;
- the objects which are manipulated to perform the task, they can be either perceivable or application objects, it is possible to specify for each role involved whether the related users can also modify it;
- some additional informal comments that can be added to further describe the task or some of its main features.

T3	Task name = ModifyTransfPar
Roles and sub-tasks	Strategic$_i$: RequestNewParameter, ReceiveNewParameter Strategic$_{(i+1)}$:ReceiveRequestNewParameter, SendNewParam.
Domain Objects	Frequency, Sector, Flight (these objects cannot be modified).
Perceivable Objects	Telephone
Role Cardinality	Strategic$_i$: Strategic$_{(i+1)}$ (1,1)
[Comments]	The strategic controller interacts with the strategic controller of a neighbouring sector in order to negotiate the parameters of one flight which is changing sector

Figure 4.22: An example of attributes associated with a cooperative task.

Figure 4.22 describes an example of a cooperative task that concerns the change of parameters of a flight when it is changing sector. It involves two strategic controllers belonging to two different sectors. Both of them can require or send new flight parameters. They interact by telephone and they cannot be interrupted while discussing.

4.10 EXERCISES

1. Specify in ConcurTaskTrees the task model describing how to cook your preferred food.
2. Specify the task model describing how to register at university.
3. Specify the task model associated with the web site of your organisation.
4. Specify the task model of a cooperative application according to the definition given in the chapter.
5. Specify the task model for a cooperative application that involves at least three roles.
6. Specify the task model of a cooperative application for electronic commerce.

5 Task-Based Design

While there are many visual environments that allow developers to easily obtain user interfaces, it is still difficult to obtain effective user interfaces. Task models can give useful support for this purpose. The purpose of this chapter is to discuss such a support.

5.1 APPROACHES TO TASK-BASED DESIGN

In many current approaches to the design of interactive applications, one of these two limitations can often be found:

- *Design completely based on ad hoc solutions and the intuition of the designer*: this can be successful in a few cases but generally designers will have to solve problems without having methods supporting elements to provide effective solutions. This implies that designers are proposing ineffective solutions or an inconsistent design where in similar situations different solutions are provided thus confusing the end user.
- *Lack of consideration for user requirements*: there are approaches oriented to the systematic structure of the data and/or the software architecture; they are useful for solving technical and implementation problems but they often overlook the introduction of user oriented elements, thus allowing designers and developers to obtain implementations which are functionally correct and engineered from the implementation point of view but still with inadequate usability.

5.1.1 Main aspects in task-based design

It is thus important to develop methods which support designers in their work by highlighting relevant aspects to take into account and giving suggestions about possible solutions. This support can be given following three different modalities:

- *manual*: where there are some predefined criteria but the designer has complete freedom on how to apply them, however this freedom may also mean that the designer has low support and so may not be able to identify effective solutions;
- *semi-automatic*: this is often the better solution as it implies the existence of an automatic tool able to highlight possible criteria and solutions still giving the designer the possibility to tailor them to the specific case study;
- *completely automatic*: where there is a tool able to take into account some criteria and to generate the final solution. However this approach seems promising when the tool is used to design a limited set of possible applications which share various features otherwise it becomes rather difficult for the tool to generate always effective solutions.

The task model can be used to drive the design of the interactive application underlying the user interface that will be used to communicate with the user. More specifically, the task model is useful for designing more user-oriented interactions because they will be structured according to the user's conceptual model of the possible activities. The task model can give useful suggestions of what information should be available and what interaction techniques should be enabled at any time in the user interface and how to design it to facilitate the user task performance.

The resulting process is described in Figure 5.1. After an informal domain and task analysis designers can structure their task model that is used, with the possible support of some tool, to derive a user interface that can be tested by end users.

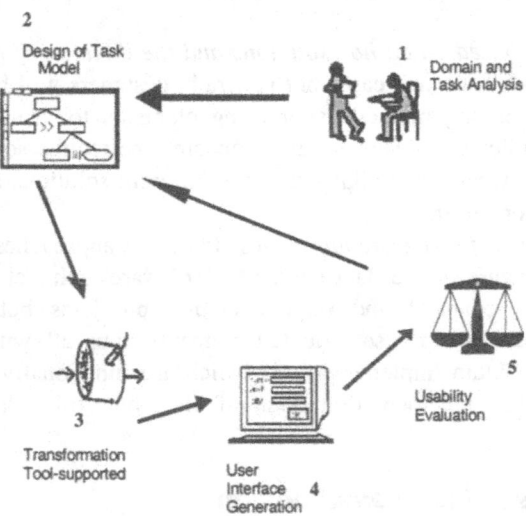

Figure 5.1: Task-based design of interactive applications.

It is possible to provide methods that allow designers to use the task model to identify the elements of an interactive application and their relationships. To this end there are different criteria to take into account:

- *Criteria for designing the presentation*: a *presentation* defines how a user interface provides a set of information to the user at a certain time. Depending on different aspects, such as the type of task, we have different requirements for choosing the media and the related interaction and presentation techniques in the user interfaces which should support the task performance.
- *Criteria for designing the dialogue*: they are mainly based on the analysis of the temporal relationships among tasks which should be supported and give indications about when to enable interaction techniques and links in the interactive application.
- *Criteria to structure the information*: they indicate how to structure the data which is contained in the interactive application.

5.1.2 Approaches to designing presentations

The design of the presentation of modern interactive user interfaces is often complex and requires in-depth design knowledge. It is thus important to identify declarative models and inference mechanisms that significantly reduce the demands on the interface developer.

The problem of designing effective presentations of information has stimulated a growing discussion over the last years. Mackinlay's APT system [M86] is a presentation tool that automatically designs static, two-dimensional graphic presentations of relational information. Mackinlay's definition of a graphical design is an abstract description of an image that indicates the graphical techniques (such as the position on the axis, or colour variation) that are used to encode information. The fundamental assumption of this approach is that graphical presentations are sentences of graphical languages, which are similar to other formal languages in that they have precise definitions of their syntax and semantics. The graphic design issues are codified as expressiveness and effectiveness criteria for graphical languages:

- *Expressiveness* criteria determine whether a graphical language can express the desired information. For this purpose it is important that the language is able to communicate, all and only, the facts that the application has to communicate.
- *Effectiveness* criteria determine whether a graphical language exploits the capabilities of the human visual system.

An example of graphical language that is not expressive according to this definition is a bar chart used to code the nationality of types of cars (car makes and models). The lengths of the bars suggest an ordering as some cars were longer or better than other cars which is not true for the nationality attribute. Unlike expressiveness, effectiveness also depends on the capabilities of the perceiver. Thus Mackinlay extended previous studies using existing psychophysical results and various analyses of the different perceptual tasks to provide a ranking of various graphical attributes to present different types of data (quantitative, ordinal, nominal). The resulting ranking is described in Figure 5.2.

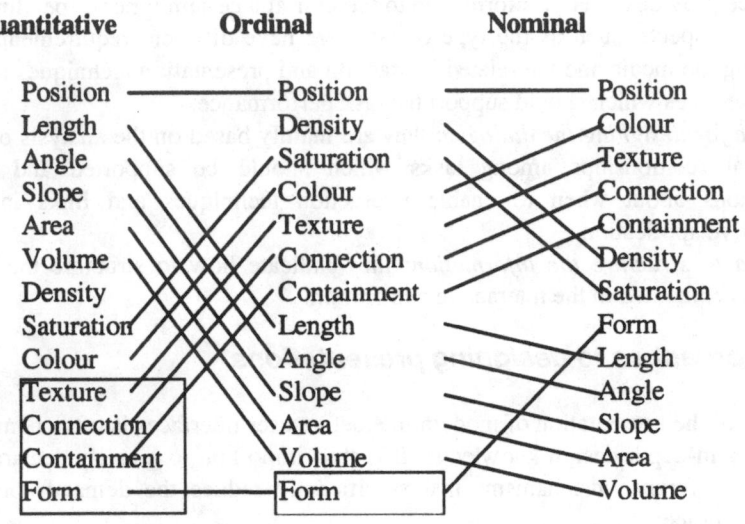

Figure 5.2: Mackinlay's ranking of graphical attributes from [M96].

The APT design algorithm is based on the analysis of the information to be presented. The data space is divided into nominal, ordinal, and quantitative data and the graphical attributes used to design the graphical representations are ranked in terms of effectiveness in presenting the type of data considered. The set of possible two-dimensional presentations which it considers is limited. Multimedia technologies are not considered in this work as they were not widely available when it was developed. Furthermore, a composition algebra is used, which composes primitive graphical languages, and generates different graphical designs. The possible compositions are limited to very simple graphical cases (such as scatter plots which refer to the same type of data), thus providing an indication of an important problem (how to compose different presentation techniques), rather than a solution to it.

Casner's BOZ [C91] is an automated graphic design and presentation tool which designs graphics based on the analysis of the task that a graphic is supposed to support. BOZ analyses a logical description of a user task and designs a provably equivalent perceptual task, by substituting perceptual inferences for logical inferences in the task description. It then designs and renders a graphic which represents data so that each perceptual inference is supported and the visual search is made easier. In BOZ every task description is defined over a finite collection of domain sets. For every logical operator in a task, BOZ generates a corresponding vector that indicates the domain sets of information manipulated by that operator. BOZ determines relationships between vectors by applying an ordered set of four rules (conjoint, parallel, orthogonal, disjoint) to the complete set of vectors in a task description. The relationships found among vectors suggest ways to present data. Information relevant to disjoint vectors should appear in different presentations, since the task does not require the different types of information to be used together.

In [RM90] Roth and Mattis show how to use data characterisation for intelligent graphics presentations. In their approach they consider data types, properties of relational structure (such as functional dependencies, relational coverage), cardinality and so on. Such an approach has been extended in the work by Roth and others [RKMG94] where they introduce three complementary modules to create graphics: SageBrush, SageBook, and SAGE. The last one is the main module; the other two are extensions. SageBrush allows users to sketch graphics so that they can explicitly specify the features which the final graphic will present. SageBook allows users to select, from a collection of previously created graphics, those which are the most appropriate for their needs. Users can thus reuse graphics to present some data or, simply, as a starting point for the visualisation of new data by extending them for new needs. On the basis of knowledge of the type of data to present and the goals of the user, SAGE generates the presentations automatically. To select the most appropriate presentation for the data and user goals, this module uses effectiveness and expressiveness criteria which are an extension of those introduced in APT. However, SAGE differs from APT and BOZ in that it can generate graphic presentations both when the user provides complete specifications for the design of the graphic presentation (by SageBrush and SageBook), and also when the user does not provide them. Further, SAGE can receive partial specifications, for each level included between the two extreme points mentioned above.

Sutcliffe and Faraday [SF94] developed a method for the design of multimedia presentations which can support user tasks. The method is based on the analysis of tasks and resources. The task analysis is performed by creating trees of subgoals. For each subgoal the following are specified: the type of information needed to perform the subgoal; the dialogue acts which are used to indicate the communication effect that the designers want to obtain; and the resource analysis, which provides a description of the resources available to the designer to present data and the possible access procedures. To select which resource to use to support a given task some information is considered, above all the dialogue acts contained in the task model. On the basis of dialogue acts and the information required, the method indicates the most appropriate presentation. This is an interesting general approach which provides useful criteria for multimedia user interface designers, however the possibility to provide automatic tool support highlighting when and how to apply such criteria is not considered.

A good collection of papers concerning the more general topic of information visualisation can be found in [CMS99].

5.2 ASPECTS TO CONSIDER WHEN DESIGNING USER INTERFACES

In designing the presentations supporting the various tasks we have to take into account many aspects, for example:

- *Task type:* we can decide the type of presentation according to the type of task, taking into account what information is required to perform it. For example, if the task has to consider a spatial relationship it is important to provide a graphical presentation which highlights the elements defining it rather than textual descriptions. Section 4.4 discussed examples of task types.
- *Cognitive effort:* there are different ways to reduce the cognitive effort required from the user. There are models for cognitive architectures, such as ICS [BM95], that allow designers to foresee possible cognitive problems. It is important to balance the use of different media, especially when they are used to support concurrent tasks, an example is when short information, complementary to that presented on the screen, is given by audio. Generally, it is possible to read a text and at the same time hear a sound or to speak, and to watch images simultaneously, whereas it is problematic to hear a long description and to read text at the same time. It is important to exploit the capabilities of our cognitive system to blend information which is perceived by different perception channels; however this blending needs to be helped, for example, by synchronising carefully information which is presented by different media at the same time;
- *Task frequency:* it is also important to optimise the resources used within a certain media to support frequent tasks or frequent sequences of tasks. Thus the interaction techniques supporting frequent tasks should be highlighted in the presentation, and have more space available, and, similarly, interaction techniques used to support tasks that are performed frequently in sequence should be close to each other, for example, if we know that the user often has to use a scrollbar and then to select a button, this control should be placed close to the scrollbar.
- *Contextual environment:* we have to take into account the context in which the application is used, for example if it is a communal area then it may be noisy and so audio or voice input are not effective.
- *User knowledge:* depending on the user's knowledge of the application domain we should present the information in a different way; for example, if the user is a beginner then a limited amount of information with clear fonts and colours should be preferred.
- *Layout optimisation:* the performance of the same task sometimes requires different amounts of information depending on the specific instances of objects involved (for example when presenting works of art, some of them may require longer descriptions). This means that the structure of the presentation remains the same (the interaction techniques and the links are in the same part of the presentation) but either to avoid leaving large parts of the screen unused, some part of the layout is automatically resized, or, when there is a lot of information,

it has to be split into multiple presentations sharing the same structure but with different information.

5.3 CRITERIA FOR GROUPING TASKS TO BE SUPPORTED BY THE SAME PRESENTATION

This section describes how to use information contained in a task model expressed in ConcurTaskTrees notation for identifying the presentations of an interactive application. The basic idea is to analyse the temporal relationships of the tasks to identify those that should be enabled at the same time and thus be supported by the same presentation of the user interface and, similarly, to identify the dynamic order among such presentations.

5.3.1 Identifying presentations

When designing a user interface usually one important aspect to consider is that there is a large set of possibilities in terms of the number of distinct presentations. The concept of enabled task set can be useful for identifying such presentations. An *enabled task set* is a set of tasks that are logically enabled to start their performance during the same period of time. One task can belong to multiple enabled task sets. If multiple tasks belong to the same enabled task set it means that they are enabled at the same time and consequently the related interaction techniques should belong to the same presentation. Generally, there are three types of approaches in identifying the presentations for an interactive application:

- *One unique presentation supporting all the possible tasks*: this is possible for simple applications, otherwise it can easily generate confusing user interfaces with a lot of interaction techniques and this high number can mean that rather limited space is allocated to each of them;
- *As many presentations as the number of possible enabled task sets*: The number of enabled task sets associated with a task model is the upper bound to the number of distinct possible presentations meaningful from the task model point of view because a higher number of such presentations would imply that the user interface imposes a sequential order on the performance of some tasks that could be enabled concurrently.
- *Intermediate solutions*: where tasks belonging to different enabled task sets are supported by the same presentation; this can be done, for example, when there are tasks that should be performed in sequence many times, and they exchange information, so they are tightly connected from a logical point of view and the related presentations could be merged. An example is the sequence between a task formulating a request and that presenting the related result. They are sequential so belonging to different enabled task sets. However, users can prefer to see both of them at the same time so that, especially in requests where there is an iterative refinement process, they can know what request has generated the current result to decide how to refine it.

The indications for designing the user interface can be generated by a visit to the task tree. This visit can be done top-down to identify the tasks that are enabled at the same time. Next, designers can take the tasks that are in the same set and indicate how to design a presentation of the user interface supporting them. These indications can be derived taking into account the temporal operators among tasks, the task types, and the structure of the tasks involved in the enabled task set. For example:

- Tasks that have to communicate information with each other should be placed in close proximity so that the user can understand immediately their relationships.
- If there is a choice among tasks to perform then we know that the related presentation should highlight what the various choices available are.
- If there is a disabling task then we know that we have a control task, which may be placed in a predefined location, whose purpose is to disable one or more other tasks.

We can try to identify whether the group of tasks considered corresponds to some predefined task pattern. Then it is possible to apply specific layout policies in order to define the structure of the overall presentation. For each basic task it is possible to identify the specific presentation using some predefined task-oriented presentation templates which take into account the semantics of the task. Basic tasks are those tasks which are not further decomposed in the task model. They correspond to the leaves of the task tree. In this analysis it is also important to consider the properties of the data that have to be presented (data type, cardinality, data relationships) in order to understand the type of presentation that they require.

In bottom-up approaches designers associate a possible presentation to each basic task and then they have the problem of composing these basic presentations to obtain the overall presentation of the user interface of the application. Associating a presentation to a basic task in isolation with respect to the design of the other basic tasks may result in low effective presentations which conflict with the type of design choices and generate bad overall presentations, whereas with top-down approaches it is possible first to make the overall design decisions and then refine each basic presentation within a common framework.

5.3.2 Identifying enabled task sets

We have seen that enabled task sets can give support to identify the presentations of an interactive application. In order to identify the enabled task sets we can define a task in terms of its subtasks and related operators. For example, the *Printing* task can be decomposed into the sequential composition of *Selecting a file*, *Selecting parameters*, and *Print* subtasks. Since the semantics of many temporal relationships depends on the first action (in our case the first subtask) of the task considered we need to introduce two functions:

- *First,* which takes a task and provides the set of subtasks that can be the first subtask to be accomplished when the task is performed (in the *Printing* example it would return the *Selecting a file* subtask);
- *Body,* which takes a task and provides the set of subtasks that are not included in the First set (in the *Printing* example it would return the *Selecting parameters* and *Print* subtasks).

With the support of these two functions we can analyse the task tree to identify the set of tasks which are enabled at the same time. Some rules to identify the enabled task sets which depend on the temporal operator are:

- independent concurrent tasks (tasks composed by the ||| operator) and communicating concurrent tasks (|[]| operator) belong to the same enabled set;
- sequential tasks (>> or []>> operator), where the task on the left (when it terminates) enables the task on the right, belong to different enabled sets;
- choice tasks ([] operator) belong to different enabled task sets except their first actions which all belong to the same enabled set;
- when there is a disabling task ([> operator) its first action belongs to all the enabled sets associated with the tasks which can be disabled and its body belongs to another enabled task set.

We can introduce this approach with a short example (Figure 5.3) where we consider the *Printing* task decomposed into three tasks (*Selecting a file, Selecting parameters, Print*). According to the rules indicated above we can apply the First and the Body functions to the *Printing* task.

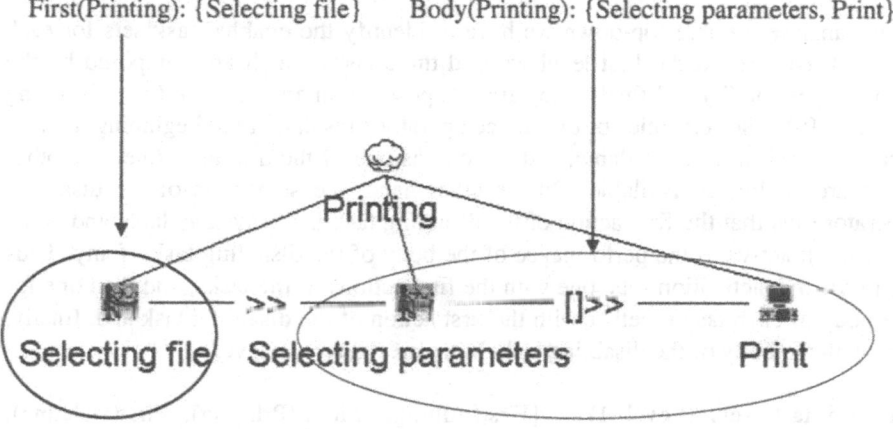

Figure 5.3: Example of application of First and Body functions.

A more extended example is provided in Figure 5.4 by a simplified task model for managing files. The abstract tasks (indicated by a cloud icon) are tasks whose performance cannot be allocated uniquely as they have subtasks that, in this case, are user interactions (indicated by a human/computer icon) or application-only tasks (indicated by a computer icon). At the beginning we have an alternative choice among *Editing*, *Printing* and *Deleting* tasks. Their performance can be disabled by the *Close* task. In the case of editing we decompose the task into opening a file followed by the parallel execution of multiple tasks (*Insert*, *Cut* and *Scroll* tasks). The *Printing* task is decomposed into a different structure as we first have the *Select print* activity (which activates a dialogue box for specifying the print parameters), followed in this case by three sequential tasks: *Select printer*, *Select pages*, and *Print*.

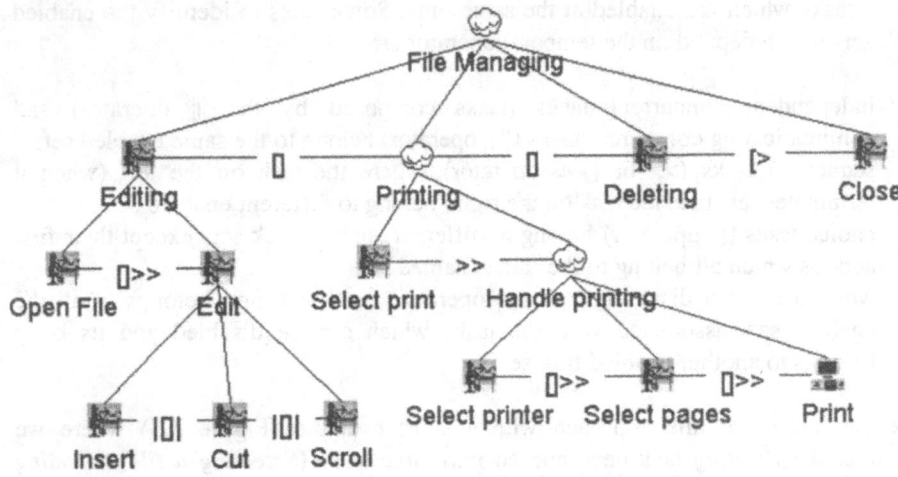

Figure 5.4: An example of a simplified task model.

If we analyse the tree top-down we have to identify the enabled task sets for each level of the tree. At the first level we find three tasks which are composed by the choice operator ([]) and finally they are composed with another task (by a disabling operator [>). The semantics of the choice operator says that at the beginning the first action of each task is available, and as soon as one of them is performed the other tasks are no longer available. On the other hand, the semantics of the disabling operator says that the first action of the disabling task is always available and when it occurs it activates the performance of the body of the disabling task, if any. Thus there are five activation sets: one with the first actions of the tasks, and then one for the body of each task together with the first action of the disabling task and, finally, one with the body of the disabling task. More precisely, we have:

Enabled task sets (Level 1) = {First(Editing), First (Printing), First(Deleting), First(Close)}, {Body(Editing), First(Close)}, {Body(Printing), First(Close)}, {Body(Deleting), First(Close)}, {Body(Close)}.

If we consider the next level, the temporal operators that we find do not need any new enabled task sets. However, we find information that can be used to give more precise definitions of the activation sets identified. For example, we know that the

Deleting task is considered as a single action task, thus First(Deleting) = *Deleting* and Body(Deleting) is empty. The same holds for the *Close* task. Similarly, we know that Body(Editing) = *Edit* and Body(Printing) = *Handle Printing*. Thus we obtain:

Enabled task sets (Level 2) = {Open file, Select print, Deleting, Close}, {Edit, Close}, {Handle Printing, Close}.

Finally, if we consider the third and last level we see that both *Edit* and *Handle Printing* are further decomposed, but *Edit* is decomposed into subtasks which are enabled at the same time and are thus still part of the same enabled task set, whereas the subtasks of *Handle Printing* have to be performed sequentially and thus each needs one enabled task set. The final definition of the activation sets is therefore:

Enabled task sets (Level 3) = {Open file, Select print, Deleting, Close}, {Insert, Cut, Scroll, Close}, {Select printer, Close}, {Select pages, Close}, {Print, Close}.

We note that one task can belong to multiple enabled task sets.

5.4 TASK-DRIVEN DESIGN OF USER INTERFACES

In the enabled task sets associated with the lowest level of the task tree, only the basic tasks of the task model are involved. The amount of basic tasks per enabled task set can differ substantially. If there are multiple basic tasks in one enabled task set we need to determine rules to indicate the most effective structures of presentations taking into account the temporal operators and the structure of the task tree. A *structure for presentation* gives an overall indication of the presentation which can be obtained leaving the definition of some details for the next phase. These structures of presentation can be represented with the support of an automatic tool so that the designer has an idea of the possible impact of the task model on the final presentation.

5.4.1 Designing layout of presentations

An important aspect within an enabled task set is the structure of the task tree which has generated the set. The tasks which are part of an enabled task set can be composed by all the operators except the enabling one. One element is the possibility of identifying both groups and subgroups, depending on whether tasks which belong to the same enabled task set share the same ancestor or parent task. If we consider the task tree, we find that the groups of tasks which share the same parent task are usually semantically closer to each other than the groups of tasks which share an ancestor at a higher level in the task tree. Figure 5.5 shows an example of a task model along with the related structure of presentation. The subtasks of the *Enter Date* task are one group of tightly related tasks. One level higher, the *Show Calendar* task and *the Enter Date* task are also grouped in close proximity, since they share the same parent. Again one level higher, the *Define Date* task and the *Enter Appointment Topic* task are grouped together.

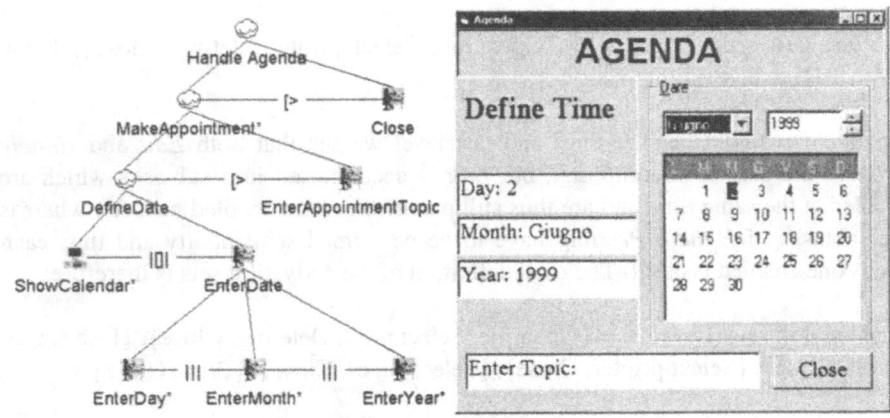

Figure 5.5: Groups and subgroups in a task model and the corresponding presentation structure.

The tasks at one level of the tree that have to exchange information (|[]| operator) are more semantically related to each other than those tasks composed by other temporal operators, thus the related interaction techniques are located closer to each other to highlight this semantic closeness.

It is possible to identify structures of presentations that are characterised by the composition of groups of certain types of tasks. These structures can be considered task-oriented presentation patterns. In some cases combinations of these patterns can be used in a task model. Examples of such patterns are [PBD98]:

- *Form*: contains combinations of Edit and Select tasks following indications from the structure of the task model such as possible groupings of tasks.
- *Control*: concerns the tasks that control the main current activities. These tasks can be triggered either by the user or the application, and they usually are in mutual choice.
- *Multiple Views*: tasks communicate with each other. There are some data which can be modified, either by the user or the application, and two or more representations of such data are updated and given to the end user.
- *Process&Present*: occurs when there are some sequential tasks that are semantically strictly connected. In this situation there is an application with some processing and results presentation. The user may want to perform these tasks several times, so s/he prefers to have them presented continuously even if they belong to different enabled task sets.

5.4.2 Considering task types for selecting user interface techniques

Once we have defined the structure of the presentation we have to define the type of presentation to associate with each basic task in the structure. In this case it can be useful to create an environment where for each task, depending on its type, there is a set of predefined presentation templates or interaction techniques which are suitable for supporting its semantics.

We now consider the basic tasks and we try to indicate their possible presentation, depending on their semantics and the type of data involved. Here we only consider single basic tasks, and thus the related presentations are not particularly structured. For the choice of the most suitable presentation some additional information might be needed about data cardinality. In the ConcurTaskTrees notation, four categories of tasks are recognised: *Abstract*, *User*, *Interaction* and *Application* task types. They are described in Chapter 4. In the enabled task sets at the lowest level of the task tree we consider only interaction and application basic tasks. The task classification needs to be further subdivided in order to give clearer indications of the semantics of the task, for this purpose there is a set of task types for each task category. Other specific information is also needed for the design of the presentation related to the task tree: the object classes manipulated to perform the tasks.

The object class can provide requirements for the type of presentation to choose. In Interaction tasks we want to consider the type of data that is the input to the application. For example, an *enter name* interaction basic task will be connected with the *string* object class. Application tasks consider the type of data which have to be presented. Thus we can take the types of tasks introduced in section 4.4 and see some examples of interaction and presentation techniques that better support them:

- *Selection* tasks: the presentation rules for selection take the data cardinality into consideration. In this case the data cardinality indicates the amount of data the user can select from. For example, if we consider a range of integer value(s) then if it is a single selection with a small amount of data then a spin button is preferable, if a large amount of data is considered, then a data slider would be better. For multiple selections from a small amount of data, check boxes are preferred, while for multiple selections from a large amount of data, a listbox allowing the selection of multiple items is the best presentation.
- *Edit* tasks: the presentation for editing is simple to determine, since it depends on the object types associated with the information that has to be given as input to the application.
- *Control* tasks: several interaction techniques can be used to trigger an action. Buttons, toolbar buttons, icons, hyperlinks and menu items can all be used to perform control tasks, directly needed by the user. Actions can also be activated by voice and gesture-based techniques. The presentation of a control technique should attract the user's attention. Colour, size and font determine the appeal of

the presentation. Another option is the use of colour to indicate that the user has already performed a certain trigger action, as with hyperlinks.

We have seen that application tasks are used to indicate that the application performs an activity. In combination with the purpose of the presentation and the data types, some presentation rules can be defined. There are various types of application tasks that can have an impact on the design of the user interface as we introduced in section 4.4:

- *Overview*: the application shows a summary of a set of data avoiding to give all the elementary data, for example giving the minimum, average, and maximum values of the data considered.
- *Comparison*: the purpose of the presentation is to facilitate the user in comparing the values of some quantities of the same type, for example the revenues of different years.
- *Locate*: the application gives detailed information on a set of data so as to allow the user to rapidly find the desired information, for example emails received by name of sender, date or topic.
- *Grouping*: there is a one-to-many relationship among two data attributes which have to be presented at the same time and this relation has to be highlighted in the presentation. For example, if the application has to present clients and sales orders the presentation should group the orders by clients.
- *Processing feedback*: the application gives information on some processing without requiring a specific request from the user, such as generating feedback on the time left before a certain event. For example, amount of time before completing copying of a file.

5.4.3 Gathering information from temporal relations among tasks

The task model can also give useful information on how to design the dynamic behaviour of the user interface of the interactive application. Depending on the temporal relationships among tasks we can decide when some interaction techniques should be available to the end user, for example when links supporting the hypermedia navigation should be included.

Temporal relationships among tasks can give useful information for structuring presentations other than the dialogues of the concrete user interface. First of all, the temporal relation called enabling (>>) indicates the border between two enabled task sets. Thus, within an enabled task set there will never be tasks composed by an *enabling* operator which indicates that when a task terminates it activates another task. Different presentations can be used to present the user interfaces related to two enabled task sets where the transition among them is determined by an enabling operator:

- The interaction techniques associated with the enabled task sets are shown in the same presentation unit. This is preferred when, for example, the iteration of the sequence of tasks occur many times or the tasks are related, exchange information, and thus having the related presentation techniques in the same presentation unit helps the user to understand their relationships.

- The interaction techniques associated with both enabled task sets are presented in separate presentation units. The first presentation unit is still visible but it may not be reactive, while the second presentation is shown in a modal state. In this case the purpose is not only to allow the user to view both the related interaction techniques but to drive them to interact with the current enabled technique.

- The interaction techniques associated with the first enabled task set are presented in one presentation unit, and those related to the second enabled task set are shown in a separate unit. The first presentation unit is no longer visible when the second presentation unit is shown. This is preferable when the sequential tasks are not tightly related and so it is useless, and perhaps confusing, keeping on the screen the interaction techniques associated with the first performed task.

- The sequential constraint is supported in other ways within the same presentation unit (for example greying out the interaction techniques associated with the disabled task or just making them not reactive to user interactions).

If a task disables another task then an interaction technique supporting the disabling task should be available. For example, if in a hypermedia supporting a museum application we have a *ShowProfiles* task is disabled by the *SelProfile* task then, when the information related to the first task is presented, a link allowing the performance of the second task and the disabling of the first one should be available to the end user.

The disabling ([>) operator suggests how to structure the presentations of the tasks belonging to one enabled task set. They indicate a kind of grouping within an enabled task set. The tasks before the disabling operator can generally be considered as one group and thus the related interaction techniques can be presented closer to each other. The control tasks, which perform the disabling, can be located so that they highlight their function of controlling the tasks which can be disabled and belong to the same enabled task set. The tasks that can be performed after the disabling task belong to different enabled task sets.

In the example of task specification in Figure 5.6 we can find one enabled task set {Enter Name, Enter Department, Submit Request} whose tasks are composed by one disabling operator and one interleaving operator. The *Submit Request* task applies to both the *Enter Name* and the *Enter Department* task.

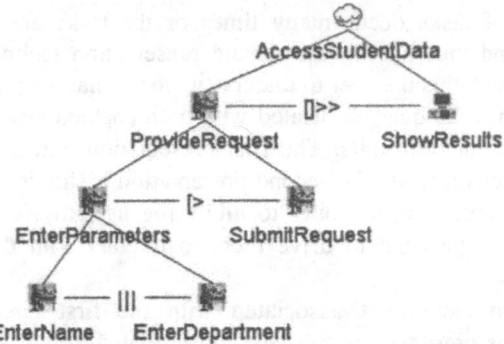

Figure 5.6: A task model containing a disabling and an interleaving operator.

Figure 5.7 shows an example of a corresponding presentation structure. The advantage of this rule is that some control tasks can be automatically identified and then placed in a part of the presentation following the designer's choice.

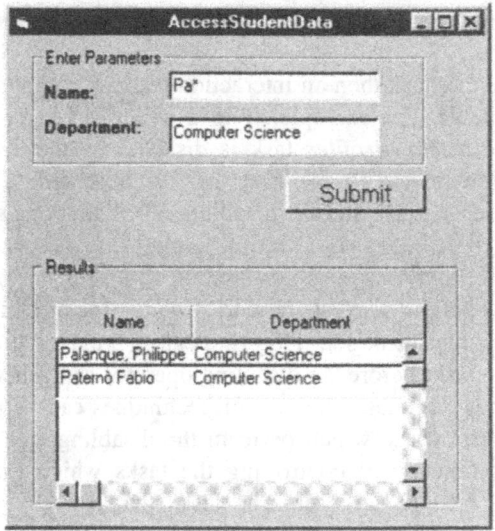

Figure 5.7: Presentation related to two enabled task sets.

The independent concurrent tasks operator (|||) does not provide any particular indication, whereas the use of the concurrent tasks with information exchange (|[]|) operator shows that we have tasks that communicate with each other and thus need to be presented close together. This often happens when there are tasks presenting some data and tasks which allow the user to modify these data, and when we want the related presentations to highlight this relationship. If two tasks are concurrent (the first action of one task can be performed before the last action of the other task) then the related presentation techniques can be available to the end user during the same period of time taking into account the criteria indicated in the section about structuring the presentation. For example, it is possible to show a video and manage the sound concurrently so that during the video presentation the user can enable or disable the sound.

When we have a choice operator the availability of the interaction techniques to support the performance of the choice depends on whether the choice is made by the user or the application. If the choice is made by the application then only the information related to the task chosen will be presented. If the user makes the choice then s/he is allowed to make at least the first action of the possible tasks that can be, for example, the selection of a link associated with each possible choice. Then depending on the user's choice, the information and the interaction techniques associated with the chosen task and, in some cases, those tasks which should be performed immediately after, will be made available while the information associated with the other choices will disappear completely. For example, the user can decide to get information about the town or about the museum. Each choice is supported by a specific link. Depending on the choice, only town-related or museum-related information will appear.

When the choice operator ([]) occurs at the lowest level of the task tree it can indicate choices that are strictly connected as they are grouped by some parent tasks, whereas if it occurs at the highest levels it can indicate activities which are not too semantically related.

5.4.4 Relationships among enabled task sets

Once we have identified enabled task sets and their main presentation structure, we have to take into account the problem of the transition between the presentations associated with the two enabled task sets.

If we find that there is an intersection among the tasks belonging to the two enabled task sets then we can have a rule indicating that the presentation of the tasks included in both enabled task sets has to be of the same type in order to keep consistency across different presentations. For example, the usual tasks allowing users to close or cancel an application should be placed in the same position with the same interaction technique. For the tasks which are no longer available, in the next enabled task set the related presentation resources can be reallocated for the new tasks introduced in the next enabled task set.

5.4.5 Structuring the information

By a top-down analysis of the task tree it is possible to determine the structure which has to be given to the available data. The tasks at the high and intermediate levels are useful for starting the structuring of the data of an application. It is possible to use high-level tasks to identify the more abstract objects of the interactive application considered. The basic idea is to associate the objects of the system with the objects relevant for the high level tasks. How to structure the entities into components depends on the subtasks at the lower levels and the objects that they need to manipulate.

5.5 AN EXAMPLE

This section gives an example of a task model, and uses it to determine the final presentation. We consider the possibility to search for some students from a database, and then select and edit the data of a particular student.

In the task model we can first identify an iterative handling task which can be disabled by a close task. Then we can search for students by entering parameters such as name and department. Once these parameters have been submitted, the application can calculate them and show the list of students satisfying the criteria given. The user can select one of them. Both searching and selecting can occur many times without constraints until the user decides to edit either one selected item of information about an employee or some new information. During editing various items of information can be given until the user saves or cancels the modification.

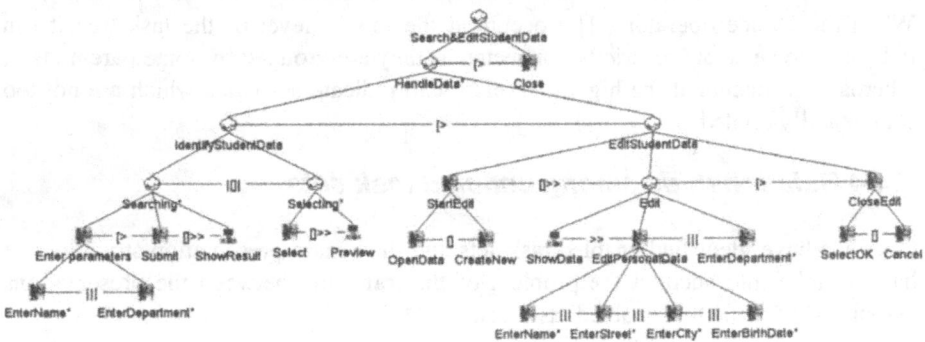

Figure 5.8: Search and edit employee task model example

In Figure 5.9 we can see the result of a tool for calculating enabled task sets according to the rules that we have introduced in this section. The tool has been integrated with the editor of ConcurTaskTrees task models. It is also possible to update the enabled task sets in case the designer changes the task model and to save the enabled task sets, and then to activate the second part of the design method which concerns the support for the design of the presentations associated with each enabled task set. Once the enabled task sets of the example are identified by applying the rules described beforehand we can start to consider how to design the presentation.

Figure 5.9: The enabled task sets of the example

The structure of the task tree highlights that there is an initial main grouping of tasks at the second level (those related to *IdentifyStudentData* and to *Edit student*). In the first group of tasks we can further decompose it into three enabled task sets. Since these enabled task sets are closely related semantically we are in the case of *Process&Present* presentation structure, and we present them all together in the same presentation structure. In this structure there are couples of tasks which have to be presented in close proximity because they often communicate with each other, such as *Select* and *Preview*.

In the second main structure there are two patterns: one *Form* which involves *Editing* tasks which can be logically grouped, and one *Control* which allows the user to determine whether or not to save the modifications.

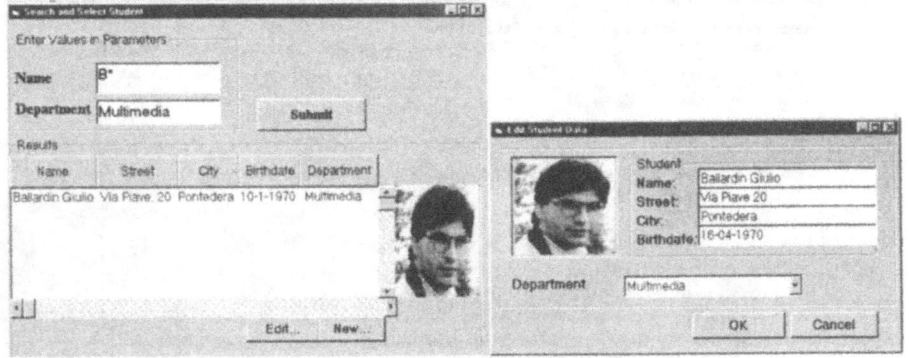

Figure 5.10: The two presentation structures obtained.

5.6 TASKS FOR ACCESSING DATABASES

Users can access an increasing amount of data, this trend is supported by the diffusion of Internet connections. Such data are often available through databases. By analysing the most frequent requests of groups of users working with databases we can identify a set of classes of high-level tasks which occur in most applications. Each class of tasks raises specific requirements for the design of the database user interface. Task knowledge can improve the process of generating effective presentations, by considering Presentation Templates which are sufficiently effective for the current task. In the task-based evaluation of templates we have to consider the semantics of the task and to what extent the template is a suitable support [ABPS98]. A Presentation Template defines the main structure of a presentation, and indicates the presentations and basic interaction techniques to use and how to compose them but leaving it up to the designer to decide how to present the specific information and how users should interact with it.

A possible classification of tasks for accessing databases is:

- *Explore Task*. In this case the user does not want to obtain information related to specific objects of the database but wants to understand its structure in order to formulate more precise queries later on. This task concerns metadata, a collection of elements which describe the structure, the relationships and the constraints in the database. In the case of queries supporting this type of task the system should support Presentation Templates which highlight the structure of the database. The user interface should also control the level of detail of the information requested, thus facilitating the discovery of the information available. In this case it is preferable to present the structure of a database graphically to make it easily perceivable and interpretable by the end user. For example, a pull-down menu or menus in cascades perform well because the dynamic activation of the various menus is suitable for highlighting the entity-attribute relationship.

- *What About Task*. This task reflects the users' need to examine the contents of the database. The formulation of the query is not detailed: the user wants to have an idea of what is available on a certain topic. The system provides a presentation which is a summary of all the information concerning the objects selected. It can contain the name, type and number of distinct values for each attribute, indexes for attributes of string type or range [min, max] for attributes with ordinal and quantitative values and constraints on data.

- *Tell Me*. Tell me implies a need for detailed information about the contents of the database: the user needs to know the values associated with a set of attributes by specifying some constraints on the requested data. The corresponding result can range from no data to a huge amount of data. The absence of an aggregation function in the query means that the user wants to consider the rough data. The resulting presentation will contain no quantitative data except for the numeric attributes.

- *What Is*. In this case the user wants to have specific information on the content of the database by applying some aggregation functions which depend on the type of information considered. Since most of the results provided by aggregation functions are numeric values, the templates which support effectively the comparison of quantitative information are good.

- *How Many*. The purpose of this task is to provide numerical information. The user is interested in either the number of occurrences of values, which satisfy a given constraint or the result of some processing. This implies a good evaluation of the templates which use graphics to highlight quantitative information.

- *Where Are*. This task is for applications which manipulate spatial data. In this case the user wants to know where one or more objects are located. To obtain effective presentations the system should have a spatial representation (map, plant, virtual representation, etc.) of the environment considered and the position of the desired object in order to present the selected information depending on the coordinate system used. The presentation should support some related tasks such as information about distances between objects or how to reach one location. Among the templates considered the most effective for this task is that using overlapping techniques: in this case the templates can use an image as background which provides the general spatial information. In this representation it is possible to provide the location of the data. These representations can be used when the user wants to have additional related spatial information.

5.7 TASK-ORIENTED HELP

Automatic help generation is widely recognised as an important feature in order to provide usable environments. However, the design of the help facility has often suffered from the same limitation as the design of user interfaces: a poor semantic support which implies a lack of semantic indications for users. In fact information which is related to perceivable features and low level actions is usually provided. Users may thus find it difficult to associate this type of information with the tasks that they want to perform. This is because the design of most of the current user interfaces and related toolkits focuses on appearance and layout, rather than on more important semantic design issues [J92b].

Using task specification to produce both the design of the software user interface and the design of help has several advantages [PP95]:

- we do not need to duplicate efforts in designing both aspects;
- the generation of help is not involved in detailed implementation issues but is automatically derived from the task specification;
- if tasks that the system should support are modified then the parts of the software architecture and help specification which have to be modified can easily be identified;
- likewise, if temporal constraints among tasks are modified, the help system gives the consequent answer simply by updating the task specification without further effort.

The first proposal for the attachment of help to points in a dialogue model was in the Syngraph system [OD83]. Then systematic work on automatic generation of help was in [SF90] which describes how it is obtained in UIDE. In this environment the logical structure of the user interface is described as a set of application objects which have pre- and post- conditions. The former indicate what is required to interact with one object, the latter indicate the effects after the interaction. This work was then extended in order to generate textual, audio and animated help. In [PBD93] there is an environment where the dialogue of the user interface is controlled by the implementation of Petri Nets. The user interactions modify the number and the location of tokens in the nets. By analysing the net it is possible to answer questions such as: What can I do now? Why is this interaction not available? How can I make that action available again. Another approach is in [MSN94] which describes hypertext-based help about data presented in application displays, commands to manipulate data, and interaction techniques to invoke commands. The authors propose a model-based design where the model consists of the commands and objects of an application, the methods for presenting these commands and objects, and the behaviour of these objects in response to input events.

More generally, we can say that if at run-time we can keep knowledge of the task model associated with the application and how the interaction techniques are related to it then, given a user interaction, we can say what the enabled and active tasks (active tasks are those started but not terminated) are. By navigating in the tree of tasks we can find out what the most abstract tasks are including the basic task considered. The help can provide information at each of these abstraction levels.

We can thus answer a set of task-related questions:

- What tasks can I perform now?
- Why is this task not allowed?
- How can I enable this task?
- How can I perform this task?

It is possible to extend the last question to ask for the actions associated with the performance of all the enabled tasks. Thus, if the user performs a disabled action, the system can give reasons for refusing to perform it in a task-oriented way saying: you have tried to perform task x which is not enabled because you first have to perform tasks y and z.

There are two ways to activate the help: either by trying to interact with a disabled interaction object or by explicit request. The answer to the question "*What tasks can I perform now*" can be found by examining the task graph and looking for enabled tasks. We are then able to provide information on the enabled tasks at the different levels of abstraction, down to the lowest level (the actual action the user has to do in order to perform a task). This kind of information would be expressed best with a hypertext system, where the user could click on a non-basic task, and be given details on its subtasks. When the user asks *How to perform a task* the first thing the system should do is to check if that task is already enabled. In this case, a short explanation on how to perform the task is generated otherwise the help system has to indicate that it is not enabled. If the user asks *How to enable a task*, again, we have to consider the task tree. Note that there may be cases where there is no way to find an enabling path for a task. This means that in the current session the task cannot be performed. We consider these situations as design faults: a user interface should not allow for one-way trapdoors.

5.8 ADAPTABILITY

When an interactive application is used by users with different goals and levels of knowledge another important aspect is to support adaptation: different users may be interested in different parts of the information contained and they may want to use different interaction techniques or links for navigation. To design adaptable applications we need to take into account that different types of users have different task models associated with them. This means that if task-based design is followed then the application should be able to adapt itself to this diversity of possible tasks depending on the user type. Different levels of adaptation can be identified. The first broad classification is into:

- *adaptable* systems that are systems that allow users to define some parameters of the system and then adapt their behaviour accordingly.
- *adaptive* system adapt their behaviour automatically.

More generally, adaptation can be done for different purposes: for supporting different types of users or different types of devices or different types of contextual environments. Interest in adaptation in user interfaces has been arisen in different areas. In [BM93] there is an attempt to provide a unifying perspective on adaptive systems in general, ranging from intelligent tutoring to autonomous agents.

In this Section we will mainly consider systems supporting adaptation for different users tailoring information to guide the user in the information space to present the most relevant material, taking into account a model of the user's goals, interests and preferences. Such an adaptation can occur at three levels:

- *Presentation*, where it is possible to differentiate the type of media, the layout, the attributes of the perceivable elements (such as font type and size) depending on the type of access;
- *Information*, where the information content can be changed, sometimes drastically, even if related to the same topic, depending on the type of user and the use foreseen;
- *Navigation*, where different links are provided, in some cases in different locations and with different appearance, determining different modalities of navigation in the information available.

5.8.1 Example of user classification

In many applications we can classify users depending on the basic knowledge of the application domain considered. However, there are also other aspects that differentiate different types of users. These aspects concern the tasks and the representations of the information more suitable to perform them.

In this section there is an example of possible classification of users for a virtual museum application. As we will see in what follows this classification has been used for the development of a real application, a hypermedia containing information of the Marble Museum (http://giove.cnuce.cnr.it/Museo.html) [PM99]. The types of users identified are: tourists, students of art, and experts.

Tourists are characterised by a low average knowledge of the topics considered. Usually they prefer to have guided tours through the rooms of the museum and the town with pictures and information about the works of art. However, linear pre-defined tours alone would be too restrictive so some degree of navigational freedom is important. Access to the information should be provided with the support of spatial representations: the museum and town maps. This allows users to have immediate information about the locations of the works. Tourists want general information on the artistic works, and this information has to be presented clearly and in a limited amount because it has to be interpreted easily. Thus a work will be presented by an image, the title, a short description, the name of the author, the material and technique used for its creation, and when it was made. Additional information about the museum and the town can be provided on request, such as the path to get to the museum from the closest railway station or airport, information (title, data, location) on further exhibitions, and historical information on the town and the museum.

Students in the artistic field who visit a museum already have some basic knowledge. They prefer to have information on a wider variety of topics than the tourists. The presentation of some images and related texts often stimulates a request for more detailed information. In this case, providing pre-defined tours is not the right answer. Instead, we let such students choose from different types of information which may concern not only the works of art but may also involve a wider spectrum of topics, so that students can improve their knowledge. Thus access to the information available is more flexible than for tourists: it is possible to call up the list of artists and historical periods, and then by selecting one of them to start the navigation in the hypermedia. Students also find technical glossaries useful. They may be interested in the life and works of an artist including in-depth information on the subject of the work, its relationships with other works, the state of conservation, related artists, the main cultural movements and artists in a specific period, etc. This information should be general (like an identity card) but it should also be possible to get more in-depth information if required.

Expert users generally know exactly what information they want and should thus be allowed, right from the beginning of the session, to make increasingly precise requests. In this case the information required may concern:

- An artist: an extended biography with the possibility to access a critique providing additional information. From here it should be possible to reach the following information: artist's work; lists of texts which discuss them, plus a short summary; a list of Internet sites which concern the artist; information on other artists who lived in the same period and in the same area as the artist selected;
- A specific work which is presented from the point of view of the critique and not purely descriptively. From the work presentation it should be possible to reach information concerning the artist who created it and also to receive in-depth descriptions;
- A specific historical period allowing the user to obtain detailed information such as how to reach the most important works in this period.

Experts are also interested in having information on works presented so as to highlight specific relationships (for example, a presentation grouping works developed in a certain period by using a specific technique and material).

5.8.2 How to support adaptation

Designing the museum application we have to take into account the indications contained in the task model. There are three task models; one for each main type of user identified (expert, tourist, and student of art).

They mainly differ from three aspects:

- *Initial access to the museum information*, the expert can specify directly very specific requests whereas the student can access only information by lists indicating the information available and tourists access information mainly by spatial representations of the museum and the town (Figure 5.11 shows the three different initial point of access);
- *Presentation of the information related to the works of art*, which takes into account the basic knowledge of the type of users and the different tasks that they are likely to wish to perform;
- *Navigation in the hypermedia*, which is more structured and pre-ordered for tourists whereas more navigational freedom has been given to expert users.

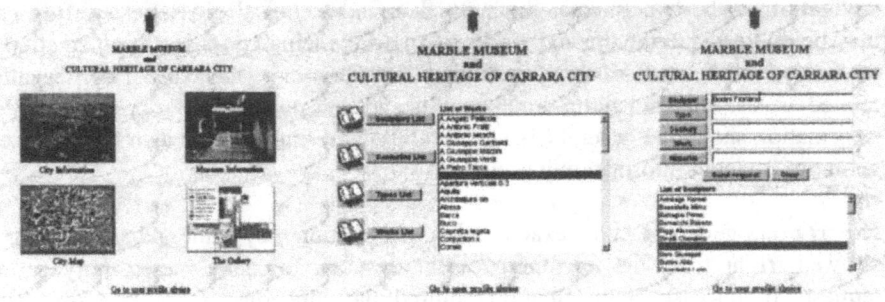

Figure 5.11: The initial access for the different types of users (from left to right: tourist, student of art, expert).

As we mentioned above, different views of the same information can be possible depending on the type of users. For example in Figure 5.12a, we can see the tourist view of information related to a sculpture. As you can see it is possible to access the next work. In this case the next work means the next work in the Modern Sculpture Section of the museum. It is also possible to access the list of works made by this material, the works performed by using different materials (wood, bronze, and others) and the museum map which drives the visit of the tourist in the museum hypermedia.

In the case of an expert user (Figure 5.12b) the information can be accessed more immediately (for example, by just giving the name of the author), it is more detailed (for example, precise dimensions and precise date of creation are given), and further information on the material, the author, the biography or other information can be accessed.

Users can change the current user profile (tourist, student, and expert) interactively during the session. Thus they can access the different views on the information available and the navigation styles without having to start a new application session.

Figure 5.12a: An example of different views, the tourist view.

The level of support provided by the adaptable hypermedia for the Marble Museum has been found satisfying because, on the one hand, users have shown they can understand it and navigate through it easily, and on the other hand, they appreciate the support it gives which enables them to access effectively the information contained in the hypermedia.

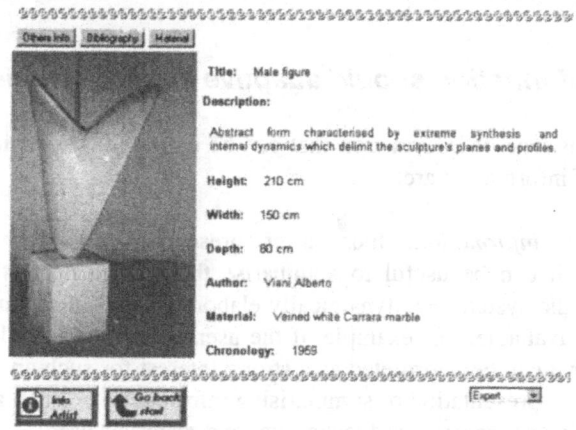

Figure 5.12b: An example of different views, the expert view.

In section 5.9.3 we discuss an interesting solution for including some adaptive features taking into account the interactions performed by users and their preferences.

5.9 ADAPTIVITY

While in the previous section we have seen an example of adaptable support, this section is dedicated to discuss adaptive support.

5.9.1 When to provide adaptive support?

As we mentioned before, it is better to leave to the user full control of the adaptive support. This can be performed in two ways:

- the user explicitly indicates when to activate such a support, for example when users are not satisfied with the current information they may want to ask for further information and the system should understand what kind of further information may be of interest in that specific context, taking into account the previously performed interactions;
- the system, taking into account the user interactions, indicates that it has some suggestions and additional information to provide and the user decides whether or not to allow it to show this information; in the latter case an agent, with some rules incorporated, is included to allow the system to understand how to dynamically present information (some information can be dynamically removed because the user does not seem interested in it or other information can be added because the user seems desiring to receive more detailed information).

5.9.2 What information should adaptive support provide?

There are various type of information that can be dynamically provided. Examples of these types of information are:

- *Summarising information*: thus, after presenting a series of pieces of information it can be useful to summarise the main aspects that have been considered; the system can dynamically elaborate some information depending on the data available. For example, if the user examines multiple works of the same author it can be interpreted as a strong interest for such an author and this can trigger the presentation of summarising information on such an author, such as a discussion of the preferred techniques and materials used;
- *Highlighting related issues*: in this case the purpose is to highlight elements that can raise curiosity, discussion or comments from the users;
- *Compare different items*: that is, giving some information that can allow the user to make the comparison or to provide directly a comparison; there are many types of information that can be analysed to provide comparisons, for

example, in a museum application, the dimensions or the date of creation of works of art;

- *Highlighting differences*: to show how a piece of information differs from the previous information considered or from a specific piece previously considered. Another possibility is to provide information by differences with respect to what has been already considered. Thus, taking into account the history of the interaction and the related information presented the system can highlight differences and contrasts to the previously viewed information while omitting any background information that the visitor has already been given. This means that the system has a logical description of the information contained and it is able to keep the history of what the user has already seen.

It is also possible to give some automatic support by making suggestions to users to change between the predefined profiles or to allow them to configure dynamically one specific profile intermediate among those predefined. We still prefer that the system suggests a possible modification explaining the reasons for this suggestion rather than it changes the current profile dynamically. For example, if the current profile is set to expert, giving the user the option to access additional information whenever a work of art is presented but the user never selects the additional information, then we can assume that probably the user is not interested in detailed information and another user profile can be more suitable for the current user. Another example is when the user starts with the tourist profile but after accessing information a certain number of times they may be interested in getting more detailed information, the system should be able at least to propose this possibility.

There are many aspects that can be adapted. We have given examples concerning change of the layout of the page according to the user's needs. Another possibility is to increase user-friendliness by adaptive ordering. For example in pages where a list of works is presented, works of art not visited before could be placed on top, while links to works of art already seen by the user could be placed below and have a different colour. In this way the layout of the page is changed to make navigation easier for the user without increasing the cognitive load. These link-level adaptations are all very simple but have the power to greatly increase the user-friendliness of the application.

Other aspects to take into account are the restrictions concerning the technical environment of the user accessing the web site. Information with high data volume (e.g., videos, high-resolution pictures) is replaced by less demanding equivalents with low bandwidth network access (e.g. via a slow modem) in order to reduce download times if required. The response time of a hypermedia system is extremely critical from the point of usability.

5.9.3 Example of adaptive presentation techniques

One aim of the application is to give the user the feeling s/he is being shown around the museum by a real human tour-guide [PMA99]. This feature should stimulate the user to spend more time with the application and consider the application as more attractive. By making reference to works earlier visited the presentation can be more coherent and less monotonous.

We can consider some examples on how exactly this earlier information can be taken into account. These examples are based on the works of Felice Vatteroni, using the "tourist" visitor profile. The Vatteroni donation consists of some 20 works of art. To the tourist all works of art are described using the following format:

<name>
<description of the work>
<artist>
<material used>
<period>

There are several dimensions on which the current work of art can be compared to the ones previously viewed, for example:

- *Differences concerning the sculptor*: when the visitor has only seen work of other sculptors and is entering the virtual Vatteroni room, some general information on the sculptor could be included in the first Vatteroni work viewed.
- *Differences concerning the material*: when the visitor encounters a work of a new material some remarks could be made about that.
- *Differences concerning the historical period*: when a user moves from works from one historical period to works from another some remarks could be made about that. For example, when a user virtually enters the modern sculpture part, some remark could be made about the differences between modern and ancient sculpture.

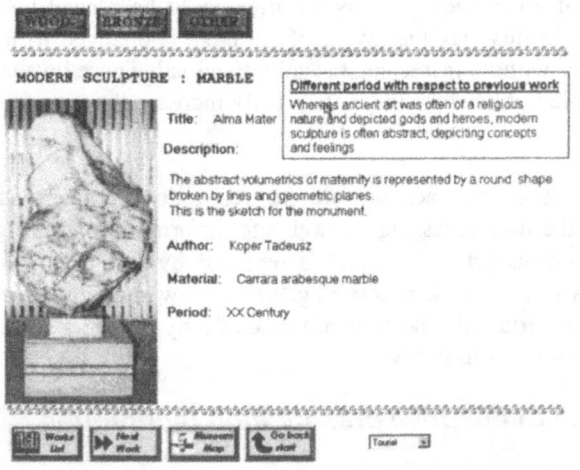

Figure 5.13: Differences concerning the historical period.

A space in the layout of the presentation of a work of art of the hypermedia can be identified to provide the additional information provided by the system agent that follow the above criteria. It can be considered the space allocated to a virtual guide supporting the visit. This space can be located in a fixed position (for example, top-right area, surrounded by a rectangle in order to highlight it). It can be useful to indicate explicitly the motivation for providing additional information. For example, in Figure 5.13 we show an example where a user accesses information concerning a work of art created in a period different from that of the previous work and some general information concerning the main differences between the periods is given.

5.10 CONCLUDING REMARKS

In this chapter we have discussed how considering tasks in order to give systematic support for deriving information from task models which are useful for the design of presentations has been shown. More precisely, we have seen how task-based considerations can be useful to support the design of presentations, what the common tasks in accessing databases are, and how to provide suggestions for task-oriented help systems. Then we have focused on how to adapt the user interface to the different tasks that can be performed by different users. We have considered both static adaptation techniques based on predefined user models and more dynamic adaptive techniques describing experiences from a museum application case study.

Note that the rich variety of possible input and output devices has generated an increasing interest in the possibility of having applications able to adapt to them.

5.11 EXERCISES

1. Identify the enabled task sets of a task model which has at least four levels and uses at least three temporal operators.
2. Identify the task types of the task model developed in the previous exercise.
3. Design a user interface using information contained in the task model following the criteria discussed in this chapter.
4. Design task models of different types of users that have to access the same type of data and analyse their differences.
5. Design different user interfaces for the different task models identified in the previous exercise.

6 Architectural Models of Interactive Applications

In this chapter topics more oriented for software engineers and designers are considered.

6.1 ARCHITECTURES FOR USER INTERFACES

6.1.1 Models for interactive systems

The problem of designing interactive applications can be described at different abstraction levels:

- the *conceptual*, where the main aspects and functionalities that should be present are identified;
- the *architectural*, where the basic components and their relationship are identified in order to carry out these functionalities.

An architectural model of an interactive application is a description of what the basic components of its implementation are, and how they are connected in order to support the required functionality and interactions with the user.

An architectural model is an important element in the design process because:

- it provides clear indications of the main components to take into account in the design of interactive systems;
- it facilitates the identification of reusable components;
- it facilitates the implementation by providing a framework which is useful for driving it;

- it defines the possible dialogues with the user (including the enabling and disabling of interaction techniques and multiple levels of feedback) thus allowing designers to reason about them in terms of their structure and the properties they should satisfy;
- it defines the input and output functionalities of an interactive system and their interconnections which may be tightly connected at various points of the architecture;
- it provides an implementation-independent description which can be easily prototyped into a corresponding implementation by using various types of toolkits for software development.

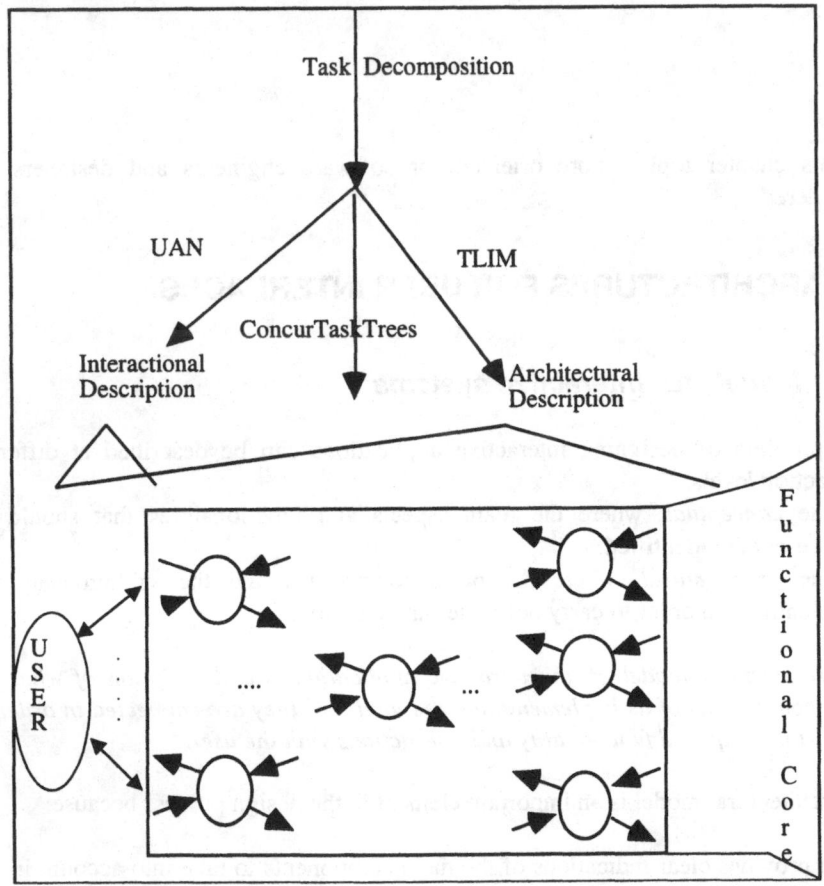

Figure 6.1: Possible relationships between tasks and user interfaces.

It is possible to describe an interactive system as a multilayered composition of interaction objects supporting input and output functionalities that can communicate with the functional core, a set of internal functionality independent from how the user interacts with the system (see Figure 6.1). This is obtained by composing interactors (the basic components of the architecture of an interactive system) hierarchically along both the input and the output flow of information with the consequent possibility to provide different levels (lexical, syntactical, semantical) of feedback to the user. This approach allows designers to describe multiple dialogues that are active at the same time using different media and devices.

One important issue is to provide a systematic method, composed of a set of precise rules, which can support the work of developers and specifiers to identify the relationships between task models and the corresponding software architecture in such a way as to obtain a direct correspondence among elements of these two levels. As Figure 6.1 shows there are different ways to indicate relationships between tasks and elements at the architectural level:

- associating tasks with user actions and feedback allowed by the system, as in UAN;
- indicating in the task specification what tasks are performed by the user, the application or their interaction, as in ConcurTaskTrees;
- deriving the basic components of the architecture from the task model as in the TIM method.

Creating an association between users tasks and interactors allows designers to obtain a more user-oriented application where the available actions can be easily mapped onto logical actions that users desire to perform. Maintaining this association at run time gives the basic information for providing contextual, task-oriented help [PP95].

More generally, there are different approaches to obtain the architecture of an interactive application:

- in [NC91] it is discussed how to derive architectures of user interface software from information concerning the user interface;
- in this chapter it is extensively discussed how to obtain architectural models from task models;
- a coevolutionary design is often used where multiple representations for supporting the design of interactive application are developed in parallel with some support to link them and to understand their relationships (an example is proposed in [BGW98]).

6.1.2 Conceptual models

The first abstraction level has been tackled at several workshops (Seeheim [P85], Seattle [O87], Lisboa [DHGL91], Arch [B91]). At the first workshop a classical subdivision of user interface systems (UIS) into three layers (presentation, dialogue, application) was proposed (with concepts from the traditional approach of programming languages, see Figure 6.2). This approach was found to be correct but too generic.

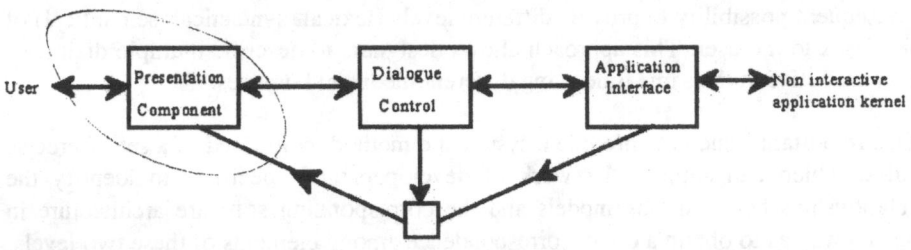

Figure 6.2: The Seeheim model.

For this reason in the Lisboa workshop a set of three types of objects were introduced: *interaction objects*, which allow the user to interact on a specific media; *transformation objects*, so that the interaction objects can be controlled and constraints on their behaviour can be defined; and *monitor objects* which can monitor relations and transactions of interaction objects and provide services such as the history of transactions. These three types of objects define a user interface system which manages communication between users and applications. Finally, a functional core was identified; i.e. the set of application functionalities independent of the media and the interaction techniques used to interact with the user.

In the Arch model the Seeheim model was revised and a further subdivision into five layers was proposed: the *interaction toolkit component* which implements the physical interaction with the end-user; the *presentation component* which provides a set of toolkit-independent objects; the *dialogue component* which is responsible for task-level sequencing, for providing multiple view consistency, and for mapping back and forth between domain-specific formalisms and user interface-specific formalisms; the *domain adapter component* where domain-related tasks are implemented which are required for human operation of the system but not available in the domain specific component and the *domain specific component* which controls, manipulates and retrieves domain data and performs other domain-related functions. With this approach several toolkits and a domain specific component can be integrated into one instance of UIS. The Slinky metamodel is a general version of the Arch model: it allows the system functionalities to shift from component to component in an architecture. A shift can depend on the goals of the developers, how they weight the development criteria and the type of systems to be implemented. Figure 6.3 shows the relationships among the layers of the three models.

SEEHEIM MODEL

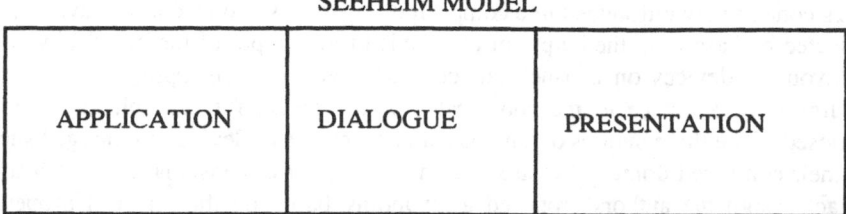

APPLICATION	DIALOGUE	PRESENTATION

ARCH MODEL

DOMAIN SPECIFIC	DOMAIN ADAPTOR	DIALOGUE	PRESENTATION	TOOLKIT

LISBOA MODEL

FUNCTIONAL CORE	Interaction, Transformation, Monitor Objects
	USER INTERFACE SYSTEM

Figure 6.3: The main conceptual models.

6.1.3 Architectural models for logical input devices

Several works have proposed models for input devices. Buxton [B83] introduced the idea that input devices are transducers of physical properties in one, two or three dimensions. Foley, Wallace and Chan [FWC84] introduced trees which relate devices to tasks.

There have been two interesting works about hierarchical composition of input devices. One developed by Mackinlay, Card and Robertson [MCR90] provides a taxonomy of input devices depending on user-related properties. They define an input device as a sextuple <M, In, S, R, Out, W> where the components of the sextuple are defined as follows: M: the corresponding physical property and the components of the sensed property; In: the input domain; S: the current state of the device; R: a resolution function that maps data from the input domain set to the output domain set; Out: the output domain set; W: a general purpose set of device properties that describes additional aspects of how the input device works.

In this context they introduce three composition operators: Connection - devices are connected by cascading the output of one device to the input of the other; Layout - the layout of devices on a panel can be described with a mapping of the local coordinates of a device to the coordinates of the panel, for example the layout composed of the three buttons of a mouse; and Merge - two devices are merged such that their combined domain sets are treated as a higher dimensional set. From this abstract design the authors proposed a taxonomy based on the physical property which the device senses; the six possible degrees of freedom (the usual 3D plus the three rotation axes) and the number of elements in the input domain set.

The other work, developed by Duce, ten Hagen and van Liere [DHL90], tried to overcome the limitations of current graphics systems where only flat organisations of input devices are possible. In this case the input device is modelled by four components: measure (M in Figure 6.4), trigger (T), control (LID), and echo (E). The result of an input device can be passed in input to the measure of another logical input device instead of the application.

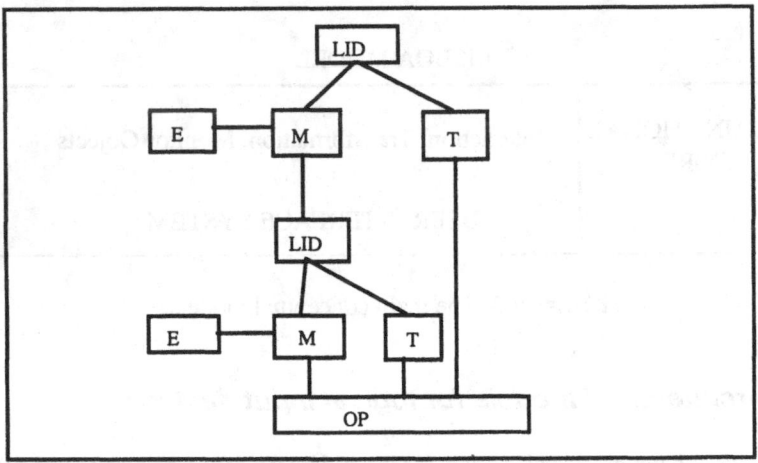

Figure 6.4: Hierarchical composition of logical input devices.

6.1.4 Architectural models for user-interaction objects

There have also been several proposals for this abstraction type. The first was Smalltalk [GR83], which proposed the model-view-controller (MVC) paradigm: the model takes the abstract description of the data to make it perceivable to users. The view performs one possible representation of the model, and the controller manages the input from the user. Another proposal was developed by Myers [M90], who indicated a small number (six) of interaction classes (menu; move-grow; new-point; angle; text; trace), each encapsulating a specific interactive behaviour, which allowed a broad spectrum of graphical interactions to be described.

Coutaz developed the Presentation, Abstraction, Control (PAC) model [C87]. In PAC each interaction object is divided into three parts (see Figure 6.5): *Abstraction*, i.e. the functional core which implements some expertise in a media-independent way so that there is an abstract description of the objects to provide to the users; *Presentation*, i.e. the perceivable behaviour: the appearance and the reception of the user input; *Control*, which links an abstraction to a presentation, controls the behaviour of the two perspectives it serves, remembers a local state for supporting multithread dialogue, and maintains relationships with other agents.

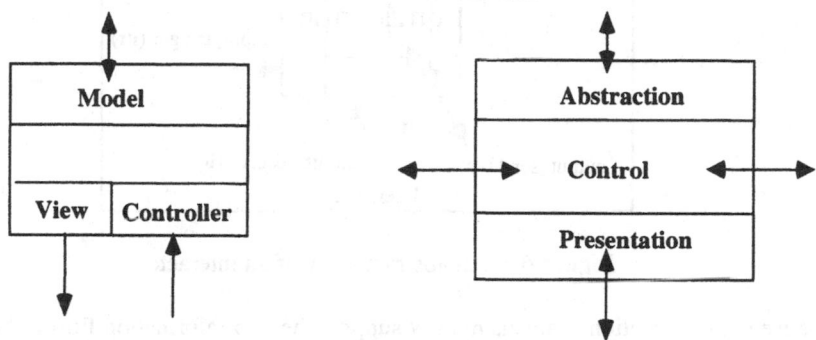

Figure 6.5: The MVC and PAC architectural models.

This model evolved into the PAC-Amodeus model [NC91] that uses the Arch model as the foundation for the functional partitioning of an interactive system and describes the Dialogue Component with PAC agents: as in Arch, PAC-Amodeus offers two-way information flows between the primary components of the arch. The nature of the connectors between the functional boundaries is left opened since it depends heavily on the case at hand. It may be procedure calls, pointers, message passing, or any other protocol suitable for the system requirements. Within the Dialogue Control component, there are two information flows: the hierarchical traversal between PAC agents, and in contrast with the original PAC style, direct links with the Domain Adaptor (DA) and Presentation components (PC).

6.2 THE INTERACTOR MODEL

An interactor is a model for describing objects interacting with users (such as scrolling lists, buttons, radio buttons, check boxes, etc.). The model described in [P94] differs from other models for interaction objects such as PAC [C87] or Myers' interactor [M90] as it structures each of them as an entity to support bi-directional communication between users and software applications. Such a model was an evolution of a previous model [FP90] which was based on abstract concepts for describing graphics systems.

Generally speaking the possible communication of an interactor can be classified into eight types of communication channels indicated in Table 6.1 and graphically represented in Figure 6.6.

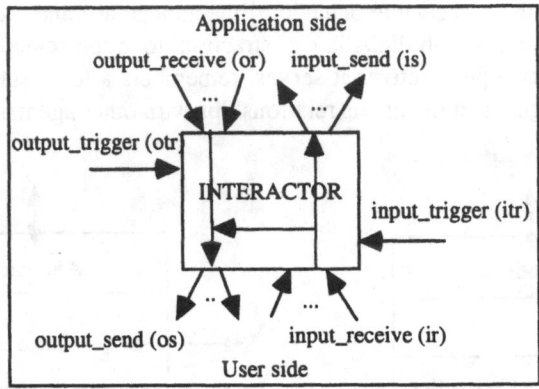

Figure 6.6: An abstract view of an interactor.

These communication channels mainly support the two information flows: the input, from the user towards the functional core, the output, from the functional core towards the user.

If the input (or output) trigger is missing in an interactor it means that there is an implicit automatic trigger. Thus, whenever there is an input in the *input_receive* (or in the *output_receive)* channel then information is automatically delivered through the *input_send* (or the *output_send)* channel.

CHANNEL TYPE	Description
input_receive	indicating *what* input can be received from the user side,
input_trigger	indicating *when* the result of the input processing of the interactor is delivered to the external
input_send	indicating *what* input information is delivered;
output_receive	indicating *what* output data it can receive;
output_trigger	indicating *when* output information has to be delivered by the interactor;
output_send	indicating *what* output information is delivered by the interactor;
enabling	indicating *when* the interactor becomes reactive;
disabling	indicating *when* the interactor becomes inactive.

Table 6.1: The communication channel types of an interactor.

We can use a small, concrete example as a pop-up menu to show how most of these communication channels are used. In a pop-up menu the output trigger event is given by the pressing of a button of the mouse. This event activates the presentation of the menu which is obtained by providing information to its *output_send* communication channel. Most of this information, such as the elements of the menu, was received from the application through the *output_receive* channel. The *input_receive* channel allows the menu to receive the cursor position currently selected by the user whereas the input trigger event is given by the event of releasing the button of the mouse. At that time the information of the current selected menu element will be provided towards the application through the *input_send* communication channel.

An interactor at the end of the architectural specification can be described by the following attributes:

- *initial enabling:* a Boolean indicating whether the interactor is enabled at the beginning of the session;
- *task:* list of tasks associated with the interactor
- *objects:* a list of objects (each of them can be either a perceivable or an application object) can be associated with the interactor;
- *for each input channel type* (see Table 6.1): a list of interactors connected by the considered type of communication channel;
- *first action:* the initial possible actions of the interactor are indicated;
- *last action:* the last possible actions of the interactor are indicated;
- *input processing*: the processing of the data received from the user side (if any);
- *output processing*: the processing of the data received from the application side (if any).

6.3 COMPOSITION OPERATORS FOR INTERACTORS

Once we have a model for a single interactor we can obtain the description of interactive applications by composing instances of such a model. To obtain a modular and flexible approach we need a set of composition operators that take into account the specific features of interactors. Hierarchical compositions of interactors can be performed along both input (and output) flows of information. Thus, each interactor may receive input from other interactors and not only from the user or the application. Besides, the compositions among interactors are not necessarily static and they can be reconfigured according to specific events. In the next sections the possible types of composition operators among interactors are introduced.

6.3.1 External composition

The external composition operator allows designers of the architecture to describe the information flow from the application side to the user side. The external composition is realised when the result of the output processing of one or more interactors is sent to another interactor.

For example (Figure 6.7), we can have two interactors each interacting with a different user in order to edit a part of a drawing. A third interactor can be externally composed with the previous two in order to receive the descriptions of the two parts, compose them into a single drawing, and then visualise the result.

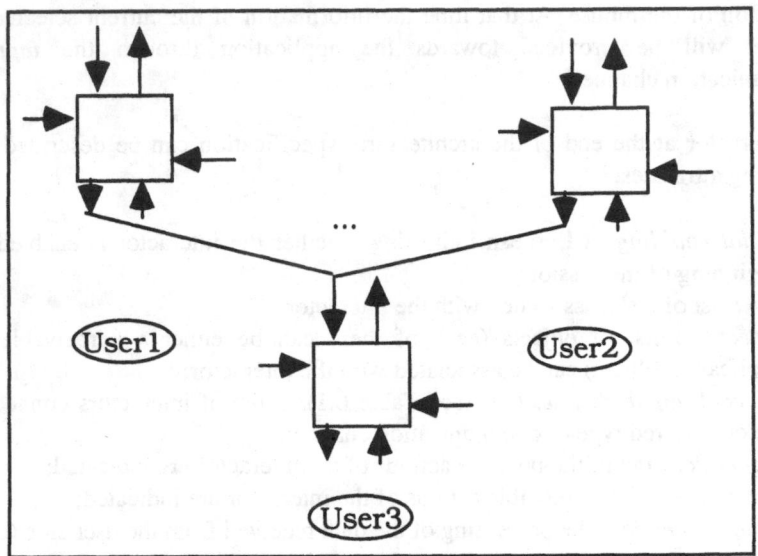

Figure 6.7: An example of the external composition of interactors.

The external composition operator can be applied also to send output information to more than one interactor. For example in a mail application the interactor that receives the new message from the functional core (the network in this case) can deliver information to a graphical icon which gets highlighted to indicate that a new message has arrived and to an audio interactor which can generate a predefined audio message signalling the new arrival.

6.3.2 Internal composition

This operator is introduced to describe an information flow which is inverse with respect to that described by the external composition operator. In this case low level input is provided to another interactor in order to perform further processing before generating the input information towards the application.

Four interactors are given as an example (Figure 6.8), where the first returns a query for a relational database (where the queries are requests for the visualisation of all the records whose content corresponds to the attribute-value pairs which are provided as input) which receives input from the other three interactors. These allow users to provide single attribute-values pairs: the first by filling a graphical form, the second by a textual shell and the third by a voice device. Once the first interactor (the query interactor) has been given enough information, if the user generates the related input trigger the request is transmitted to the data base application.

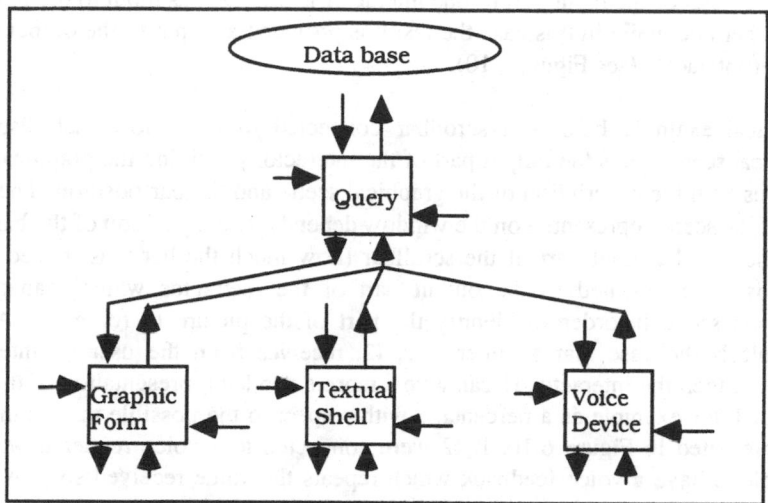

Figure 6.8: An Example of Internal Composition of Interactors.

Another example is in the case where we have one interactor, I2, which receives input from a graphic tablet and another one, I3, which receives input from a mouse. Both interactors receive input in coordinates depending on the device, translate them in a logical coordinate system and provide the result to the I1 interactor which will process them without considering the original coordinate system.

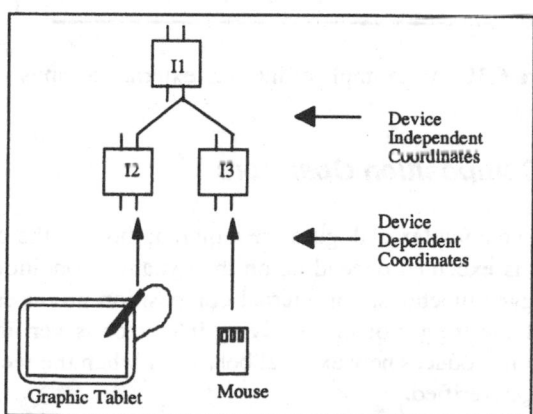

Figure 6.9: Another example of the internal composition of interactors.

6.3.3 Internal-External Composition Operators

With the internal-external composition operator it is possible to communicate the result of the input part of an interactor to the output part of another interactor. It differs from the internal composition operator because in the internal composition case the result of the input part of one interactor is provided as input to the input part of another one while in this case the result is provided as input to the output part of another interactor (see Figure 6.10).

A typical example here is a scrollbar connected to a window that displays a graphical scene. Thus the output part of the interactor providing the graphical scene receives both the description of the graphical scene and the bar position. The actual part of the scene represented on the window depends on the position of the bar. Thus the result of the input part of the scrollbar (how much the bar was moved by the user) is communicated to the output part of the interactor which manages the graphical scene in order to identify the part of the picture to represent. Another example is the case that an interactor, I2, receives from the user an integer by keyboard then the interactor I1 can give a more extended representation of the value provided, for example as a percentage with respect to the possible maximum value as represented in Figure 6.10. If I2 were connected to a voice render it would be possible to have a voice feedback which repeats the value received so providing a feedback additional to that produced by the I1 interactor.

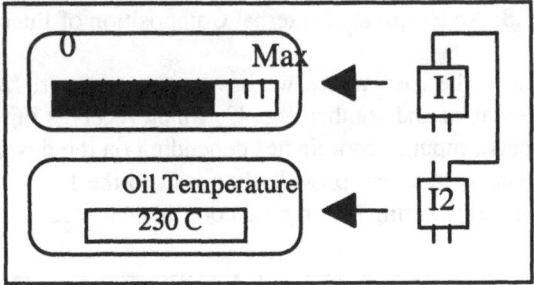

Figure 6.10: An example of internal-external composition.

6.3.4 Control Composition Operators

Especially if multiple complex dialogues are required: most of the processing of the interaction objects is executed depending on the dynamic conditions that are associated with the trigger functions. An internal composition produces a result on the application side, if the trigger of the receiving interactor is verified. Likewise, an external composition produces new external behaviour when the receiving interactor has the output trigger verified.

Thus we also need another particular case of composition. We can call it *control composition*: when the result of an interactor is an event which is used for triggering the processing of another interactor. Specifically, two new composition operators have to be introduced in order to distinguish whether the input or the output trigger are generated. In the internal control composition the result of the processing of a interactor generates an input trigger for another interactor. An example of internal control composition is when we consider an input form where the user has to fill various fields in textual ways and then to select a button to send the information to a database. In Figure 6.11, I1, I2, I3 allow the user to provide input, I4 composes them and when it receives the trigger event from I5 (which is associated with the Submit button) it sends the information stored to the internal database.

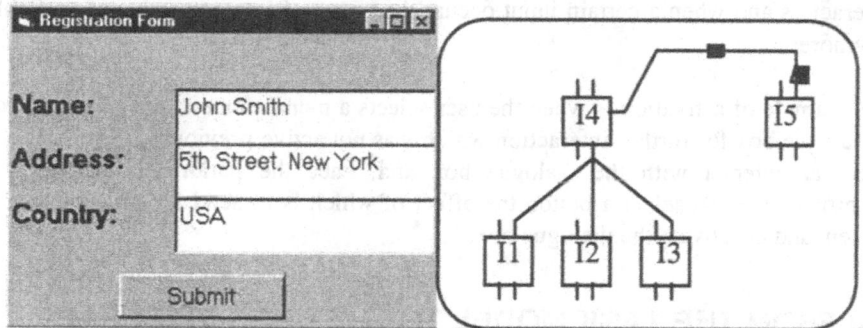

Figure 6.11: An example of internal control composition.

Similarly, in the external control composition the result of the processing of an interactor generates an output trigger for another interactor. The triggers events may also be directly generated by users or applications. Figure 6.12 graphically represents the five types of composition operators considered.

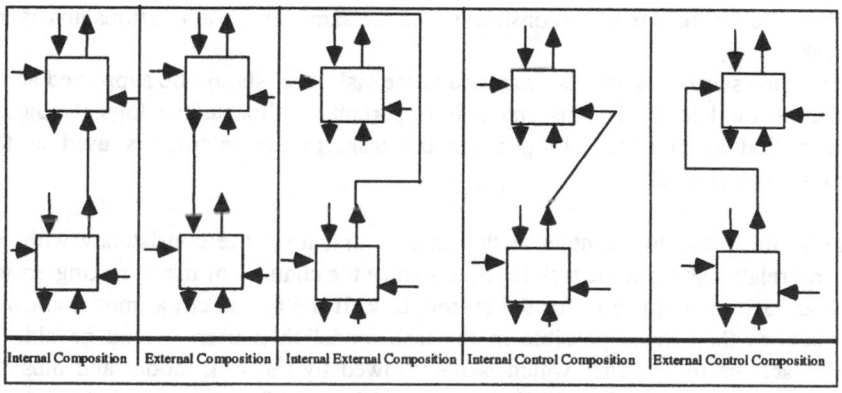

Figure 6.12: The set of possible composition operators.

6.3.5 Activation and deactivation composition operators

The previous operators allow us to describe even very complex networks of interactors, but always static organisations of interactors. While observing user interfaces it is easy to recognise that usually the set of active interactors is dynamic because it may happen that when performing some events some interactors are deactivated and others activated. For this purpose one activation and one deactivation composition operator have to be introduced.

In the activation case we have one interactor that, having received an input, can activate a set of interactors whereas in the deactivation case we have more interactors and when a certain input occurs then a set of interactors is not available anymore.

An example of activation is when the user selects a menu element and this activates a dialogue box for further interaction which was not active previously. Similarly the user can interact with the dialogue box and, once the parameters desired are specified, s/he can select a button the effect of which is to send a command to the system and deactivate the dialogue box.

6.4 FROM THE TASK MODEL TO THE USER INTERFACE ARCHITECTURE MODEL

In deriving an architectural model from the task model there are some important elements:

- a precise association between tasks and software objects for interacting with users (*interactors*) should be performed;
- the architecture should be consistent with the same temporal relationships as the task model;
- the same semantics effects described at the task level should be supported at the architectural level. To this end it is important to allocate the logical objects, identified as necessary to perform the task, to the interactors used at the architectural level.

It can be important to maintain at the architectural level the consistency with the temporal relationships at the task level, to reduce the chances of users making errors, which are actions not useful for the current task. If the architectural model allowed more actions than those possible in the task model then users would be able to perform actions in an order which is not allowed by the task model and thus we would have erroneous and possibly damaging actions. In fact, suppose that two tasks must be performed in sequence because the second task needs information processed by the first one. If the user interface allowed the performance of the second task before the termination of the first, this would mean that it would be performed on the wrong set of data thus providing the wrong result. For example, imagine that we have two tasks: one formulating the values for providing a request to a telephone numbers database, and the other to send the query. There is a sequentiality constraint between these two tasks that can be identified at the task level. If the corresponding user interface would relax this constraint it would introduce the possibility for the user to make an error: trying to send a request without having formulated its parameters first. This can only generate an error message indicating that an incomplete request has been formulated.

On the other hand, if the architectural model did not allow actions that are possible in the task model, this would imply that it is too rigid and introduces limitations which have no motivations from the application domain point of view.

Another reason for identifying precise rules for tasks-to-interactors transformation is that once they have been precisely defined they can be incorporated into an automatic tool whose main purpose is to support the designer's work when passing from one model to another. *This transformation cannot be done completely automatically if we want optimal solutions.* However, a tool incorporating knowledge of these rules can give relevant information which can optimise the designers' work and highlight the important aspects that they have to take into account.

This approach can be used both to design and develop new systems and to analyse existing ones. In the latter case it is useful because it gives better insight into the dialogue that is supported by the application considered, how it is supported and, what the main components are.

The starting point is the task model whose main aspects can be represented formally in the following mappings:

Decompose: Task → Tasks, decomposes one task into other tasks (one-to-many relationship);
ActionsObject: Object → Actions, returns the set of actions associated with one given object (one-to-many relationship);
ObjectsTask: Task → Objects, returns the set of objects associated with a given task (one-to-many relationship);
TasksObject: Object → Tasks, given an object the function indicates the tasks which manipulate it.

We assume that Interactor, Object, Task, Action are the finite sets indicating the available interactors, objects, tasks and actions respectively. Interactors, Objects, Tasks and Actions are the power set of the elementary sets (the set of all the possible sets obtainable by the elementary elements).

In this section we consider the problem to transform, following the TIM method, the task specification into an interactor architecture which is represented by the following mappings:

InteractorObject: Object → Interactor, returns the interactor associated with one given object, which is the interactor that contains the description of the given object. Each object is associated with one and only one interactor;

ObjectsInteractor: Interactor → Objects, returns the set of objects associated with a given interactor,

ActionsInteractor: Interactor → Actions, returns the set of actions which are performed within the given interactor. Each interactor can have many actions associated with it. The actions of an interactor are the actions of the objects associated with that interactor.

Note the difference between the TasksObj and the IntObj functions: in the former, given an object we can find one or more tasks associated with it, whereas in the latter, given an object we can find one and only one interactor associated with it. The difference is because the task model addresses mainly the user activities which are abstract entities and it is possible to use the same object for two different tasks (I can use the phone both to speak with a colleague of mine and to get an alarm call). On the other hand, in the architectural models we give a structure for the application components. Each object can be allocated in only one place (while still maintaining the possibility to support more tasks).

This transformation makes it possible to obtain at the end the following mappings in addition to a complete architectural specification:

TransTasktoInt: Task → Interactors, given one task it returns the set of interactors associated with a given task.

TransInttoTask: Interactor → Tasks, it provides the set of tasks associated with an interactor.

It is possible to have various cases: one task associated with one interactor, one task associated with various interactors, and various tasks associated with one interactor. If we consider an abstract task then the related interactors, at the end of the transformation process, are those associated with the basic tasks obtained from the decomposition of the considered task. As a consequence of a systematic transformation method it is possible to have an automatic tool that, after the transformation is performed, is able to allow designers to select one task, in the list of the tasks supported by the application, and show what the interactors required to support the performance of that task are.

Actions can be associated with objects. They allow objects to receive and send information. Thus in order to identify them designers should think about what exchange of information should be performed among the objects of the task level considered when the tasks are performed. This level of detail of specification of the task model is useful when the designer wants to derive an architectural model consistent with the requirements of the task model.

6.5 THE TRANSFORMATION ALGORITHM

In the tasks-to-interactors transformation there are some key elements:

- the identification of the interactors and the association of each of them with one or more objects required to perform the tasks;
- the identification of the connections among interactors so as to allow the information flow needed to perform the tasks;
- the interactor-based architecture should comply with the temporal relationships defined at the task level.

In the transformation it is possible to build an architecture for each level of the task tree. When we move to build the architecture associated with the next level of the task tree we use two inputs: the architecture of the previous level and the indication of what the tasks at the next level of the tree (and their relationships) are. When moving from the architectural description associated with a level of the task tree to the architectural description associated with the next task level, the interactors of the previous architecture may be transformed into two modalities:

- *interactor refinement* occurs when in the task decomposition an object which has already been allocated to the interactor considered is refined and this may entail new connections for the corresponding interactor too;
- *interactor decomposition* is performed when the associated task is decomposed into a set of tasks which operate on different objects (some of them are new).

We start to consider subtasks top-down in a level-by-level approach. For each task at the same level in the task tree we consider the set of objects associated with it. There are mainly three possibilities for the identification of the interactors:

R1) The set of objects of the task considered have already been associated with interactors. If there is a refinement of these objects, the related interactors may have new connections to support the new actions.

R2) For each set of objects associated with *more than one* task and not yet allocated to any interactor, we have to introduce one new interactor. We have in this case an *object-driven* allocation of interactors.

R3) If there are sets of objects which are used *only* by one task and not yet allocated to any interactor then a new interactor is introduced for each of them and is associated with all the objects of the set considered. In this case we have a *task-driven* allocation.

For example, if we have the *Send request to flights database* task decomposed into three subtasks (*Select departure town, Select arrival town, Send request*), with the *Select departure town* task associated with the *current request, list of departure towns* objects, the *Select arrival town* task with the *current request, list of arrival town* objects, and the *Send request* task with the *Current request, button for sending request* objects and all these objects have not yet been allocated to interactors. Then we need four interactors, one for each task, as the *list of departure town, list of arrival town, and button for sending request* objects are allocated to different tasks (R3) and one for the *current request* object which is manipulated by all tasks, but in each case coupled with a different object (R2). This means that it is not strictly connected to any of them, and so we need one interactor for it too.

6.6 CONNECTING INTERACTORS TO SUPPORT THE INFORMATION FLOW

Once all the objects of the task level considered are associated with interactors, the input and output actions of the objects are used to define composition operations among interactors. These compositions define connections among interactors which, at the implementation level, can be performed as calls to the related methods.

To identify the connections among interactors we consider the input and the output actions associated with the objects belonging to the interactors considered. We follow the following rules for the identification of the connections among interactors:

R4) If the input action is from the user then there is an *input_receive* type from the user.

R5) If the input action is from an object of another interactor then there is an input connection from the interactor associated with that object. There are four possible types of connections allowing the interactor to receive information (beforehand they were called *input_receive, input_trigger, output_receive, output_trigger*). The choice is made depending on whether the information received affects the output or the input flow of information in the interactor considered, and on whether the input provides data information or just a control event.

R6) In the case of output actions we have to identify the object with the corresponding input action, and then follow the above rules. If the output action is towards the user then there is an *output_send* type of action.

If designers want that the temporal relationships defined at the task level are supported at the architectural level as well, they need to analyse the operators used at the task level and create connections among operators which operate on the disabling and enabling gates. What usually happens is that the first or the last action of a task generates an event for the enabling or disabling gate of an interactor.

We can follow the following rules for defining temporal relationships at the architectural level which are consistent with those at the task level:

R7) If two tasks are independent concurrent tasks (||| operator) then the related interactors should be active at the same time and independent without any composition among them.

R8) If two tasks are concurrent with information exchange (|[]| operator) then the interactors related should be composed in such a way as to support communication among them (the previous set of rules defines more precisely how this communication should be performed).

R9) If two tasks are composed by the sequential enabling operator (>>) then the last action of the interactors associated with the first task generates an enabling event for the interactor associated with the second task.

R10) If two tasks are composed by the disabling operator ([>) then the related interactors should be enabled at the same time and the first action of the interactor(s) associated with the second task should generate a disabling event for the interactor(s) associated with the first task (or the last action of the interactor(s) associated with the first task should disable the interactor associated with the first task).

R11) If two tasks are composed by the choice operator ([]) then the related interactors should have the first action available at the same time and once one of them has been selected then the interactors associated with the other tasks are made inactive.

R12) If a task and its ancestor tasks are not iterative then the related interactors once terminated are deallocated.

R13) If a task is iterative then the related interactors are iterative too.

R14) If two tasks are composed by the sequential enabling operator with information passing ([]>>) in addition to the connection indicated in R9 there should be another connection supporting information passing from the enabling to the enabled interactor.

When we move to consider a new level in the task tree and we build the related architectural description some interactors of the architectural specification associated with the previous level of the task tree can be decomposed into two or more interactors. The new interactors inherit some elements from the abstract one.

R15) Initial enabling. At any level only the interactors associated with the tasks enabled at the beginning are those enabled at the start of the session.

Iteration at the parent task. When the parent task is iterative (see for example Figure 6.13) then the interactors associated with the subtasks require additional connections depending on the temporal relationships among subtasks:

R16) In the case of sequential enabling (Figure 6.13) we have first the performance of the B task and then that of the C task, however if the parent task (A in the example of Figure 6.13) is an iterative task, then when the C task terminates then the B task is enabled again.

R17) In the case of disabling, when the C task terminates or if the B task terminates without any action of the C task occurring then both B and C are enabled again.

R18) In the case of choice, when one of the two tasks terminates then B and C are enabled again.

R19) In the case of interleaving, both tasks have to be terminated before being both enabled again.

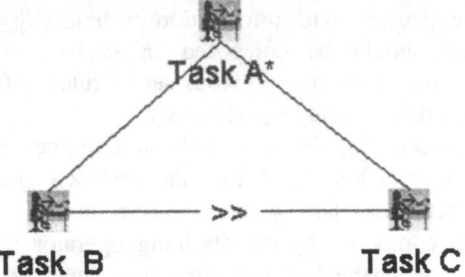

Figure 6.13: An example of a parent iterative task.

6.7 AN EXAMPLE OF APPLICATION OF THE TRANSFORMATION

We can further discuss how the TIM method works by considering the specific case study introduced before (an application for interacting with museum information).

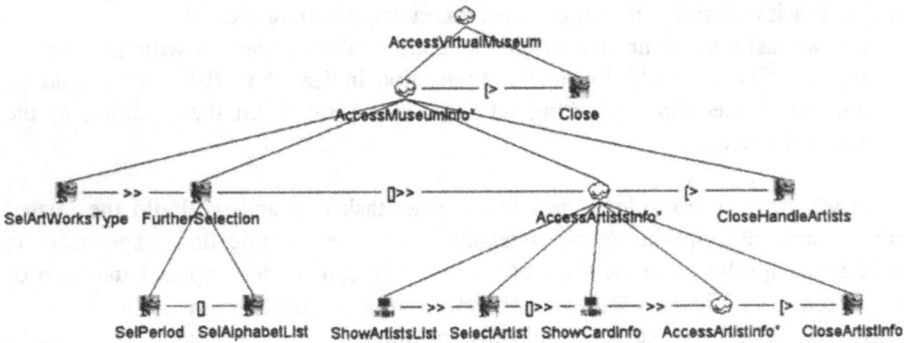

Figure 6.14: An example of task specification.

Let us consider the example task tree in Figure 6.14 which was introduced in chapter 4. The information related to the first two levels of the task tree is given in Table 6.2. At the first level we have an abstract task (*AccessMuseumInfo*) that requires three abstract objects: to receive information from the user (*Pres_in_sel*), to provide information to the user (*Pres_out_sel*), to contain the application information on the museum (*Museum_info*). The *Close* task only requires a perceivable object to allow the user interaction (*Pres_close*).

At the next level we have four tasks. *SelArtWorksType* requires a perceivable object to specify the type of work of interest (*Pres_type*) and the application object containing the current user request (*Req_info*). Similarly, the *FurtherSelection* task manipulates two objects. The *AccessArtistsInfo* task manipulates three objects: that containing the application information on the museum (*Museum_info*), that containing the user request (*Req_info*) and that presenting the list of artists selected by the user (*Pres_list*). *CloseHandelArtists* is similar to the *Close* task.

The transformation starts from the first level of the task tree and it associates the two tasks (*AccessMuseumInfo* and *Close*) with one interactor for each because each task has its own set of related objects (R3). Then, since the two tasks are composed by the disabling operator, the first action of the interactor associated with the second task should generate a disabling event to the interactor associated with the first interactor (R10).

	Task name	Object name	Type	Input Action	OutputAction
L	**AccessMuseumInfo**	Pres_in_sel	Perc.	Inf. from User	Inf. to Museum_info
e		Pres_out_sel	Perc.	Inf. from Museum_info	Inf. to User
v		Museum_info	Appl.	Inf. from Pres_in_sel	Inf. to Pres_out_sel
e					
l					
1	**Close**	Pres_close	Perc.	Inf. from User	
	SelArtWorksType	Pres_type	Perc.	Inf. from User	Inf. to Req_info
		Req_info	Appl.	Inf.fromPres_type/ Pres_list/Pres_artist/Pres_selcri	Inf. to Museum_info
L	**FurtherSelection**	Pres_selcri	Perc.	Inf. from User	Inf. to Req_info
e		Req_info	Appl.	Inf.fromPres_type/ Pres_list/Pres_artist/Pres_selcri	Inf. to Museum_Info
v					
e	**AccessArtistsInfo**	Museum_Info	Appl.	Inf. from Req_info	Inf. to Pres_list/ Pres_artist
l		Pres_list	Perc.	Inf. from Museum_info/ User	Inf. to User/Req_info
2		Req_info	Appl.	Inf.fromPres_type/ Pres_list/Pres_artist/Pres_selcri	Inf. to Museum_info
	CloseHandleArtists	Back_sel	Perc.	Inf. from User	

Table 6.2: Specification of objects and actions associated with tasks.

At the next level a set of interactors are created which replace the first abstract interactor associated with the *AccessMuseumInfo* task. We consider the subtasks of such a task and apply the rules previously introduced for identifying the new interactors. In this case, for each object at the task level considered we allocate a new interactor because each object is either handled by only one task (R3 - task-driven allocation) (this is the case of *Pres_type*, *Pres_selcri*, *Pres_list*, and *Back_sel* objects) or it is manipulated by more than one task at the level of the tree considered, each time together with different other objects (R2 - object-driven allocation) (this is the case of *Req_info*).

Then the designer has to consider the actions of the objects in the task model to create the corresponding connections among interactors. Thus, for example, in the *SelArtWorksType* task there is a *Pres_type* object which has an output to the *Req_info* object. The *Pres_type* object is in the interactor associated with the *SelTypeArtWorks* task since it is not used by any other task whereas the *Req_info* object is in another interactor because it is used by various tasks. Thus we need to create a connection between these two interactors [R5]. In this case if tool support should be provided then the tool should provide a message to the designer asking to transform this action in a connection between the two involved interactors (see for an example Figure 6.15). The message shows the current state of the architecture under construction. In this case the tool proposes to create a communication channel that connects the *input_send* channel of the interactor containing the *Pres_type* object with the *input_receive* channel of the interactor containing the *Req_info* objects. The motivation of this indication is that there is an output action from the *Pres_type* object with a corresponding input action to the *Req_info* object, and as the *Pres_type* object receives information directly from the user then it will provide it through the input_send type communication channel to the interactor containing the *Req_info* object. Likewise a connection between the interactors containing the *Pres_selcri* object with the interactor containing the *Req_info* object will be created.

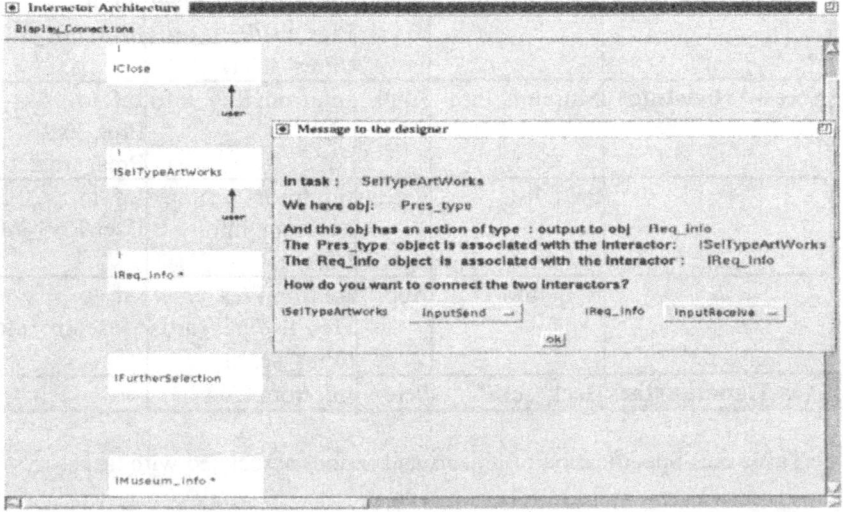

Figure 6.15: An example of tool-supported definition of interactor's composition.

In this way we will find also that the *input_send* channel of the interactor containing *Req_info* sends information to the interactor containing *Museum_info* and that this last interactor sends information to the *output_receive* channels of the interactors containing the *Pres_list* object which will then present this information to the user by the *output_send* channel (R6).

Since the *SelArtWorksType* and *FurtherSelection* tasks are composed with the enabling operator it means that the related interactors (those handling the *Pres_type* and the *Pres_selcri* objects) once performed (following R9) are deactivated until the parent task (*AccessMuseumInfo*) is started again. The interactor associated with the *CloseHandleArtists* task will deactivate the interators associated with the *AccessArtistsInfo* (R10).

When we complete the task model by applying the transformation algorithm iteratively to all the levels of the task model, it is possible to obtain a final detailed description of the software architecture identifying basic components (in this example about 50) and their connections. Once the final architecture has been obtained it is possible to know, for each interactor, what the corresponding task is. It is useful to understand the interactors involved in the performance of a given task because, in case of modifications of the task tree, we thus know immediately which parts of the software architecture have to be modified.

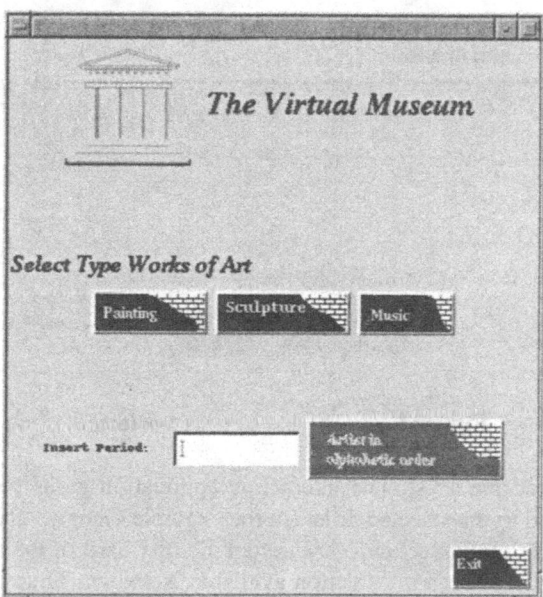

Figure 6.16: The initial layout of the resulting user interface.

It is then possible to generate the user interface consistent with the task and architectural models. The concrete interface can be obtained associating specific presentation and interaction techniques with the abstract objects indicated in the architectural description. This association is performed taking into account the requirements raised by the corresponding task. In Figure 6.16 the layout associated with the *SelArtWorksType* and *FurtherSelection* tasks is presented. Since there is a sequentiality constraint between these two tasks, from a temporal point of view, the interaction objects (a text input field and a button) associated with the second task will be enabled only after the termination of the first task (selection of the type of art of interest for the user).

After the first request is provided to the application a list of artists will appear (see Figure 6.17). At that time the *CloseHandleArtists* and *Close* tasks are also enabled (they are associated with two buttons).

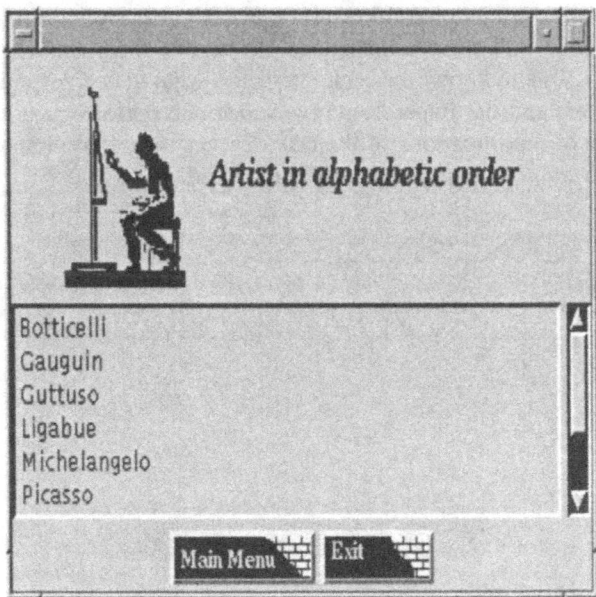

Figure 6.17: The list of artists selected.

The user can select one artist. The interactive application gives the option to have information related to the selected artist (in the example Gaugin) and his life (Figure 6.18) by using multimedia techniques. First an identity card of the artist is provided and next a list of the related information available is shown. Thus the enabled tasks are *AccessArtistInfo*, *CloseArtistInfo*, *CloseAccessArtists* and *Close* tasks. The *AccessArtistInfo* task is decomposed into various subtasks that, for example, allow the user to select the list of available videos about Gaugin, and finally select and activate one of such videos.

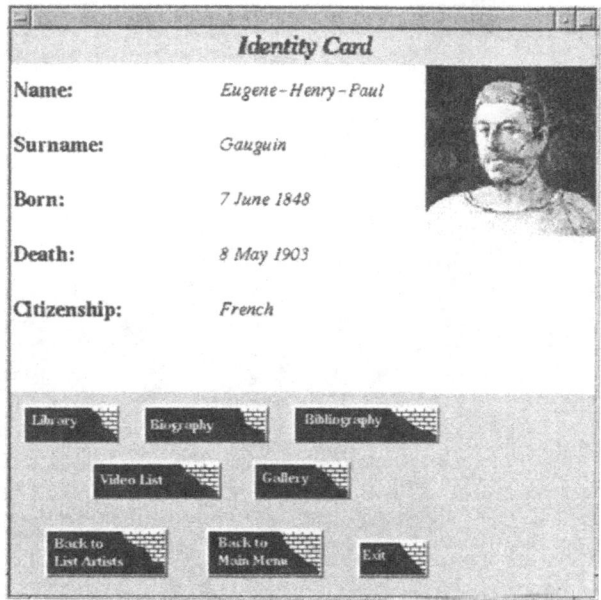

Figure 6.18: Presentation of information concerning an artist.

6.8 EXERCISES

1. Consider an application that you are familiar with and identify what aspects belong to each of the three layers of the Seeheim model.
2. Develop an interactor-based description of the software architecture of a graphical editor.
3. Develop an interactor-based description of the software architecture of a web-based application for electronic commerce covering also client-server communication.
4. Develop the task model of an application for access to a tourist kiosk and then develop the corresponding architectural description and finally a corresponding user interface.

7 Patterns in Interactive Applications

7.1 INTRODUCTION

There is a growing interest in the possibility of using patterns [GHJV95] in user interface design, development and evaluation. For example, they can be a good way of capturing and communicating design solutions that can be reused in many areas [PM97a]. In general terms they can be used for both descriptive and prescriptive purposes. In the former case they capture a recurrent aspect (it can be a recurrent behaviour or system structure or presentation structure) whereas in the latter case they can be used to indicate a solution for a recurring problem.

In the human-computer interaction field there are many candidates for their application [ET97], for example, embodying HCI guidelines as patterns or using patterns for process and organisation design. Another possibility, described in [C97a], is to use them to represent usability problems and related solutions. In that work three types of usability patterns are identified: simple patterns, where one usability attribute dominates and solutions are easy; intrinsic patterns, where multiple usability attributes conflict or support - these may pose difficult problems; and circumstantial patterns, where usability attributes must be achieved but external factors constrain the solution - these may be very difficult as the constraints may be unique and require a novel solution.

In this book we have considered different viewpoints on the dynamic behaviour of an interactive application and the activities that it has to support. At the task level we focus on the logical actions, whereas at the software architectural level we consider the available interaction techniques and the software components that support the performance of logical actions. Each of these two representations can be provided at different, more refined, abstraction levels which provide different details. An additional advantage of a two-level approach is that it is possible to create a link between them. This allows designers and developers to use task patterns as a more conceptual and easy to manipulate and interpret representation of software which can be reused in different contexts.

7.2 PATTERNS

The pattern approach to design was first defined by the architect, Alexander [A77]. Although the books he wrote relate to urban planning and building architecture, they are applicable to many other disciplines, including software development. The main elements in Alexander's patterns are: the name, context, forces (which require solutions), problem (growing from the forces), and solution.

Patterns have been used in many areas of software engineering including development organisation, software processes, project planning, requirements engineering, and software configuration. In [BMRSS96] the *Design patterns* are grouped into categories of related patterns:

- *Structural decomposition*: this category includes patterns that support a suitable decomposition of subsystems and complex components into co-operating parts. An example is the *Whole-Part pattern*. This pattern helps with the aggregation of components that together form a semantic unit. An aggregate component, the Whole, encapsulates its constituent components, the Parts, organises their collaboration, and provides a common interface to its functionality. Direct access to the Parts is not possible.
- *Organisation of work*: this category comprises patterns that define how components collaborate together to solve a complex problem. An example is the *Master-Slave pattern*. A Master component distributes work to identical Slave components and computes a final result from the results these Slaves return.
- *Access control*: such patterns guard and control access to services or components. An example is the *Proxy pattern*. This pattern makes the clients of a component communicate with a representative rather than with the component itself. Introducing such a placeholder can serve many purposes, including enhanced efficiency, easier access and protection from unauthorised access.
- *Management*: this category includes patterns for handling homogenous collections of objects, services and components in their entirety. An example is the *Command Processor pattern*. This pattern separates the request for a service from its execution. A command processor component manages requests as separate objects, schedules their execution, and provides additional services such as the storing of request objects for later "undo".
- *Communication*: patterns in this category help to organise communication between components. For example, the *Forwarder-Receiver pattern* provides transparent inter-process communication for software systems with a peer-to-peer interaction model. It introduces forwarders and receivers to decouple peers from the underlying communication mechanisms.

In [GHJV95] there is a catalogue of design object-oriented patterns which are classified using different criteria. One of them, called purpose, divides patterns into groups depending on what each of them does. In this case patterns can have either a *creational, structural, or behavioural* purpose. Creational patterns concern the process of object creation. Structural patterns deal with the composition of classes or objects. Behavioural patterns characterise the ways in which classes or objects interact and distribute responsibility.

Patterns in the object-oriented technology suffer from the same general limitation of object-oriented approaches: they are more useful to design the internal system components. This can be overcome with task patterns that are more useful to support the design of user interfaces because they are closer to the conceptual models of end users that are usually structured in terms of activities to perform.

7.3 HOW TO REPRESENT A TASK PATTERN

The representation of a pattern depends on what kind of pattern we are considering and the purpose of the pattern. In [BPS97] some possible task pattern candidates are described by using ConcurTaskTrees. Here a more systematic description of one of them is given by following a specific list of indications for patterns. The purpose is to show how designers can apply pattern-based methods to dialogue design.

In choosing how to represent a pattern one must take into consideration the need to give both precise information with a sufficient level of formality, and informal information useful to grasp intuitively the characteristics of the pattern. Important aspects are:

P1. **the name**: to identify them in short;

P2. **the problems they address**: what kind of design problems they help to solve;

P3. **the specification of task relationships**: this is performed using ConcurTaskTrees. The hierarchical structure of ConcurTaskTrees specifications has two advantages: it provides a large range of granularity allowing large and small task structures to be reused, and it enables reusable task structures to be defined at both a low and a high semantic level.

P4. **the specification of the objects manipulated by the tasks**: in this case we can use tables indicating for each task the objects it needs to manipulate;

P5. **a scenario of use**: this is useful to give a precise example of an instance of pattern;

P6. **possible subpatterns**: it is possible to have structured groups of patterns which share a specific feature additional to those which characterise the pattern;

P7. **the aspects that can be modified in an instance**: since a pattern identifies the main element which defines the solution there are some minor aspects which can be modified by instances of patterns;

P8. **the applications where it is likely to be used**: this is useful to suggest where the pattern could be most suitably applied.

7.4 AN EXAMPLE OF A TASK PATTERN

To clarify this approach we can focus on one specific pattern, the search pattern, and we present it by following the above indications.

P1. Name: the Search Task

P2. Problem: the search for specific information via navigation in which the next query is based upon the results of the previous one. The pattern is used whenever the user has no precise ideas about how to search for the desired data and so can find the information needed just by refining the query depending on the result of the previous query.

P3. Task relationships: As we can see in Figure 7.1, we first have a distinction between the *Iterative Search* task which can be repeated several times (this is expressed by *) until the *Close* task disables ([> operator) the session. When we start a search, we define a first query (*DefineQuery* task) and only after the performance of this task ([]>> operator) application tasks will perform the query and show the result. Then the user can refine the query several times until s/he decides to perform the *Close Refinement* task. At that time it will be possible to start another completely different search without closing the session. We introduced an additional user task (*Decide Refinement*) which receives information from an application task (*Show Query Result*) and produces input for the next interaction task (*Refine Query*).

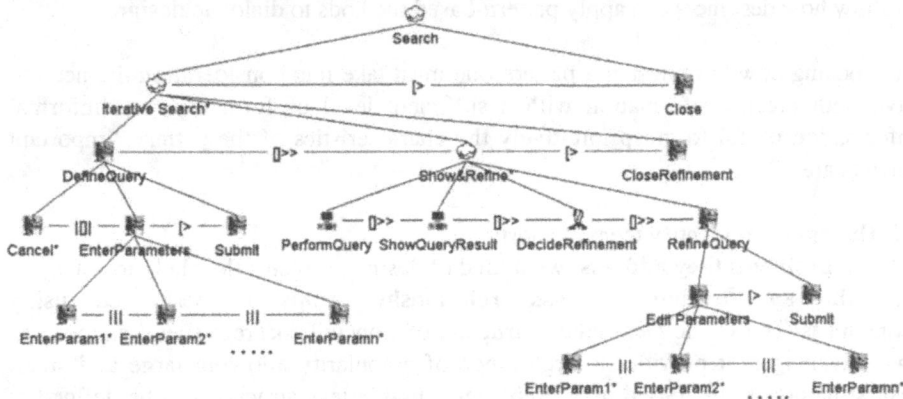

Figure 7.1: Search pattern specification.

P4. Objects manipulated by the task: Objects are entities which are manipulated to perform tasks by the associated actions. There are user-perceivable and application objects, which are both manipulated to perform the tasks by using the associated actions. The following table indicates objects and actions associated with the tasks.

In the task decomposition some objects at higher levels of the task tree are decomposed into multiple objects when we consider more refined task descriptions. For example, at the first level in the *Iterative Search* task we introduce an abstract presentation object (*Pres-refinement*). Then, at the tasks of the next level, this object is refined into objects which are used to provide input (*Pres-define)* and objects to present results (*Pres-show*). We can see at the third level that the perceivable object for input data can still be decomposed into objects which allow the user to provide input data (*Pres-parameters*, which is finally decomposed depending on the number of data attributes to edit) and the object which controls the delivery of input to the application (*Pres-submit*).

The following table aims to describe additional information contained in the task model in a compact way. As we have seen in Chapter 6 it is useful in the transformation from a task model to an architectural model. To make it easier to keep track of the relationships among objects, beside the name of the objects there is a column indicating when they are new objects introduced in the task model (N) or objects obtained as refinement of objects introduced in previous levels (R) or if they are just objects already introduced at previous levels (blank).

P5. Scenario of use: Silvia is looking for interesting papers on patterns. She makes a request to the on-line CNR library by giving the name of the topic as parameters of her request, and indicating that she is interested in papers written in English. The order of providing these two parameters is not important. She receives a long list of references. As she is interested in recent contributions she adds a further constraint in the request so that she receives information only on papers published in the last five years. The new list of publications is more manageable. She understands that the works by Gamma are very relevant. She would like to have them grouped so that they are presented together. Thus she makes a new request adding the constraint that the author has to be Gamma. The result is the information that she was looking for. Now she can move to another request for another topic.

P6. Describes or refers to variants and subpatterns: There are different ways to identify subpatterns. Here we introduce one that depends on the skill of the user performing the tasks. The interaction between user and system can result in a different manner depending on the user's skill. There can be various user typologies: expert users - users who have used the system several times and so want to interact with it in the fastest way or want to customise some tasks; or beginners - this type of user has no idea how to use the system and so needs to use the system in an easy way even if it is not the fastest way to use it.

Task name	Objects name		Obj. type	Input Action	Output Action
Iterative Search	Pres-refinement	N	Perc.	Inf. from user Inf. from Database	Inf. to user Inf. to Database
	Database	N	Appl.	Inf. from Pres-refinement	Inf. to Pres-refinement
Close	Pres-close	N	Perc.	Action from user	
Define Query	Pres-define	R	Perc.	Inf. from user	Inf. to Database
Show&Refine	Pres-data	R	Perc.	Inf. from Database	Inf. to user
	Pres-define	R	Perc.	Inf. from user	Inf. to Database
	Database		Appl.	Inf. from Pres-define	Inf. to Pres-data
CloseRefining	Close-refining	N	Perc.	Action from user	
Enter Parameters	Pres-parameters	R	Perc.	Inf. from user Control from Pres-submit Control from Pres-cancel	Inf. to Database
Submit	Pres-submit	N	Perc.	Action from user	Control to Pres-parameters
Cancel	Pres-cancel	N	Perc.	Action from user	Control to Pres-parameters
PerformQuery	Database		Appl.	Inf. from Pres-define	Inf. to Pres-data
ShowQueryRes	Pres-data		Perc.	Inf. from Database	Inf. to user
Enter Param1	Pres-param1	R	Perc.	Inf. from user Control from Pres-submit	Inf. to Database
Enter Paramn	Pres-paramn	R	Perc.	Inf. from user Control from Pres-submit	Inf. to Database

Table 7.1: Specification of objects and actions associated with tasks.

We can have different patterns depending on this distinction between users. They can vary in terms of the number of tasks or different temporal operators between the same tasks. In the first case the pattern for beginners can have less tasks than that for expert users, allowing them to do only the primary functions. There is also the opposite case, where the pattern for beginners has more tasks than the other. This is because beginners need to do more steps to accomplish the goal than experts. In the second case, there may be the same number of tasks but different temporal operators. For example, a beginner needs to do some steps in a sequential manner while an expert can do them without temporal constraints.

The above search pattern includes the basic operations which are necessary to accomplish a search. In the next example we show how we can extend it to support features which can be useful for expert users.

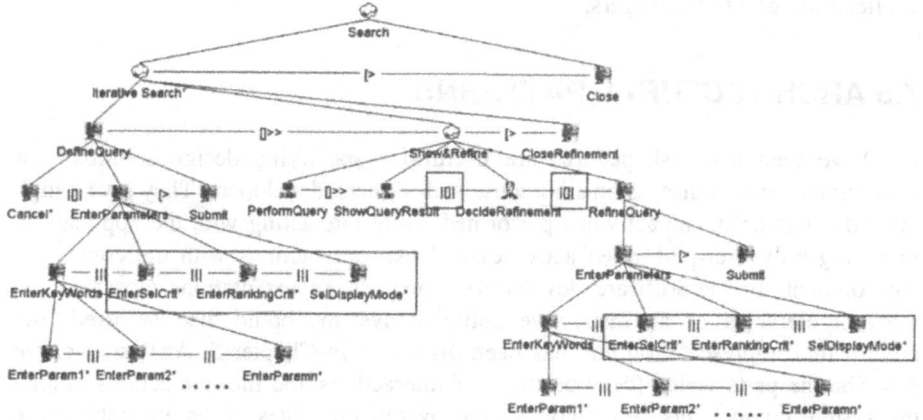

Figure 7.2: Search task pattern for expert users.

In this search pattern, we have more tasks than in the previous one (see the dashed rectangles in Figure 7.2), because the expert user can customise the research in the following manner:

- The *EnterSelCrit* task allows the user to insert the criteria to search for the parameters inserted. For example, the user can add some logical operators such as AND/OR/NOR, to combine the parameters specified.
- The *EnterRankingCrit* task allows the user to specify the weight of the parameters in the research, that is, for example, which one has to be found first.
- The *SelDisplayMode* task allows the user to decide how to visualise the query result.
- The *EnterKeyWords* task simply does the same operation as the *EnterParameters* Task shown in the SearchPattern for beginners.

There are also different temporal operators between the *ShowQueryResult*, *DecideRefinement* and *Refine Query* tasks with respect to the model given for beginners. In fact, while expert users are waiting for the *ShowQueryResult* task to end, they can get some idea of what the output will be and so can decide the refinement while the previous task is in progress and can start to insert new parameters at that time.

P7. Aspects that can be modifiable: The details which can vary in this specification are the instance of the presentation objects which can be used to interact with the application. For example, the global structure of the task specification (for instance, the results can be shown only after a query has been specified) cannot be modified.

P8. Applications where they are likely to be used: This search task can be applied in many applications where searching is needed, like search engines, database query applications, and file managers.

7.5 ARCHITECTURAL PATTERNS

We have seen that task patterns are useful for specifying design solutions for communication and discussion among users, designers, developers. They give a high level description of the activities performed while interacting with the application, including only user-performed activities and user interactions with the contextual environment. In the software development process, representations closer to the relevant elements of an interactive software system should also be used: the architectural representation that has been discussed in Chapter 5. At this level we describe the parts which focus on the user interactions and the interactions among the system components which control the overall dialogues. Thus an architecture representation has to take into account the main features of the system components used to support dialogues with the user, irrespective of the implementation language.

In [BMRSS96] there is a discussion of both design and architectural patterns. In the architectural patterns their application to interactive systems is considered. However, this is done in a rather limited approach because they consider architectural models (MVC [KP88] and PAC [C87]) for single interaction objects. Instead, we believe that one important element is to identify patterns associated with compositions of interaction objects which support solutions for dialogues occurring across many applications because they can give compact representations of large software components which can be reused in different applications. In [CCN97] the authors view PAC as a style and within the PAC style they have identified patterns of PAC agents.

We can exploit the rules previously described to associate tasks with the corresponding interactors to obtain high-level task patterns as easy to interpret and manipulate representations of pieces of reusable software. The basic idea is to identify patterns with compositions of interactors associated with good solutions to recurring situations and thus giving a more powerful possibility of reuse than patterns associated with single interaction objects.

We need a different representation for an architectural pattern. We still need the name and indication of the problem addressed, but the solution is represented in a different way: a graphical structure where there are boxes indicating basic components and arrows indicating how they communicate with each other. This representation is useful to have an idea of the structure of the interactive system and of how the dialogue is supported. We then also need an example of the layout associated with the architectural patterns to allow the designer to understand what kind of presentation it can generate to the end user. It has the same purpose of the scenario in the task pattern representation: to give an example of a specific instance which complies with the requirements of the related pattern.

7.6 AN EXAMPLE OF AN ARCHITECTURAL PATTERN

We will now show an example of a software architecture pattern which is associated with the task pattern example previously presented. This allows us to show the different purposes of these two representations. This pattern is based on the interactor concept [P94]. An interactor, as it has been described in Chapter 5, is a model for describing software objects interacting with users.

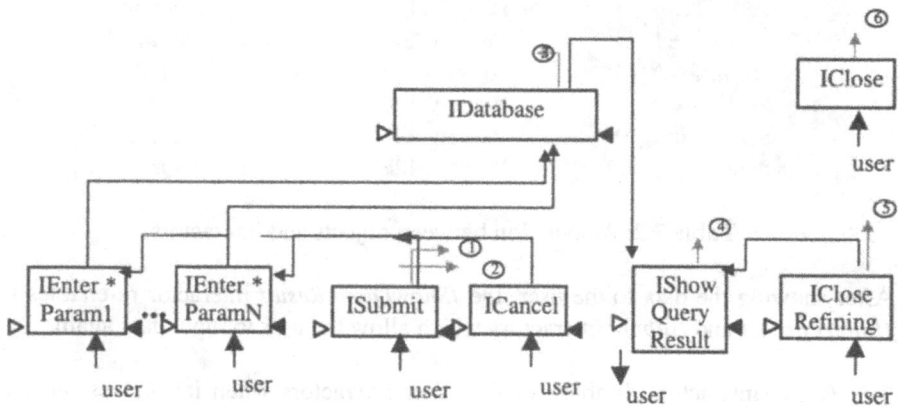

① Input_send to the disable_gate of: IEnterParam1.....IenterParamN, ICancel
② Input_send to the enable_gate of ICloseRefining, IDatabase
③ Input_send to the enable_gate of IShowQueryResult
④ Input_send to the enable_gate of : IEnterParam1, IEnterParamN, ISubmit
⑤ Input_send to the trigger_gate of: IEnterParam1......IEnterParamN
⑥ Input_send to the disable_gate of all interactors

Figure 7.3: The search task software architectural pattern.

P1. Name: Search Architectural Software

P2. Problem: We want an architecture in terms of software objects which describes the same dialogue described by the search task pattern and provides an indication of the software components needed to support it.

P3. Interactors Relationships: Each task can be managed by one or more interactors. The objects identified at the task level will be associated with interactors following Table 7.2 and actions among objects have been used to identify the composition among interactors. The resulting architecture is described in Figure 7.3.

For each task of editing a data attribute we have a corresponding interactor (for example, *IEnterParam1*), which receives input data from the user and sends them to the Database. It does not send these data immediately: it has to wait for the control event (input_trigger) from the *Isubmit* interactor which provides it when it receives the input from the user and disables it. The Database sends the result data to the *IShowQueryResult* interactor which presents them to the user.

Object name	Type	Interactor associated
Pres-param1	Perceivable	IEnter Param 1
...	...	...
Pres-paramN	Perceivable	IEnter Param N
Pres-submit	Perceivable	ISubmit
Pres-cancel	Perceivable	ICancel
Database	Application	IDatabase
Pres-close	Perceivable	IClose
Close-refining	Perceivable	ICloseRefining
Pres-data	Perceivable	IShowQueryResult

Table 7.2: Association between objects and interactors.

After showing the data to the user, the *IShowQueryResult* interactor re-enables the *IEnterParam1* and *Isubmit* interactors which allow the user to input data again.

The *IClose* interactor disables all the other interactors when it receives an input from the user. The *ICloseRefining* interactor allows the user to start a new search, so it sends an input_trigger to the *IEnterParam1* and IShowQueryResult interactors to cancel the data associated with the previous query. Table 7.2 shows how the objects associated with the basic tasks are allocated to the interactors identified. The interactors will manage the access to the related objects.

P4. Presentation layout of the architectural pattern: Figure 7.4 provides an example of a presentation layout which can be supported by the software architecture pattern considered. It shows how the presentation objects are associated with the interactors.

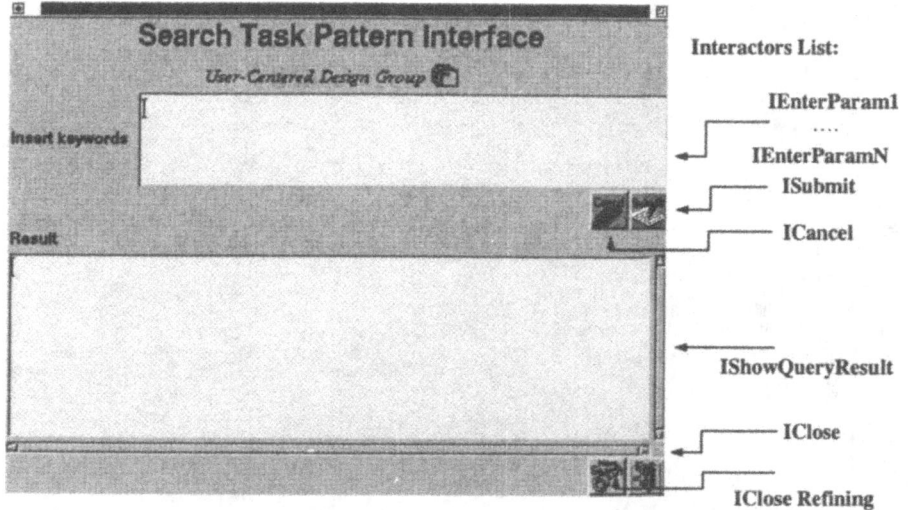

Figure 7.4: An example of a presentation layout.

P5. Modifiable aspects: The architectural patterns shown in Figure 7.3 can be expanded by adding new interactors which support the editing of new addition data attributes. These possible new interactors will receive an input from the user, send data to the database when receiving input triggers from the Isubmit interactor and will be disabled by the same interactor.

The connections described in the architecture cannot be modified if designers want to keep its dynamic behaviour consistent with that described in the task pattern.

7.7 RELATIONSHIPS BETWEEN TASKS AND ARCHITECTURAL PATTERNS

Chapter 5 described how it is possible to create an association between tasks and interactors. The aim of each interactor is to manage accesses to one or more objects defined at the task design level: each input and output action among objects provides indications on how to compose interactors.

The rules indicated allow designers to obtain architectural specifications which comply with the temporal constraints indicated in the task model. This is obtained by considering the operators used at the task level, the objects associated with each task and their relationships. The temporal relationships defined at the task level provide further information about how to compose interactors.

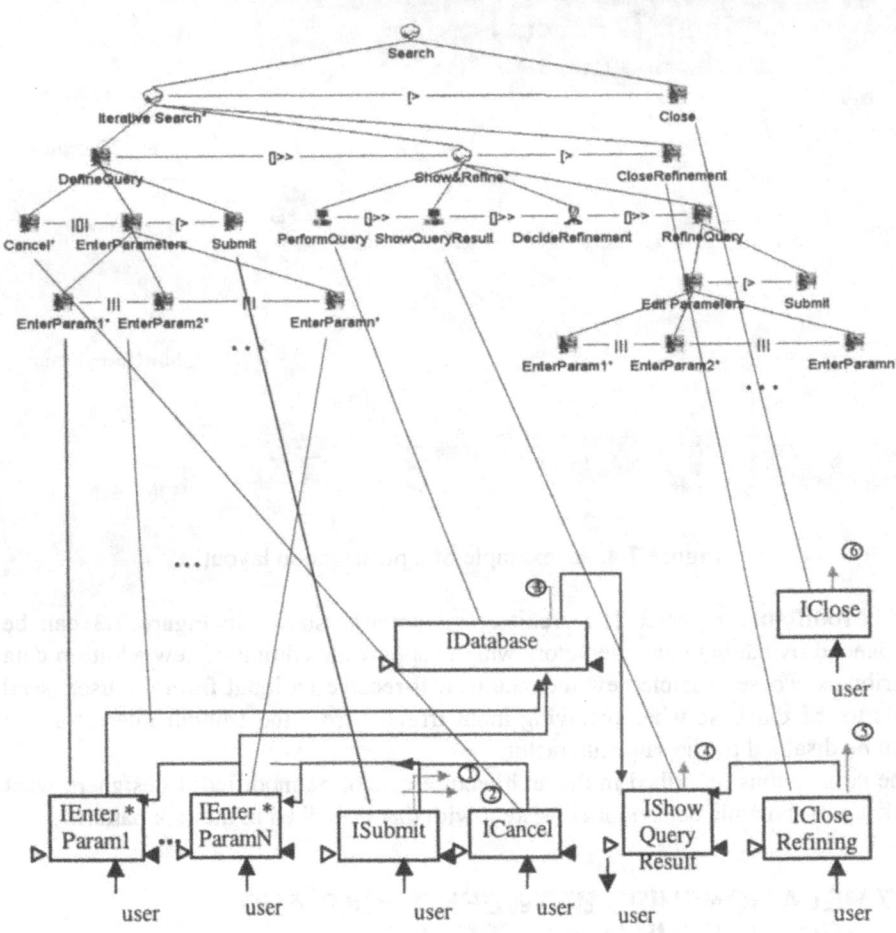

Figure 7.5: Tasks-to-interactors association.

The resulting representation can give information indicating what interactors are required, how they communicate, the purpose of their communication (exchanging data, disabling or enabling interactions, control data delivery).

The result of the task-to-interactor association in the example considered is shown in Figure 7.5 which indicates the interactors associated for each task. Generally, the relationships between tasks and interactors can be flexible. There may be cases where one task is performed by one interactor, others where we need several interactors to perform one task (this happens especially with high-level tasks) and further examples where one interactor supports the performance of several interactors.

7.8 TOOL SUPPORT FOR PATTERNS

We have seen how it is important to have automatic tool support for designing user interfaces, their task and architectural models because it allows designers to edit, modify, analyse and reuse specifications more easily. Tool support can be helpful also for patterns. An example of possible tool support is to extend an editor for task models so as to include support for task patterns.

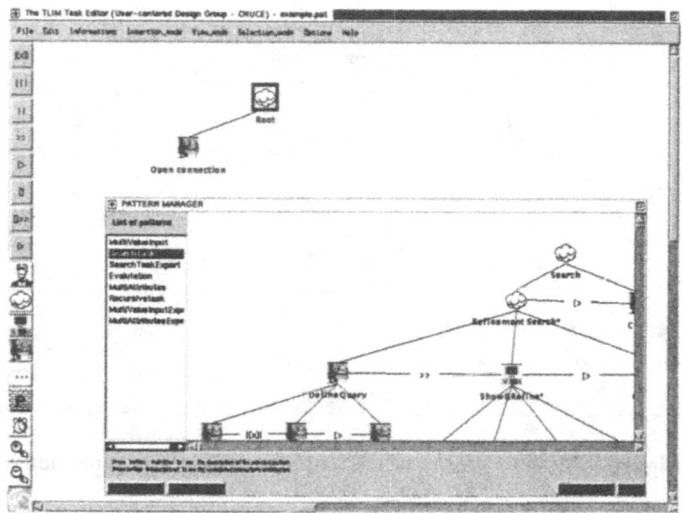

Figure 7.6: Browsing the available patterns.

Suppose we want to create a task tree to design a session using a web browser. First of all we specify an interactive *open connection* task. After that, we assume the user can perform a search task, which corresponds to a pattern which was previously designed. Thus it should be possible to allow (see for example Figure 7.6) the designer to browse the patterns available. After the selection is performed the pattern should be shown on the right side of the new window.

The editor lets the designer retrieve all the information needed about the selected pattern, such as the specific information related to the points previously introduced. Once designers are sure they have selected the right pattern, they can insert it into the task tree which is being designed. The editor should allow the pattern to be shown in a symbolic way or the user can decide to expand the pattern thus obtaining the result shown in Figure 7.7.

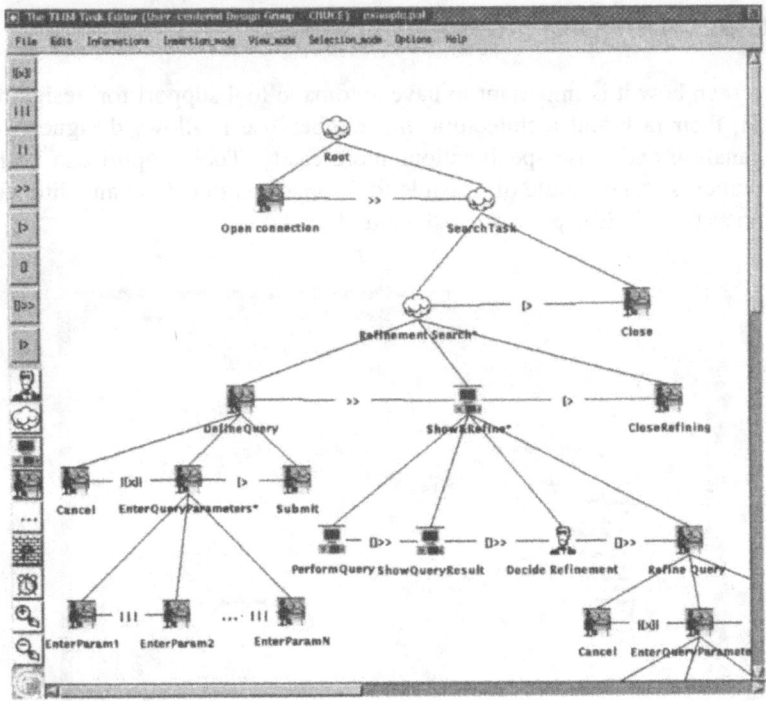

Figure 7.7: The pattern inserted into the task tree is expanded.

7.9 COMMENTS ON PATTERNS

In [BPS97] other possible patterns at the task level have been identified which describe recurring situations, such as the Evaluation Task Pattern which is used to model each situation in which a user selects a set of data to be evaluated and inserts the parameters that are needed during the evaluation. An example is a system which allows house evaluations such as pricing, history, mortgage, and size. Another example is the Recursive Activation Task Pattern which makes available an initial task whose main purpose is to allow the user to activate new instances of another task. An example can be a word processor which, whenever a specific technique is selected, allows the editing of a new file.

We have shown an approach for representing dialogue patterns at both task and architectural level. They are useful to represent design solutions of common problems. Furthermore, by creating a relationship between these representation levels we can design an environment which allows developers to use high-level, semantic-oriented representations of software components to support reuse across various applications thus making the development process less expensive or to support the use of guidelines incorporated in the patterns applied. This approach opens up the possibility to create environments for user interface design and development which are more powerful than current toolkits which usually provide libraries that allow only the reuse of classes associated with specific behaviours of single objects.

7.10 EXERCISES

1. Identify at least three task patterns that, with different parameters, can occur in different applications.
2. Design the architectural patterns corresponding to the three task patterns identified.
3. Represent the patterns identified in the format described in this chapter.
4. Propose a way to use and represent patterns in the HCI area different from those indicated in this chapter.

8 Usability Evaluation

A key concept in the human computer interaction field is *usability*, which is concerned with making systems easy to learn and easy to use. An important step towards the goal of usability is the evaluation of the user interface. The results from the evaluation should provide information to the designer about how to improve the user interface and thus achieve good usability.

Usability is a multi-dimensional concept. It involves more than just "easy to use" and "easy to learn". For example, if the users cannot carry out all the tasks they want, because a feature is missing in the system, it is not likely they will agree that the system is usable. A broader definition is therefore preferable, a definition that at least includes the following:

- The *relevance* of the system, how well it serves the users' needs.
- The *efficiency*, how efficiently users can carry out their tasks using the system.
- The users' *attitude* to the system, their subjective feelings.
- The *learnability* of the system, how easy the system is to learn for initial use and how well the users remember how to use the system.
- The *safety* of the system, giving the users the right to "undo" actions and not allowing the system to act in a destructive way.

The important thing to know when evaluating a user interface is what usability means for the current application. This is why an analysis of users and their needs is important. If we do not know what the user wants and needs, we cannot know which tasks s/he must be able to perform. Thus, usability depends on the application area considered. For example, if we consider a video game, a banking system and an air traffic control application, we can easily recognise that each of them raises different requirements in terms of usability. For video games it is very important that they are easy to use and that they engage the users. For banking systems efficiency is very appreciated. In air traffic control application an effective integration of safety and usability is strongly required. Another distinction used often is between formative and summative evaluations. Formative evaluations are performed early and continually throughout the design process whereas a summative evaluation is performed when it is complete, or almost complete.

The importance of usability has started to be recognised even though it has not yet penetrated in the industrial practise. It is also considered into some standards of the International Standardisation Organisation (ISO). For example, in ISO 9241-11 usability is defined as *the extent to which a product can be used by specified users to achieve specified goals with effectiveness, efficiency and satisfaction in a specified context of use.*

Efficiency is defined as the resources expended in relation to the accuracy and completeness with which users achieve goals. *Effectiveness* is indicated as the accuracy and completeness with which users achieve specified goals and *satisfaction* is a subjective measure concerning the freedom from discomfort, and positive attitudes towards the use of the product.

Usability engineering [N93] is an area in HCI which aims to achieve usable systems by applying different methods at different stages of the design and development process in a structured and systematic manner.

Before an evaluation is performed it is important to know what the goal of the evaluation is. Evaluation can be performed at different times in the development process. In the early stages of the design process usability evaluation is used to sort out alternative user interface designs and to predict the resulting design. Later on, evaluation is performed to determine whether the design meets its requirements and improving the user interface.

This chapter gives an introduction to the possible results of usability engineering and user interface evaluation, and discusses some evaluation approaches and a comparison among them. Then it explains how to use task models for user interface evaluation paying particular attention to the RemUSINE method. Finally we discuss the costs and benefits of such approaches and provide some suggestions for future work.

8.1 CRITERIA FOR USER INTERFACE EVALUATION

The main purpose for performing an evaluation is usually one of the following [PRSBHC94]:

- Engineering towards a target: is the design good enough?
- Comparing alternative designs: which is the best?
- Understanding the real world: how well does the design work in the real world?
- Checking conformance to a standard: does this product conform to the standard?

In usability engineering you try to operationalize "your" definition of usability for the current system to make measurable goals. This means that you have to define usability in terms of measurable factors, for example:

- User performance on specified tasks, measured in terms of task completion rate, completion time or number of errors;
- Users' subjective preference or degree of satisfaction;
- Learnability, measured in task completion rate, completion time, number of errors, or use of documentation and help desk.
- Flexibility, how well the system can change when the requirements change.

These factors and others similar can be the result of an evaluation of a user interface. The benefits of having measurable terms are, among other things, as follows:

- It is likely that the resources put into designing for usability will increase. This means that if you have measurable goals of usability that you must reach, it is likely that you will work to fulfil these goals.
- You will know how much more work is required on usability.
- It will be easier to compare requirements of alternative designs.

It is important to consider task-related aspects in the evaluation of the user interface. Generally speaking an evaluation of a user interface after performing a user test should include the following:

- *The tasks the user was able to perform.* When testing the user interface the user should be given different tasks s/he should be able to perform. If the user succeeded in performing the tasks it is likely that the interface is usable. But there is also a risk that the tasks you specified were too easy.
- *The tasks the user was not able to perform.* These tasks are important because they indicate problems the user had with the user interface. It is likely that the user needs some help to perform these tasks.
- *How many times each task was performed.* If a task is performed frequently it could be implemented as a shortcut or a macro. This is useful when users are not performing a predefined list of tasks.
- *In which order the tasks were performed.* The designer often has an opinion in which order the user will perform the tasks. If the user wants to break this order it could signify that the designer must make it possible to perform the tasks in a different order. Another issue is whether the user always chooses to perform one task before another. Then the second task could be executed automatically when the first one is performed.
- *The different errors the user made.* The user errors can be of different types. If the user does an unnecessary action in performing the current task this is, in most cases, an error. However, there is also the possibility that the user wanted to go backwards in the interaction to a previous step. The reason for this could be the user wants to be sure s/he is on the right track before continuing. For

example, before the user decides to delete some selected files s/he may want to be sure that s/he has made a correct selection, i.e. so only the files meant to be deleted are selected. A common type of error is an action performed belonging to the task, but the user has failed to do some actions needed before. For example, if the user tries to print a file without specifying the name of the file. In this case the user performed the right action (pushing the print button) but the *precondition* of the task (specifying the name of the file) was not satisfied. An error could also arise if the user inputs something to the program that is not correct. For example, if the user is trying to divide a number by zero, then the user lacks information about the current domain.

- *The user's subjective opinion of the user interface*. The user's opinion is important because if the user does not like the interface it is not likely that s/he will use it. The user can give useful information to the designer as to which part of the user interface s/he liked or disliked. However the quality of this information depends on the user's knowledge of computer science and experience of user interfaces.
- *How much help the user needed*. If the user needed a lot of help it is possible that the user interface was too difficult, i.e., this is a measure of how easy the user interface was.
- *How many times the user had to restart from the beginning*. This measures how difficult it was to navigate within the program.
- *How long it took the user to perform the tasks*. If time is an important factor of the specification of the software, which is often the case, then it is necessary to measure the time.

This is a non-exhaustive list of information which should suggest to the designer what improvements could be made to the user interface, however it gives a useful indication of aspects to take into account.

8.2 INTRODUCTION TO APPROACHES TO USABILITY EVALUATION

Usability engineering concerns the development of systematic methods to support usability evaluation. Various types of approaches have been proposed for this purpose. We can classify them in various groups of methods: model-based approaches, empirical evaluation, inspection-based evaluation, and metrics. In this paragraph we introduce these families of approaches and then we will discuss more specific examples of methods belonging to these families.

8.2.1 Model-based evaluation

Model-based approaches to usability evaluation use some models, usually task or user models, to support such evaluation. They often aim [JK96] to produce *quantitative predictions* of how well users will be able to perform tasks with a proposed design. Usually the designer starts with an initial task analysis and a proposed first interface design. The designer should then use an engineering model (like GOMS) to find the applicable usability problems of the interface.

It is important to find a method that allows designers to apply meaningful models to some empirical information. An attempt in this direction was USAGE [BWSFK94] that provided tool support to a method where the user actions required to execute an application action in UIDE are analysed by the NGOMSL approach. However this information is still limited with respect to that contained in the logs of the user actions performed during work sessions by users.

While model-based evaluation is useful to highlight relevant aspects in the evaluation, it can be limiting not considering empirical information because the possible predictions in some cases can be denied by the real user behaviour.

8.2.2 GOMS-based evaluation

Often models aim to produce *quantitative predictions* of how well users will be able to perform tasks with a proposed design. The goal is also to capture the essence of the design in an inspectable representation. Usually the designer starts with an initial task analysis and a proposed first interface design. As we have seen in Chapter 2 a GOMS model is a representation of the *procedural knowledge* the user must have in order to carry out tasks, their "how to do it" knowledge. One of the purposes of GOMS is to *predict* the *execution time* which is simulated by executing the actions required to perform the tasks. Each action is divided into smaller parts until the remaining action is a simple keystroke or a mouse click. The times for all actions are then counted and summed up into a prediction of the time it will take to perform the whole task. The detail of the evaluation is very extreme, down to keystrokes. Therefore it is also called the "keystroke-level analysis". This method makes it possible to predict the time needed to complete a task within a 20 per cent margin [LR93].

Next the KLM method has been introduced to support performance evaluation associated with a GOMS analysis. The basic idea is that given a task (decomposed into subtasks) the language of the commands of the system, the parameters giving the motorial capabilities of the user considered, the response time of the system, the method used to accomplish the task it allows designers to predict the time taken for the user considered to perform the task. The underlying cognitive theory (the Human Processor Model) is used to associate temporal values with the possible user actions (examples are in Tables 8.1 and 8.2).

This approach has been shown to be useful to predict the quality of an existing system, and to check the consistency of the methods (where consistency means that similar goals are achieved by similar methods). It can be used to check that more frequent goals are achieved by fast methods or as an evaluation technique to compare different design solutions. This approach can be applied to analyse the user interface before its implementation to reduce the need for modifications that are more expensive when they have to be done on the implementation.

Operator	Duration
Point	1100
Click down	100
Click up	100
Point	1100
Type 2.5	600
Click down	100
Click up	100
Total	**3400 ms**

Table 8.1: An example of KLM analysis without a mental operator.

Operator	Duration
M	1350
Point	1100
Click down	100
Click up	100
Point	1100
Type 2.5	600
M	1350
Click down	100
Click up	100
Total	**5900 ms**

Table 8.2: An example of KLM analysis with a mental operator.

GLEAN [KWAH95] is a tool with the purpose of allowing interface designers or analysts to easily develop and rapidly apply GOMS model techniques in order to evaluate a user interface. The GLEAN user (the interface designer) will develop a GOMS model for an existing or proposed interface and supply a representative task and a description of the interface behaviour. GLEAN will then simulate the user interaction and generate usability metrics such as the learning time for the task. The most important factor of GLEAN is that it automates the tedious calculations required to generate usability predictions from the GOMS model. The GLEAN tool also supports the reuse of GOMS methods, making it possible to use the same GOMS methods with a later revised version of the interface. However, the designer still needs to perform a task analysis to determine what goals the user is trying to accomplish. Another advantage of GLEAN is that it makes the GOMS model notation more readable and easier to understand.

Recently there has been a growing interest in providing automatic support for GOMS-oriented evaluations. One recent relevant contribution is EPIC (Executive-Process/Interactive Control) [KSM97] which provides a framework for constructing models of human-computer interaction by taking into account results on human perceptual/motor performance, cognitive modelling techniques, and task analysis methodology implemented in the form of computer simulation software. Starting with a description of the system interface and a task analysis, designers construct an EPIC model by writing the production rule program for performing the task using the proposed interface. They also program a module that simulates the relevant behaviour of the interface at an abstract, symbolic level. Then by running the model in a simulated interaction they can obtain statistics that predict human performance with the actual system. This approach is interesting, however the automatic support provided is limited and it is not easy for designers to use, one reason being that they used ad hoc techniques.

More recently, work has been started on using logs of user events to build GOMS models. The goal is to overcome the problems related to performing a KLM-like evaluation by hand. The problems are that often people forget to include physical operators required to perform the task, it is difficult to place mental operators in a consistent way and it can be very time consuming. In the solution proposed in [HJKB99] mental operators are included following a small set of heuristics such as when users start to work with a new interactive object or when start a different form of input to the current object (for instance, switch from pointing and clicking to typing in a text box).

8.2.3 Empirical evaluation

In *empirical testing* the behaviour of real users is considered. It can be very expensive and it can have some limitations too. It requires long observations of users' behaviour. In *usability testing* [DR94] the designer studies the user performing some tasks and gathers data on the problems that arise. The problem with usability testing is that it is based only on observational data and to be able to interpret the data some user interface experience is needed and some problems may still not be identified. There is also the problem of cost, you take up the time of the users and the observers, and the problem of getting the appropriate users for the current test.

Often these observations are supported by video that can be annotated by some tool. Even observing video describing user behaviour, either in work places or in a usability laboratory, can take a lot of time to designers (a complete analysis can take more than five times the duration of the video) and some relevant aspects can still be missed. Other support for empirical testing is to use think aloud techniques [L82] where users have to express their thoughts while interacting so that the evaluator can better understand where and when they make mistakes. Another support to empirical testing can be given by logging tools: they are able to automatically store all the user-generated events so that it is possible to know them even without being physically present during the user session. In the next section we discuss a technique based on the use of this information.

When developing an empirical test it is important to define some parameters (such as tasks to give to the users, time available to perform them, type of support to give them during their session, criteria to evaluate the session) in order to make the experiment meaningful.

8.2.4 The MUSiC method

The *MUSiC performance measurement method* [MBB94] was developed by the European MUSiC (Metrics for Usability Standards in Computing) project to provide a valid and reliable means of specifying and measuring usability. The method gives useful feedback on how to improve the usability of the design. MUSiC also includes tools and techniques for measuring user performance and satisfaction. The basic outputs of the MUSiC performance measurement method include measures of:

- *Effectiveness* - how correctly and completely goals are achieved in a certain context;
- *Efficiency* - effectiveness related to cost of performance (calculated as effectiveness divided by the time).

Together with the DRUM tool, which supports the analysis of a video recording of a usability test, the full (video supported) method also includes the following measures and diagnostic data:

- *Relative User Efficiency* - an indicator of learnability; how easy the system was to learn, relating the efficiency of users to that of experts;
- *Productive Period* - the proportion of time the user spent not having problems;
- *Snag, Search and Help times* - time spent overcoming problems, searching unproductively through a system, and seeking help.

These measures provide data about specific areas where the design fails to support the users' performance. The method provides suggestions for causes of the problems. A benefit of these quantitative data is that they enable a comparison of alternative designs. The diagnostic information of the full method also gives help in identifying where improvements to the user interface have to be made.

8.2.5 Inspection-based evaluation

In inspection-based techniques to usability evaluation, designers analyse a user interface or its description. There are variations of these techniques, such as heuristic evaluation, cognitive walkthrough, and software guidelines. In *heuristic evaluation* [N93] user interface designers study the interface and look for properties that they know lead to usability problems. Evaluators with good experience are likely to find many problems with this approach although non-experts can also find some problems. The use of multiple independent evaluators is recommended. It can be performed both on an early prototype or a specification and on the final system. Examples of possible rules are those indicated by Nielsen:

- Simple and natural dialogue
- Speak the Users' language
- Minimise User memory load
- Consistency
- Feedback
- Clearly Marked Exits
- Shortcuts
- Good Error Message
- Prevent Errors
- Help and Documentation

The problem is that usually the list of identified problems is useful to improve the current design but can overlook other relevant usability problems. In cognitive walkthrough the designer tries to capture what the possible thoughts and problems of the users can be.

Guidelines [SM86] are used in large companies because they provide indications about how to use possible interaction techniques and evaluators have to check how much the user interface is complying with them. They tend to facilitate the reuse of design solution and code and guarantee a consistent environment, however they tend to create resistance to the introduction of innovations in the use of new interaction techniques.

These inspection-based techniques have been found useful but limited because they are dependent on the ability of the evaluator, they may require multiple evaluators, or they may miss some relevant problems [JMWU91].

8.2.6 Cognitive walkthrough

Unlike the MUSiC method, *cognitive walkthrough* [WRLP94][LR93] can be performed very early in the design phase. Cognitive walkthrough is an evaluation method mainly focused on how easy a system is to learn, especially through exploration. Users often prefer to learn a program by exploration instead of taking a course or reading the manual. The users tend first to learn how to perform the tasks important for their work and then learn new features when needed.

The idea of cognitive walkthrough comes from "code walkthrough" used in software engineering. In code walkthrough the sequence of code is stepped through to find bugs and to check the quality of the code. The aim of cognitive walkthrough is to get the users' thoughts and actions when using an interface for the first time. A brief description includes the following. First of all it is necessary to have a prototype or a detailed design of the interface as well as facts about the users, who they are and which tasks they have to do in their work. Then a relevant goal that the design is intended to support is chosen. After this you try to tell a believable story about each step and action the user has to do to accomplish the task. To make the story believable you have to motivate every action the user performs, based on knowledge about the user and the feedback the user gets from the system. If you cannot tell a believable story about an action, you have found a problem with the interface. For this purpose, as the walkthrough proceeds the designer asks the following four questions:

- Will the user try to achieve the right effect?
- Will the user notice that the correct action is available?
- Will the user associate the correct action with the effect trying to be achieved?
- After the action is performed, will users understand the feedback they receive?

8.2.7 Metrics-based evaluation

A metric provides a specific value as a result of the evaluation of a specific design aspect. In this area there was some work [CM96] aimed at applying previous metrics to evaluate the usability of presentations containing various graphical objects. However empirical experiments did not find those specific metrics particularly useful.

In [KF93] Kim and Foley showed how it is possible to propose an automatic tool that incorporates metrics and allows designers to develop graphical user interfaces that are effective and consistent. This tool is divided into two parts: an organisation manager using a top-down approach that supports the structuring of the user interface allowing designers to select appropriate interaction objects and their dimensions and a presentation manager that supports the location of the objects incorporating some metrics. AIDE [S95a] is a tool that develops such an approach and uses "simple task descriptions" to guide the design and evaluation of an interface. The aim of the tool is to assist designers in creating and evaluating layouts [S93] for a given set of interface widgets. It is based on five metrics; efficiency, alignment, horizontal balance, vertical balance and constraints. The *efficiency* evaluates how far the user must move a cursor to accomplish a task. The basic idea is to identify more frequent tasks and associate them with interaction techniques that are close to each other to improve the performance of such frequent tasks. The issue of checking consistency is addressed by SHERLOCK [MS97], a family of consistency analysis tools, evaluating visual and textual properties of user interfaces. The authors demonstrated the harmful effects of inconsistency by conducting an experiment that showed that inconsistent interface terminology slowed user performance by 10 to 25 percent. Thus the tool provides an automatic support for the analysis of the interaction techniques and terminology used allowing designers to check better their consistency.

8.3 COMPARING METHODS FOR USABILITY EVALUATION

Comparison between usability evaluation methods is a complicated topic as it is demonstrated in [GS98] where Gray and Salzman discuss the limitations of some important studies that used experimental methods to compare different usability evaluation methods.

Here only a few issues are outlined. In [JMWU91] there is a comparison among four evaluation techniques: heuristic evaluation, software guidelines, usability testing and cognitive walkthrough. They found that cognitive walkthrough misses general and recurring problems. For walk-up-and-use systems, where it is especially important that the user can quickly and easily use and understand the interface, cognitive walkthrough still remains a good alternative. One must remember though that cognitive walkthrough does not test real users on the system. Therefore you must be aware that it is unlikely you will find all the existing problems of the user interface with this method.

Empirical testing, for example testing used in the MUSiC method, consists of iterative testing and design revision where real users test and help to find usability problems. The involvement of real users makes it more expensive but at the same time more reliable, at least from the users' point of view. The major disadvantage with this method is that it is expensive. This is because you use the time of the users, thus preventing them from carrying out their *real* work. It is also a problem finding the necessary numbers of users who are both domain experts and who belong to the target group. Because of this, "discount methods" [N93] and "inspection methods" (e.g. cognitive walkthrough) have been developed, for assessing the usability of an interface design more quickly and at a lower cost. The lower cost is due to the fact that you do not use real users in the methods.

Approaches such as GLEAN are methods best used early in the design to predict the execution time. It is not easy to use for non-experts. There is hope, though, that future versions of similar tools can reduce the evaluation time. Another disadvantage of models like GLEAN, is that they presume an error-free behaviour of the user when performing the task. This means that you do not take user errors into consideration.

The measures from MUSiC are good if you want to compare different interface alternatives, but they are hard to use in order to improve the user interface, which is the purpose of our evaluation method. Cognitive walkthrough and GLEAN do not directly involve users in the evaluation.

8.4 REMOTE USABILITY EVALUATION

In the last years there has been an increasing interest in remote usability evaluation [HCKKN96]. It has been defined as usability evaluation where evaluators are separated in time and/or space from users.

This approach has been introduced for many reasons:

- the increasing availability and improvement of network connections;
- the cost and the rigidity of traditional laboratory-based usability evaluation;
- the need to decrease costs of usability evaluation to make it more affordable.

A remote support for usability evaluation can be performed in various ways:

- users self-reporting critical incidents encountered in real tasks performed in their normal working environment [HC98];
- use of teleconferencing tools to observe user behaviour in real-time from a remote location;
- instrumented or automated data collection for remote evaluation, where tools are used to collect and return a journal or log of data containing indications of the interactions performed by the user. These data are analysed later on, for example using pattern recognition techniques; however, usually the results obtained are rather limited for the evaluation of an interactive application. For example, use of logging tools to store user events such as keystrokes and mouse movements or web pages selected and then this information is analysed. This can be done using various techniques, for example, in [SE91] pattern recognition techniques are used to identify where usability problems have occurred.

8.5 THE REMUSINE METHOD

If we consider current approaches, briefly summarised in the previous section, we can note that there is a lack of methods that are able:

- to give the possibility to support the evaluation of many users without requiring a heavy involvement of designers;
- to support the evaluation gathering information on the users' behaviour at their work place without using expensive equipment;
- to apply powerful and flexible task models in the evaluation of logs of user events, thus linking model-based and empirical evaluations. Current automatic tools, such as ErgoLight [H99], that support usability evaluation by task models, use simple notations to specify such models, thus still requiring a strong effort from the evaluator.

These three relevant results are obtained by a new method (RemUSINE – Remote User Interface Evaluator) following an approach that is summarised in Figure 8.1 where ovals represent data files and rectangles represent programs. As you can see it is possible to have one evaluator and N users who are located in different places.

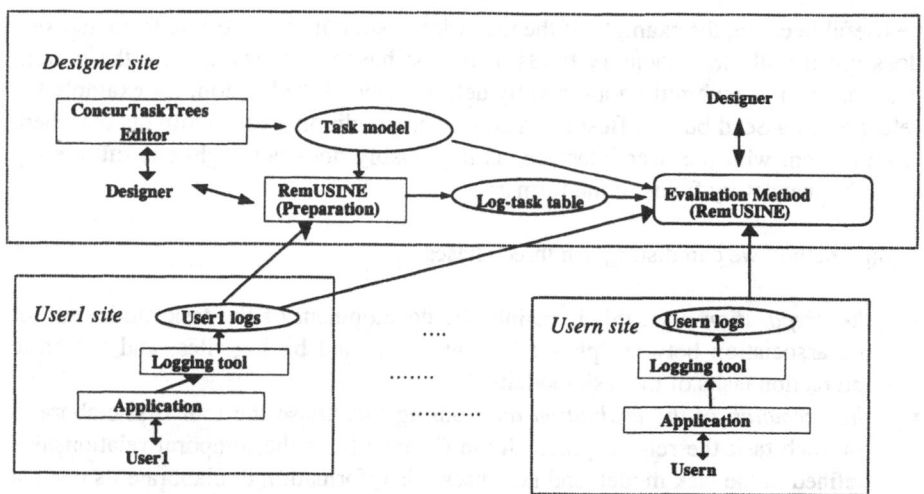

Figure 8.1: The architecture of the RemUSINE approach.

We have one application that can be used by many users. Then we have the RemUSINE tool (that has been developed at the HCI group at CNUCE) with the following input:

- *the log files with the user interactions*: by the support of a logging tool it is possible to automatically generate a file storing all the events performed by a user during a work session. One or more of these files have an additional use that is the creation of the log-task table;
- *the log-task association table*: the purpose of this table is to create an association between the physical events, that can be generated by the user while interacting with the application considered, and the basic interaction tasks (the tasks that cannot be further decomposed in the task model and require only one action to be performed). This association is a key point in the RemUSINE method because through it we can use the task model to analyse the user behaviour;
- *the task model*: it is developed using the ConcurTaskTrees notation by the editor available at http://giove.cnuce.cnr.it/ctte.html.

The user interactions are captured by logging tools that are able to get this information without disturbing users during their work. These logs are useful to identify user errors such as attempts to activate an interaction that was not allowed because some precondition was not satisfied or selections of elements of the user interface that were not selectable.

A user error mainly depends on the current user task. An action is an error if it is not useful to support such a task. One problem is how to identify automatically the tasks that the user intends to perform. To this end the knowledge of the user actions can be useful because, for example, if the user tries to submit an electronic form and s/he does not fill all the mandatory fields, it is possible to understand what the current user intention is (submitting a form) by detecting the related action, for example the selection of a Send button. Besides, a similar precondition error highlights that there is a problem with the user interface, as it probably does not highlight sufficiently what the mandatory fields of the form are.

In this method we can distinguish three phases:

- *the preparation part*: this is mainly the development of the task model and of the association between physical events, extracted by log files, and the basic interaction tasks of the task model;
- *the execution of the evaluation tool*: during this phase the tool first elaborates for each task the related precondition (if any) from the temporal relationships defined in the task model, and next uses this information to elaborate its results: the errors performed, task patterns, duration of the performance of the tasks and so on;
- *the analysis of the results of the execution tool*: in this phase the designer can provide suggestions to improve the user interface by using the information generated by the RemUSINE tool.

8.5.1 The preparation part

There are various tools available to collect automatically data on the user-generated events during an interactive session, for example, JavaStar (http://www.sun.com/suntest/JavaStar/JavaStar.html) or QCReplay(http://www.centerline.com/productline/qcreplay/qcrplay.html).

They are able to provide files that contain indications of the events that have occurred and when they occurred. The events considered are mouse click, text input, mouse movements, and similar. When interaction techniques such as menu, pull-down menu are selected they are also able to indicate what menu element was selected. The resulting files are editable text files. Similarly, using the ConcurTaskTrees editor it is possible to save the task model specification in a file for further modifications and analysis.

This information is used in the preparation part whose main purpose is to create the association between logs of user events and the basic tasks in the task model. This association will be used to analyse the user interactions with the support of the task model.

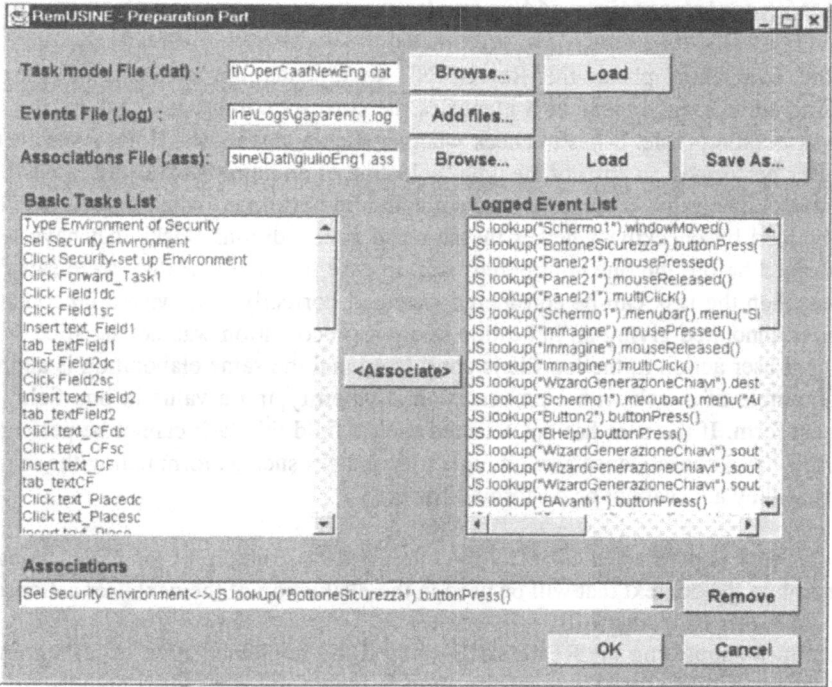

Figure 8.2: The tool supporting the preparation phase.

In the preparation part (as you can see in Figure 8.2) the evaluator can load one log file and one file with the task model. The lists of elements contained in the two files appear in two different, parallel columns. In the task-related part only the basic tasks appear, as they are the only elements that can be associated with logged events. The application designer then has to select one physical event on one side and the corresponding basic task on the other side and then add this association to the table containing all of them by the related button. Once a basic task has been associated with the related event it will disappear from the list of tasks that thus indicates only tasks that still need to be associated with the related event by the designer. The associations performed can be displayed by the *Associations* pull-down menu. In case of mistakes the designer can remove elements from such a list by the *Remove* button. The associations can be saved in a file and loaded later on for further expansions or for the evaluation phase. A one-to-many relationship usually holds between tasks and user actions because the action required to perform a basic task can occur many times during a session.

This association needs to be done only once to evaluate as many user sessions of an application as desired because it contains the information required by the evaluation tool. Only the log file to analyse has to be changed for the evaluation of each session.

8.5.2 The elaboration of the tool

In the evaluation phase the RemUSINE tool scans the elements of the log considered. For each element it identifies the corresponding basic task by the log-task association table. It has to check whether such a task exists, if not it means that the user performed an error of the type "selection of an item that was not selectable". If it exists then it has to check whether it could be performed when it occurred. This is obtained by checking whether the task had preconditions (tasks that have to be performed before the one considered) and, in case they exist, if they were satisfied. If yes, then the task can be considered executed correctly otherwise a precondition error is annotated giving an indication of what precondition was not satisfied. Then the next user action in the log file is considered and the same elaboration is applied. An example of a task with a precondition is when typing a value in one field of a request form. If the user has not selected such a field this task cannot be performed and this has a consequence also on higher level tasks such as formulating the request because they also cannot be performed correctly.

When a task is performed correctly the internal data structure of the tool is updated to maintain the context that will be used in the evaluation of the next user actions.

In the tool supporting the RemUSINE method the implementation of an algorithm that takes a ConcurTaskTrees specification is incorporated and it is able to provide the preconditions for all the tasks at all the levels of the task tree. Such preconditions indicate the tasks that have to be performed in order to complete the accomplishment of the task considered.
The method for finding the preconditions and creating the precondition table searches through a traversal of the task tree.

The main elements that have to be considered in identifying the preconditions are:
- For every non-optional task we check if its *left brother is an enabling task* (a task on the left of the >> operator). If so we know that the left brother is the precondition of the current task and write this (the task and its precondition) to the result.
- If the current task is a high-level task then the left enabling brother is a precondition also for the children of such a task that are available at the beginning of its performance. The children available at the beginning of the performance of the parent task are those which are on the left of the leftmost enabling operator.
- If the current task (a child of a task) is an optional task, because of its type, the task does not need to be performed; it is not counted as a necessary precondition and thus is not included in the results.
- If there are tasks composed by the choice operator ("[]") or the disabling operator ("[>") we will add these tasks as a precondition to their parent but on different lines (because the performance of only one of them is sufficient to satisfy the precondition).

- If the current task is the rightmost and has the enabling operator on the left we will add this task as a precondition to its parent. This is because in this case the current task has another precondition that must be performed first, and we only want the strictly needed preconditions of the parent of the current task.
- If the current task is on the left of the rightmost enabling and has a right brother that is optional we must select the current task as a precondition to its parent. This is because we do not know if the optional task will be performed or not.
- If the children of the task are composed by the interleaving operator (|||) then we will add them as a precondition. When all the children have been performed then this precondition is verified.
- We can have multiple tasks that share the same left enabling task, which thus have the same precondition.
- In any case when we consider a non-basic task (a task that is not a leaf in the task tree) we have to search for its preconditions which are among its children. While searching the method collects the results.

More specifically, if we consider the example in Figure 8.3 we will find, for example, that *SendbyButton* is a precondition of *AccessVirtualMuseum* because only when this task terminates will the parent task be considered completed and its sibling task (*SpecifyRequest*) is composed of iterative subtasks and thus it never terminates unless it is interrupted by the disabling operator. At the next levels of the task tree we can find that *PresList* is a precondition of *SpecValue* which has *ShowValue* as precondition. Then we can find that *SpecifybyTyping* has as a precondition *TypeValue* which has *SelField* as a precondition.

Another element that we have to take into account is that sometimes the performance of one task has the effect of undoing the effects of another task thus falsifying a precondition that beforehand was true. For example we can have a deselect task that makes false a precondition requiring a certain selection.

8.5.3 An example of an analysis of a small log

Figure 8.3 provides an example of a ConcurTaskTrees specification [PB99]. It concerns a museum application. The related user interface is shown in Figure 8.4. In this specification we did not consider user tasks (tasks associated with internal cognitive actions such as recognising a visual element in the interface or deciding how to carry on a set of tasks) because we want to focus on interaction tasks that can be associated with the user actions stored in the log files and application tasks that are closely related to them.

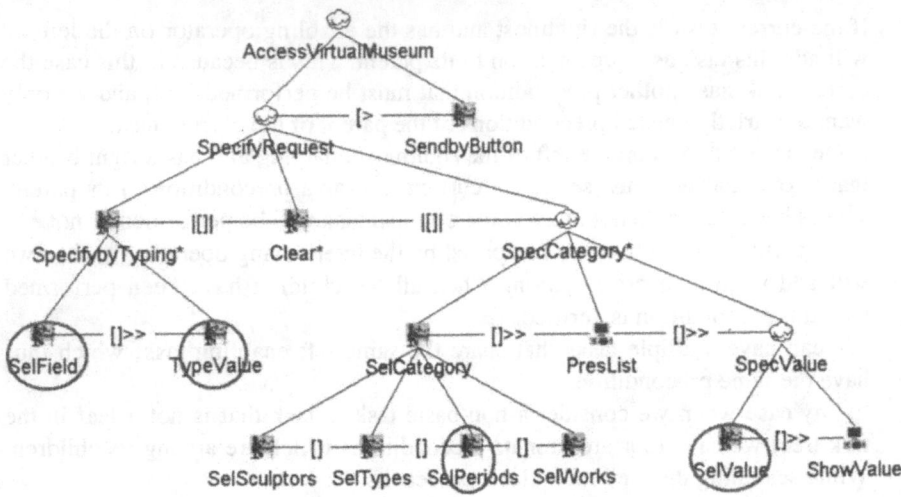

Figure 8.3: An example of a task model.

At the first level there is a distinction between the part to specify the request (*SpecifyRequest* task) and that for sending the request (*SendbyButton* task) that can disable ([> operator) the first one. *SpecifyRequest* has iterative children tasks (iterative tasks are indicated by the * symbol) as they can be performed multiple times. These tasks support specifying and clearing the request and they are concurrent communicating tasks (indicated by the |[]| operator) disabled by sending the request (*SendbyButton* task).

More specifically, specifying a request can be performed either by mouse selection (*SpecCategory* task) or by typing (*SpecifybyTyping* task). They are communicating because a specification done in one way can override a specification done in the other way beforehand and viceversa. The specification by mouse requires first to select a category (*SelCategory* task), next the application presents the list of related values (*PresList* task) and then the user can select a value (*SelValue* task) and the application shows it in the related field (*ShowValue* task). These are sequential activities with information passing ([]>> operator). Selecting a category is decomposed into the choice ([] operator) among different tasks, each one associated with a specific category of request (by sculptor, by type of work, by historical period, by work name).

Once the list of values is presented the user can activate another request for another field by selecting another category. Specifying by typing requires first to select the field of interest (*SelField* task) and next to type the value (*TypeValue* task).

The cloud icon is used to indicate abstract tasks; i.e. tasks that have subtasks whose performance is allocated differently (either user, application, or interaction tasks).

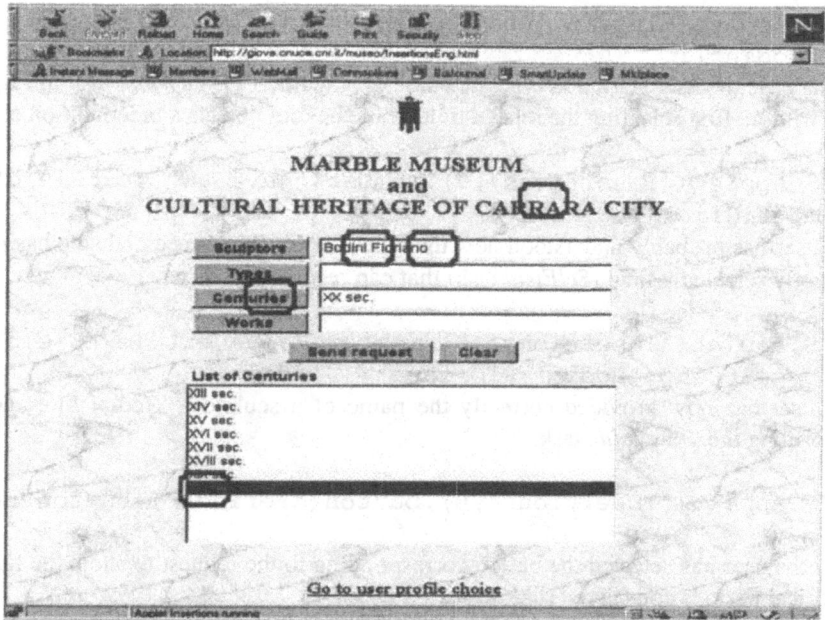

Figure 8.4: The user interface corresponding to the example.

It is important to remember that for the RemUSINE analysis it is required that the task model is refined so that each possible user action, supported by the user interface considered, can be associated with one interaction basic task (that are leaves in the task tree). We can consider an example of a small log taken using JavaStar applied to the museum application in Figure 8.4 to better understand how our method works once it has calculated the preconditions for all the tasks. In the log we have removed the information useless for our tool. In Figure 8.4 there are circles to indicate where the interactions indicated in the log occurred and in Figure 8.3 the corresponding tasks (if any) are likewise highlighted by circles. We consider seven events in the log file:

```
1)JS.applet("Insertions",0).member("NewPanelSfondo2").mu
ltiClick(124,93,16,1);
```
The tool detects that the user has selected an area that does not correspond to any interaction technique, it provides the position where it occurred, in this case it corresponds to the name of the town. Probably the user thought it was selectable and tried to receive some information about it.

```
2)JS.delay(7310);
```
Between each couple of actions an indication providing the time passed among their occurrence is provided in milliseconds. We will not report the other occurrences of similar actions.

```
3)JS.applet("Insertions",0).button("Sculptors").typeStri
ng("Bodin");
```
In this case the user started to type the name of a sculptor (*TypeValue* task in Figure 8.3) without first selecting the related field, thus the tool detects a precondition error

```
4)JS.applet("Insertions",0).member("java.awt.TextField",
0).multiClick(0,8,16,1);
```
The user has probably understood now the type of error performed and s/he has now correctly selected a field (*SelField* task) that can receive text input.

```
5)JS.applet("Insertions",0).member("java.awt.TextField",
0).typeString("Bodini Floriano", 0, 0);
```
The user has now provided correctly the name of a sculptor ("Bodini Floriano"), performing the *TypeValue* task.

```
6)JS.applet("Insertions",0).button("Periods").buttonPres
s();
```
Now the user has selected the button corresponding to the request to show the list of historical periods considered (*SelCatPeriod* task).

```
7)JS.applet("Insertions",0).member("NewPanelSfondo2").me
mber("java.awt.List", 2).select(4,"XVIII sec.");
```
Finally the user has selected the historical period of interest (*SelValue* task) from the list dynamically shown by the application.

8.5.4 Results obtained by a RemUSINE analysis of a single session

By a task model-based analysis of the logs of user events a wide variety of results that can be useful for the evaluator can be derived. It is possible to obtain some general information on the user session (such as duration, number of tasks failed and completed, number of errors, number of scrollbar or windows moved), more detailed information for the tasks considered, and some graphical representations of such results. There are two main types of information that RemUSINE provides:

* *interactive analysis of a log of events*, it is possible to interactively simulate the execution of the log of events with RemUSINE. For each event the tool is able to indicate what task is associated with it (if any), what other tasks were enabled when it occurred, if the task associated had preconditions verified when the event occurred, and, in case such preconditions were not satisfied, what tasks had to be performed in order to satisfy them.

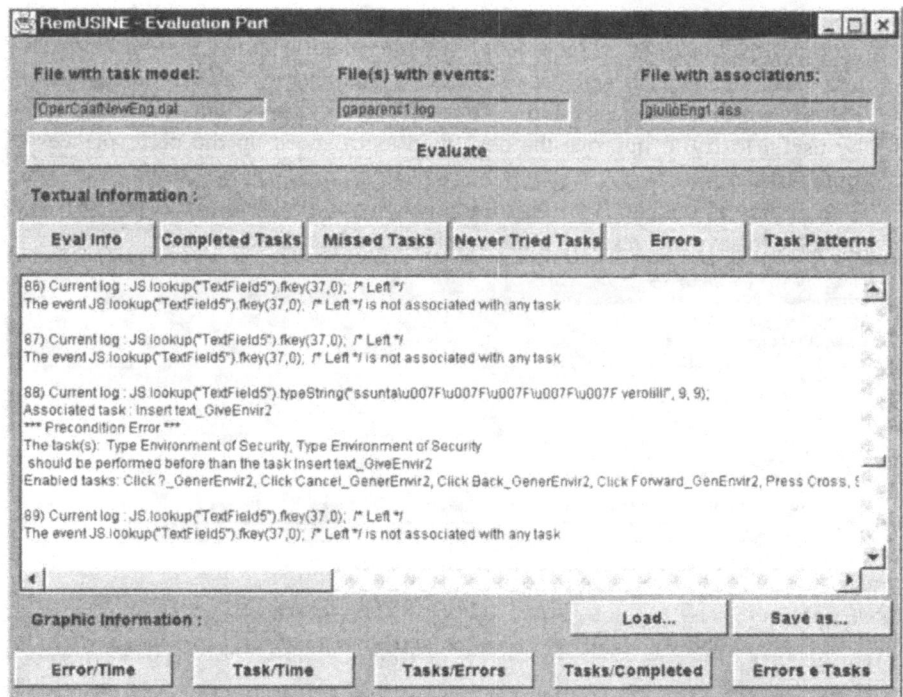

Figure 8.5: An example of interactive analysis of a log.

- *summary and statistical information on the user sessions*, such as duration, number of tasks failed and completed, number of errors, number of scrollbar or windows moved, more detailed information for the tasks considered, and some graphical representations of such results. When tasks are counted we consider all the tasks in the ConcurTaskTrees specification thus including both basic and high levels tasks.

The more detailed information about the tasks include:

- The display of the accomplished tasks and how many times they are performed. The frequency of the tasks is useful when deciding the layout of the interface. To make the interface more efficient the interaction techniques supporting tasks performed frequently should be clearly highlighted.
- The display of the tasks the user tried to perform but failed because their preconditions were not satisfied, and how many times each task failed.
- The display of the tasks the user never tried to perform. This information can be useful to identify parts of the user interface that are either useless or difficult to access for the users; this result is more difficult to obtain with other approaches based on observations.
- Display of all the errors divided into precondition errors and others.

- The display of the task patterns found (specific sequences of tasks) among the accomplished tasks (see Figure 8.6). The presentation shows first the frequency and next the pattern, and orders them by frequency. Patterns are useful to identify sequences of tasks frequently performed by users. This information can be useful to try to improve the design so as to speed-up the performances of such tasks.
- The display of the entire result from the evaluation in temporal order. It is also possible to save this result in a file and load at a later time.

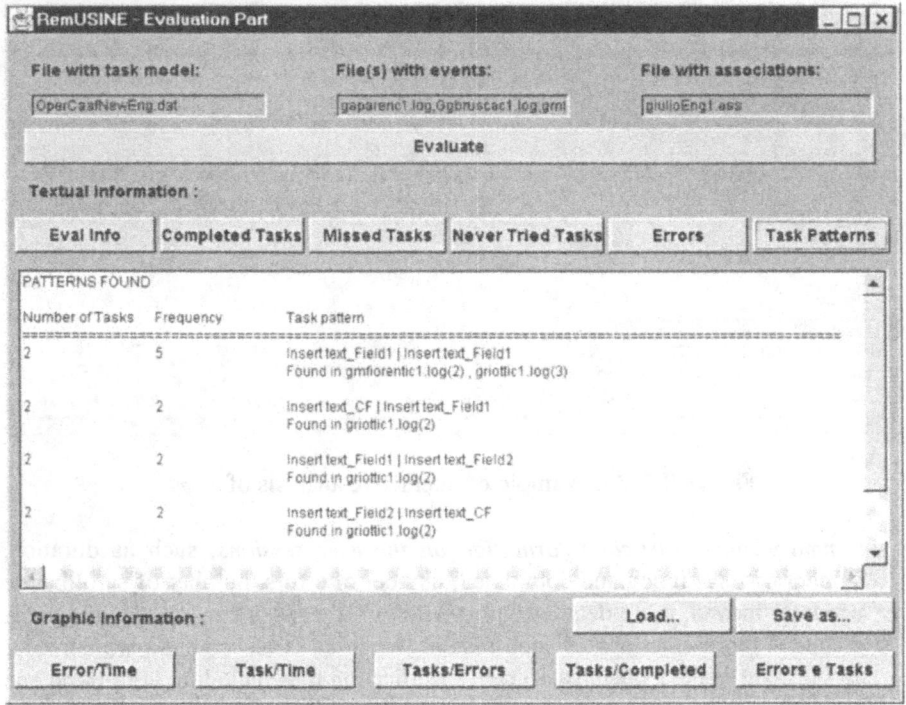

Figure 8.6: An example of task patterns detected.

The different graphs showing the data from the evaluation in different manners are:

- The *Tasks/Time* chart graph with the tasks on the x-scale and how long they took to perform on the y-scale. It is possible to have distinct presentation of basic and high level tasks.
- The *Errors/Time* graph with the number of errors on the y-scale and the time on the x-scale.
- The *Tasks/Errors* chart graph containing the number of precondition errors associated with each task.
- The *Tasks/Completed* chart graph containing the number of times the tasks were performed.

- The *Errors & Tasks* pie chart containing the different types of errors and their percentage, and another containing the number of the tasks accomplished, the tasks missed and those never attempted (see Figure 8.7).

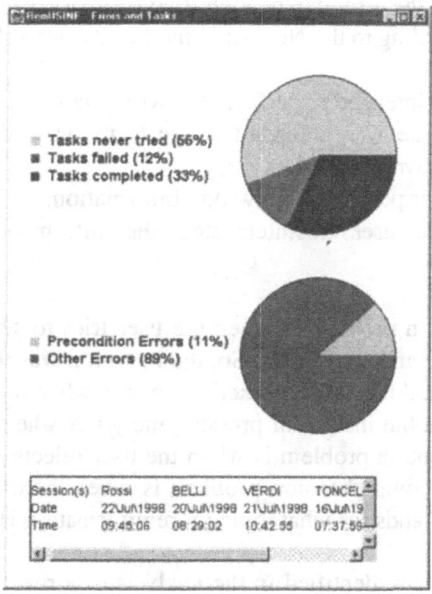

Figure 8.7: Tasks and errors related percentages.

8.5.5 How to interpret the results

Identifying errors in the analysis of the logs indicates a mismatch between the user behaviour and the task model associated with the application. The reasons for this mismatch can be various: in some cases the user interface imposes constraints that are not motivated from a logical point of view so it has to be changed in order to support a more flexible task model closer to that of the user. In other cases the task model associated with the interactive application describes the desired behaviour but the design of the user interface is not sufficiently effective and the user has problems in understanding how to perform the desired task, thus changes have to be introduced, for example using more explanatory labels.

We found it useful, for each error identified, to prepare a short report structured in four fields:

- *the problem*: an indication of the problem highlighted by the error identified;
- *the identification*: a description of how the error has been identified;
- *the cognitive motivation*: a description of the possible cognitive problems that can have generated the problem;

- *the solution proposed*: an indication for improving the user interface design so as to avoid new occurrences of the problem detected.

The cognitive cause of the error can be identified by analysing the possible phases of a user interaction according to the Norman's model (Norman, 1988), in particular:

- *Intention*, the user intended to perform the wrong task,
- *Action*, the task the user intended to perform was correct but the actions supporting it were wrong,
- *Perception*, the user perceived the wrong information,
- *Interpretation*, the user misinterpreted the information provided by the application.

An example of intention problem is when the user tries to send an electronic form without filling all the mandatory fields. So, the intention was wrong according to the state of the application. An example of action error is when the user wants to answer positively to a question but instead of pressing the y key s/he selects the t key which is just beside. A perception problem is when the user selects an image which is not interactive whereas a comprehension problem is when there is a More Info button but the user misunderstands for what topic more information is available.

An example of a problem identified in the analysis of a real application [PB99b] is described in the excerpt of a log that is in table 8.1. The user had to fill all the fields of "User Information" Frame (see figure 8.8). More precisely, the user types the first part of the code (action 1). Between each couple of user actions the logging tool provides information on the amount of time passed (action 2), we will not show the other similar information for sake of brevity. Then the user selects the Identify Number field (action 3) and provides the identify number (action 4). Similarly then the user selects address and user type fields and provides the relative values (actions 5-6-7-8) and, finally, selects the forward button (action 9) and s/he gets an error message (action 10).

```
1   JS.lookup("Code").typeString("501d636", 0, 0);
2   JS.delay(55690);
3   JS.lookup("Identify_Number").multiClick(4,12,16,1);
4   JS.lookup("Identify_Number ").typeString("BPLL-001-HMF", 0,
    0);
5   JS.lookup("Address").multiClick(3,10,16,1);
6   JS.lookup("Address").typeString("Street H. Smith, 111
    London", 0, 0);
7   JS.lookup("User_Type").multiClick(3,11,16,1);
8   JS.lookup("User_Type ").typeString("d10", 0, 0);
9   JS.lookup("Forward").buttonPress();
10  JS.lookup("Screen1").dialog("cli..",
    "Error").button("OK").buttonPress();
```

Table 8.1: Example of log.

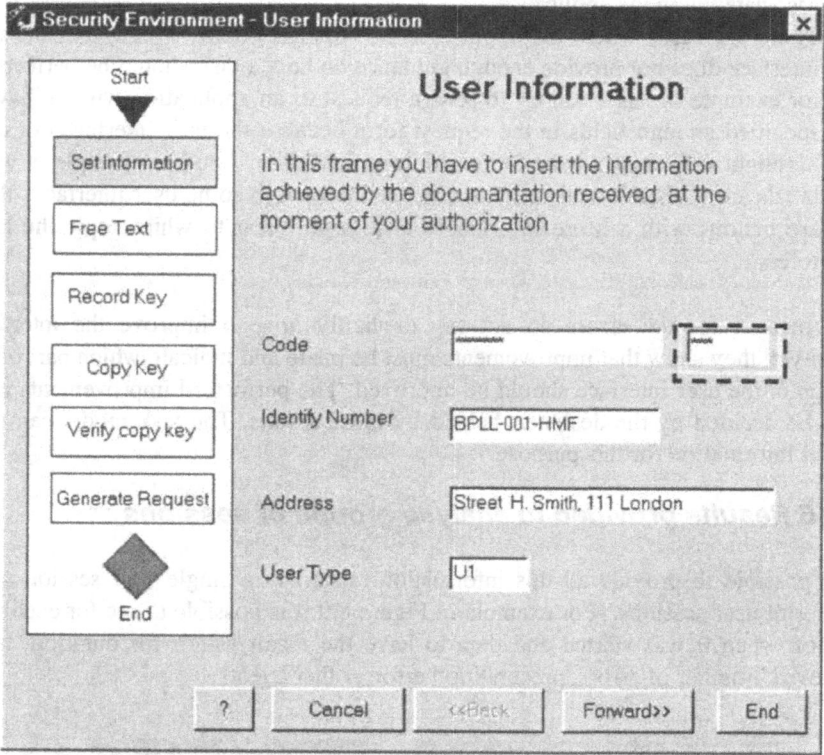

Figure 8.8: Example of usability problem report and related interface.

To summarise, the problem was that the user did not fill the second field of the code highlighted in Figure 8.8. RemUSINE detected the error because the user selected the *Forward* button without first filling both the fields associated with the code as indicated in the task model. This was an interpretation problem. The user did not understand that both fields should have been filled. A possible solution is to add a label indicating that it is mandatory to fill both fields of the code.

We can notice that RemUSINE is able to identify where there are problems in the user interface design, in general the causes are:

- Task model mismatch: the task model of the application (how the application implies that the user should perform task) is different from the task model of the user. Thus, the user interface imposes constraints in performing tasks which are too rigid for the user who wants to perform a task in a different way. For example if a movie database application allows only to select a cinema and next the movies projected in the selected cinema, and finally indicates when the selected movie is projected it can be found too limiting by users who want to know what movies are projected at a given time. In this respect, the analysis of logs of user events can be considered also a way to validate the task model associated with the application.

- There are cases where the application task model could be okay but the user interface does not provide enough guidance on how a task should be performed, for example the user can try to send a request to an application without having specified enough fields in the request form because the user interface does not highlight sufficiently what the mandatory fields are. Another example is when labels are not sufficiently explicative, for instance in some user interfaces there are buttons with a More Info label but it is not clear to which topic the label refers.

The reasons for the errors do not say explicitly *how* to improve the interface. However, they show that improvements must be made and indicate which part of the design of the user interface should be improved. The performed improvements must then be decided by the designer, helped by these results. The task model can give useful information for this purpose.

8.5.6 Results provided to analyse groups of sessions

It is possible to provide all this information related to a single user session or to groups of user sessions. For example in Figure 8.9 it is possible to see for each user session when it was started and then to have the mean values for duration, tasks achieved, number of errors, precondition errors, other events.

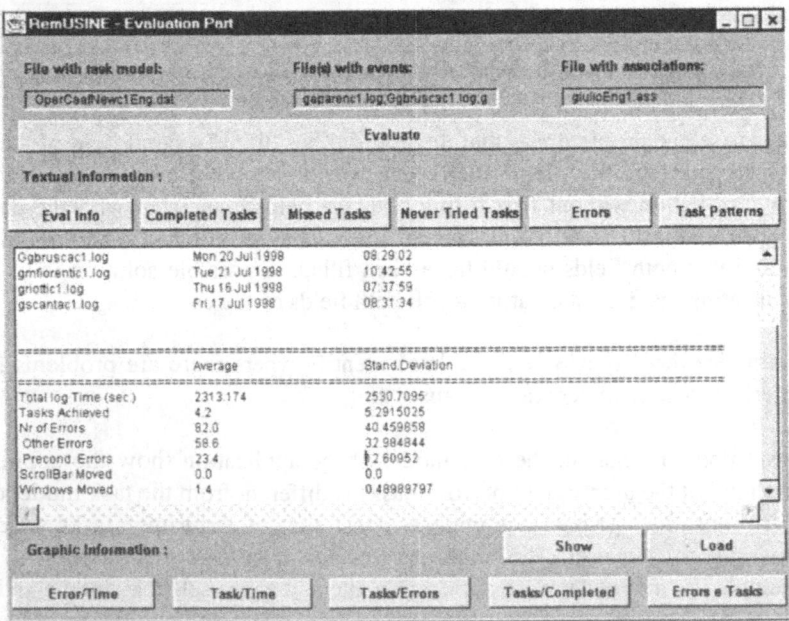

Figure 8.9: An example of information on a group of sessions.

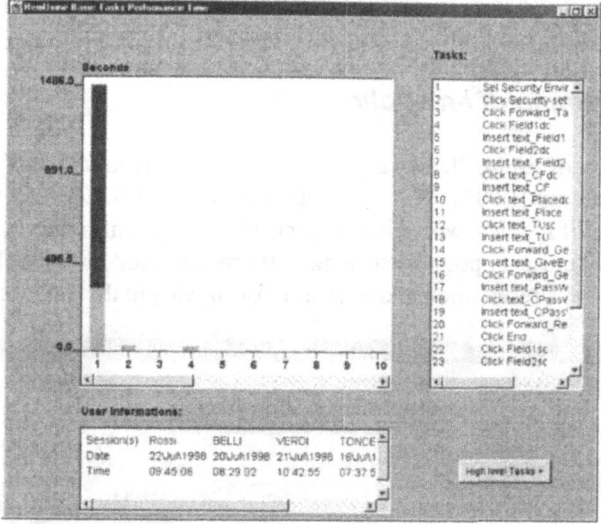

Figure 8.10: An example of a graph produced by the tool.

Another advantage of analysing groups of sessions is that in this way it is possible to immediately identify if in any session there was some abnormal behaviour. For example, a task could have taken a long time to perform just because the user was interrupted by external factors during its accomplishment. Figure 8.10 shows a task that has taken a particularly long average performance with respect to the other tasks.

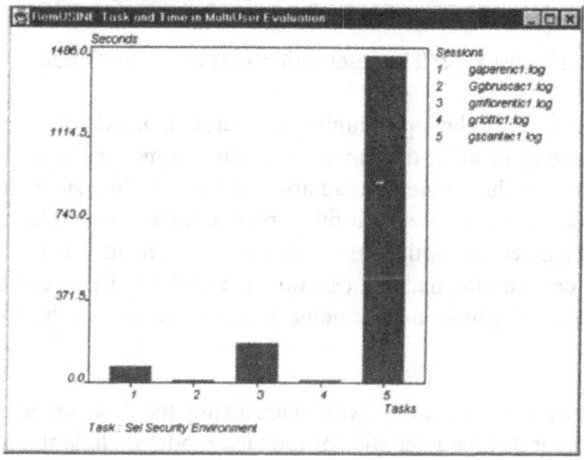

Figure 8.11: A graph indicating when errors occurred.

However, Figure 8.11 shows the time performance for each session revealing that the problem is located particularly to one session. This means that this result is likely to be affected by some external interruptions (for example, a telephone call) and does not indicate a problem that occurs regularly.

8.5.7 An example of an application

An early version of RemUSINE was used to evaluate the *MovieGuide* application by Lecerof and Paternò [LP98]. This application (see Figure 8.12) consists of one part with a database of movies, where it is also possible to get information about movies, and one part where it is possible to make reservations for movie tickets. It is also possible to cancel a reservation and to search for movies in the database.

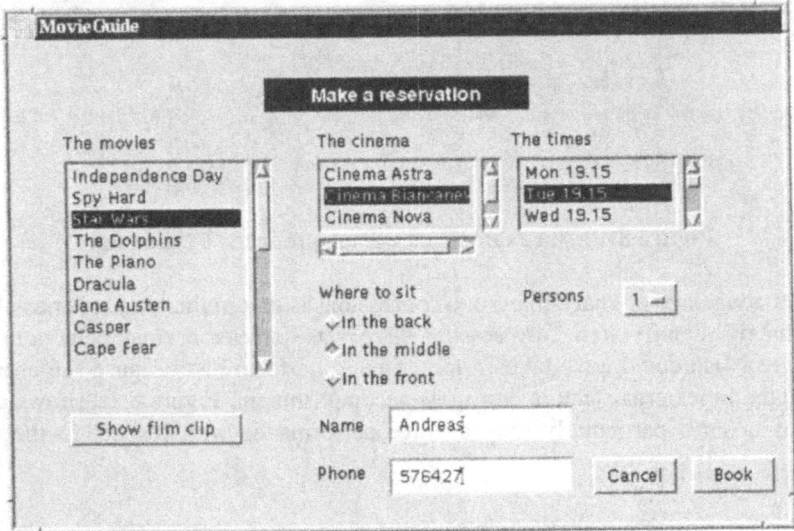

Figure 8.12: The reservation part of MovieGuide.

The database part gives the opportunity to search a movie by director, by first openings, by category or all at the same time. When a movie is chosen it is possible to see a film clip from the movie, to read about the movie (the story, the actors, etc.), to vote for the movie and to see what other people have voted. The reservation part (see Figure 8.12) gives the option to choose a movie from a list and then make a reservation at a certain cinema, at a certain time and for a number of people. It is also possible to decide where in the cinema you want to sit - at the front, the middle or the back.

The task model of the application was made using the ConcurTaskTrees notation described in Chapter 4. Characteristics of the task model include the following:

- The *Quit* task disables the whole session of the application.
- The *Session* task is divided into four parts with the choice operator between the parts. The different parts are: *Cancel reservation*, *Making reservation*, *Search* and *See database part*.

- The effect of the choice operator is that when one of the children of *Session* is performed their sibling tasks are not available any more.
- The *Cancel reservation* and the *Send query* tasks are not derived completely in the task model because they were not evaluated in this example. That is, it is not necessary to include parts of the user interface, not being evaluated, in the task model. Thus the designer only has to specify the parts that s/he wants to evaluate.
- To be able to perform the *Book* task the user has to fill in necessary data before. These data include the movie, the cinema, the time the movie is shown, the name and the telephone number. *CancelBook* disables the possibility to perform the reservation (the booking).
- After the view style is chosen (*Choose viewstyle* task) it is possible to perform the *Choose a movie* task, enabling the *Requesting Info* optional task.
- Some tasks are optional, e.g. *Where to sit* and *Nr of persons*. This means the user does not have to perform these tasks. For example, the *Nr of persons* task, has the default value "1". If the user is satisfied with "1" s/he will not do anything, i.e. no interaction with the interface will occur.

The user test of the application was performed by computer science students aged from 24 to 26 who had never seen the application before and were therefore total beginners. The users received written instructions on paper and an opportunity to ask any questions they liked before the test started. When the test had started questions were not answered directly, instead they were answered with a question. For example, if the user asked "What do I do now?" the answer would be of a general type like "What do you think you could do"? No further help was given during the test. The test consisted of three tasks the user had to perform. The tasks were chosen to force the user to examine different features of the application. During the user test the logs were recorded using the Replay tool. After the test the users answered three questions concerning their impression of the application.

The purpose of the evaluation was to improve the user interface. The aim was also to see which tasks the user performed and the errors s/he made. We did not specify any particular usability goals before we started the evaluation because we were not testing *towards* a quantitative target, for example to see if the application was good enough.

The evaluation of the application was performed following two different approaches. The first approach was based on observations made during the performance of the user tests. An advantage of performing a user test is that you actually see the user using the application which can give you additional information about how to improve the user interface. The second approach, using the *task model* and the USINE *method*, the early version of RemUSINE, was performed considering the logs generated by the user tests. We discuss below the benefits of the two approaches and their results. The first results from the evaluation, however, consist of the users' answers to the questions, asked immediately after a test was finished.

It was found that all users accomplished all the tasks described in the instructions. This indicates that the user interface was easy to use. The time it took the users to perform the tasks was too long though. This means that some sort of built-in help could be motivated. The task that took the longest *time* to perform was the *Select/insert data* abstract task, i.e. inserting the different data required for a reservation. Another fact detected was how many *times* each task was performed. It showed that the *Choose a movie* and *Choose cinema* tasks were performed most. The scrollbars were used frequently and the window was resized a few times. This could indicate a readability problem, i.e., the user had problems with reading and finding the wanted information.

The most frequent precondition errors, i.e. the tasks causing the users problems were *Choose Time, More info, Send Vote* and *Book.* To understand better what the problems with these tasks were we can look at the results from the evaluation to see which precondition the user failed to perform before the current task. The reasons for the precondition errors (failed tasks) can guide designers to improve the user interface, e.g. where to provide better information and more help.

The approach is thus to see which precondition (or preconditions) was not satisfied when the user failed to accomplish a task. The task (or tasks) associated with the unsatisfied precondition then indicates where improvements should be made to the user interface. The reasons for the precondition errors follows below, together with the improvements that could be made to prevent the errors:

- For *Choose Time* it was because the user had to choose a cinema before it was possible to choose the time. However, one of the tasks to perform given to the users was *Making a reservation for watching Independence Day or Sleepers on Saturday 9.30 p.m..* Thus the users obviously tried to choose the time before the cinema was chosen. An improvement of the interface could thus be to make it more obvious that a cinema must be chosen before a time. Or to show a cinema **and** a time after a movie has been chosen.
- The error of *More info* was due to the fact that no movie was chosen before it was selected. To improve the interface a default value could be provided, e.g. a certain movie that is always chosen, together with more information and help as to how to perform the task *More info*. For example it could have been written that you must choose a movie before you can view *more info*.
- The errors of *Send Vote* were due to the fact that no name had been inserted before sending the vote. Here there is a lack of information. It should be more obvious that a name must be inserted before a vote can be given.
- The *Book* task failed because the user did not fill in the required fields like name, telephone number, and so on. The improvements in this case could include message boxes occurring each time the user tries to make a reservation. The messages should include exactly what field or fields are missing in order to perform the reservation. This task has many preconditions. To make it easier for

the user to perform the required actions, a possibility could be to highlight the fields that must be completed.

Among the never tried tasks we found the *See a film clip* task located in the reservation part. We noticed that we had an inconsistency between the *Trailer* task in the "More info" window and this task. These tasks are in fact the same. This failure in design could be very confusing for the user, who may wonder what the difference is. We decided therefore to remove this task as it does not belong to the other tasks in this part. That is, it is not a part of the tasks you normally perform when you want to make a reservation.

The other errors were mainly caused by clicking on images. This was probably caused by, as mentioned above, a lack of feedback when moving the mouse. In other words, the mouse pointer should be of one kind when moved over buttons, and of another kind when moved over a "non-clickable" area.

Among the *task patterns* we found that the user always chose a cinema after s/he had chosen a movie. This is an indication that the application should automatically provide the cinemas after the user has chosen a movie.

Based on the evaluation above and the answers to the questions it was decided to change the user interface as follows:

- To make the difference between buttons and images more distinct.
- To make a default choice of a cinema and a time after the user has chosen a movie.
- To provide some feedback when moving the mouse over "clickable" and "non-clickable" objects.
- To make the information visible in all the present lists from the beginning.
- To make the lists bigger.
- To allow double-click on list items.
- To add more labels and messages, providing useful and helpful information.
- To take away the option of seeing a film clip in the reservation part.

This information did not change the user interface drastically. That is, we did not perform major changes, like changing the structure of the program. Instead we made smaller changes (as mentioned above) that users will notice when they actually use the application. The most visible changes were made in the reservation part (see Figure 8.13). The changes can be seen in the bigger lists and the removal of the "See film clip" button. Other changes include some (default) information always shown in the lists and a couple of instructive labels.

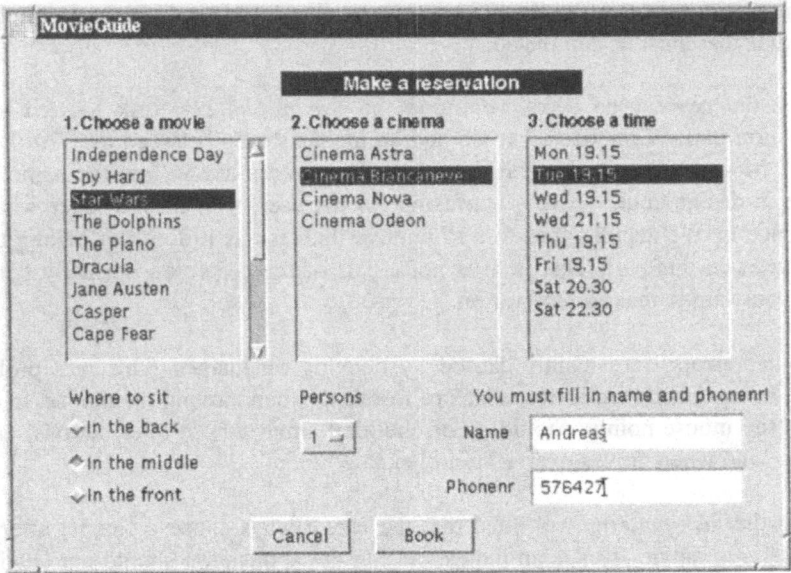

Figure 8.13: The new version of the reservation part, after the evaluation

8.6 EVALUATION OF REMUSINE

One reasonable question is whether the benefits of this approach justify the extra time and effort involved.

The time required for applying RemUSINE (which will be indicated as $t_{RemUSINE}$) can be divided in five parts:
- Record of logs using a logging tool such as *JavaStar* or *QCReplay*. It will be indicated as $t_{Logging}$;
- Developing of the task model, indicated as t_{Build};
- Solution of problems in using RemUSINE, problems can be caused by incomplete task models, or incomplete association between logs and basic tasks, or other problems, $t_{Problems}$;
- Generation of the results $t_{Results}$;
- Analysis of the results provided by RemUSINE, indicated as $t_{Analysis}$.

Consequently we have that:

$$t_{RemUSINE} = t_{Logging} + t_{Build} + t_{Problems} + t_{Results} + t_{Analysis}$$

Now we can consider each of these times. The $t_{Logging}$ time is only the time required by the operator to perform the tasks, it does not require effort from the evaluator but only from the user and the test designer (if any). The users sessions can be run in parallel whereas with video-based evaluation evaluators have to observe the users and so if only one evaluator is available then s/he has to run the tests sequentially.

The t_{build} depends on the designer/evaluator (often the same person has the two roles). It has to be spent only once to build the task model of the application considered. It is independent from the number of users that will be used in the test phase. It depends on the complexity of the application, the knowledge of the application that has the person developing it and the experience in task modelling of such a person. Often the task model is built before the evaluation phase to support the design phase. In these cases it does not require new additional time. In our experience having the application available (we consider medium-large applications) the time requested for developing 95% of the corresponding task models can vary between half day or a week. We say 95% of the model because often during the evaluation of the applications evaluators may discover that some small refinements are necessary.

It is difficult to give a quantitative indication of $t_{Problems}$. In our experience all the problems are removed after an analysis of 2-4 sessions that lasts as long as the 2-4 sessions.

$t_{Results}$ can be neglected as RemUSINE can give its results in a few minutes.

$t_{Analysis}$ depends on the ability of the evaluator and it is proportional to the number of users. On average it has the same duration than the session because the tool helps in identifying the problematic parts.

Thus, we can conclude that: $t_{RemUSINE} \cong t_{build} + t_{Problems} + t_{Analysis}$

As we can see the total time depends only in a limited way on the number of users, only for the third factor. Now we can compare the time required by our method and that required by video-based analysis. In [N93] the time required for video-based analysis is between 3 and 10 times the session duration. We can indicate with **K** ($3\leq$ **K** ≤ 10) these factor. In our case study it was 5 times.

Indicating with T_{Reg} the time required for the evaluation we obtain the evaluation time is: $T_{VideoAnalysis} = K * t_{Logging} *$ **number of sessions**

Note that we do not report any fixed time to compare our method with the best case of the video-based method.

If we compare the time requested by the two methods we can see that RemUSINE is preferable when at least 10 users are considered.

However, the time requested is not the only parameter to take into account when comparing evaluation methods. For example, with RemUSINE it is possible to have more reliable evaluations of the application as no action to be analysed can be omitted (for example experiences have shown that sometimes it is not possible to detect clicks on the screen by a video analysis) and the approach is also valid for large applications. Additional results like tasks never tried are provided. When

RemUSINE gives similar results to those obtained by observing users, it has some advantages because in our case we can run various user tests in parallel and then let the automatic tool evaluate the results whereas in the other case we need an evaluator to follow sequentially each user and analyse manually his/her behaviour with great effort in terms of time from both the user and the observer and less reliability of the results especially when user interactions evolve fast.

The video-based analysis is also more expensive in terms of money as it requires a usability laboratory with the relative equipment and the commercial software for supporting analysis of videos.

Regarding user testing, RemUSINE can give the evaluator more specified and concrete results as the tasks and errors are performed. It does not, however, give explicit recommendations for the evaluator on how to improve the user interface, but, it can give support when deciding which improvements must be made and where in the interface they should be made. This is possible due to the precondition errors pointing out those tasks that caused the user problems. Thus, RemUSINE is worth using with graphical applications with a well defined set of tasks to support and the application considered has many dynamic dialogues and a consistent complexity. It complements and strongly reduces the need for evaluation done by observing and interviewing users which can be limited only to an additional analysis of the parts of the user interface which are found problematic by our method. As it was indicated before, its use is justified when at least ten users will be analysed. For less users the cost of the preparation phase does not justify the use of the approach.

One problem in using this approach for evaluating temporal performance is when either remote applications or applications requiring heavy processing are considered; in that case it is necessary to distinguish between the time spent by the user and the time because of network delay. One technique for addressing this problem with Web applications is indicated in [FR96].

Possible evolutions of this type of approach include the possibility to automatically generate usability reports that could be further annotated by remote users. They could be multimedia reports including audio information with users' comments, for example gathered with think aloud techniques during users sessions, and screen dumps associated with the parts of the user interfaces found complicated.

8.7 EXERCISES

1. Develop a GOMS-KLM evaluation to predict the performance for achieving a goal in two different user interfaces supporting the same task.
2. Apply the cognitive walkthrough method to evaluate the same interface and compare the results obtained with those obtained with the previous exercise.
3. Apply Nielsen's heuristic evaluation to the design of the web site of your organisation.

4. Download an application for logging events (for example JavaStar) and log events generated by the interactions of a group of users with another application. Then compare these events with the task model of the application to identify possible problems.

9 Conclusions

9.1 SUMMARISING THE RESULTS DESCRIBED

The book has given an extended discussion on how models, in particular task models, can be useful in the design and evaluation of interactive applications. The approach discussed implies a deep revision of current practice for various reasons:

- current automatic tools for supporting user interface development allow easy production of user interfaces with various interaction techniques but they do not give support to take into account user knowledge and intentions in generating effective user interfaces. Besides, we have seen that task models can be useful to support design and development of multi-user applications;
- on the one hand it is important that task models require interdisciplinary groups for their development so that they incorporate all the meaningful requirements and capture the main relevant aspects and, on the other hand, their development requires notations with formal foundations in order to obtain structured and rigorous models that can better support the software generation phase;
- we have seen how it is possible to bridge the gap between the task model and the concrete design of the user interface, whereas often people have problems in making the information contained in task models support the concrete design;
- another important aspect is to provide automatic support to move from informal descriptions to formal models and vice versa, for example using material contained in informal descriptions such as a textual scenario or a use case for building a task model;
- it is important that task models are flexible and able to describe interactive dynamic environments where users can perform various tasks concurrently, with the possibility of interruptions, and different possible modalities that can be followed to achieve their goals;

- the use of patterns for HCI can open new effective ways to support design and evaluation of user interfaces and improve their development;
- in usability evaluation it is possible to develop approaches that combine model-based and empirical testing trying to take the best aspects of each of them and avoid the respective limitations.

9.2 SUGGESTIONS FOR OPEN AREAS OF INTERESTS

As it is easy to imagine there are still many open problems and areas with possibility of further development. This is a field that has generated a lot of interest, it is continuously evolving, and thus it is easy to foresee many new developments that will further address such issues very soon. In this section some of them are mentioned:

- In software industries the use of object-oriented approaches, such as UML, for modelling and design software is well established. However these approaches are not adequate to capture effectively aspects important for the design of the interactive part of an application whereas task-based approaches can better address such an issue. Thus a systematic integration of these two types of approaches would be very important to improve industrial practice.
- One of the advantages of the task-based environments that we have discussed is that they can be used to develop applications directly even if the developer of such models does not have a specific background in programming. This opens the possibility of obtaining environments where end users can directly develop their applications.
- Our computers are changing their forms, they are penetrating everywhere we go and every object we manipulate. They are increasingly invading our cars, our pockets, our houses. A rich variety of screen dimensions are appearing: from small screen of PDAs (Personal Digital Assistants) to flat very large screens. This means that there will be an increasing need for applications able to exploit these possibilities and tools supporting their design and development. There will be a strong need for context-dependent applications, where similar tasks are supported but taking into account the devices used [TC99], the contextual environment [SDA99] where the user performs them, the position where the user is located thus optimising the information provided and the possible interactions, and other information such as awareness of identity of the persons that are close to the application, light, noise, time constraints.
- While virtual reality has been successful for specific application areas, augmented reality where the objects that we manipulate are enriched with additional intelligence seems to be a more pervasive technology. It will be important to identify methods that help the design of these new enriched artefacts that add new functionality to our familiar objects using various types of sensors and devices.

- Emotional aspects are important when people interact with applications, thus it is important to design them to take this into account. This means that designers should be able to incorporate similar aspects in their specifications.
- In modern society there are various applications that can be considered interactive safety-critical applications, where a user error can threaten human life. The design of such applications requires more rigorous methods to create environments able to support both usability and safety requirements. For example, flexible environments should be provided but warnings able to catch the user attention when deviations with potential dangerous effects occur should be systematically introduced and designed so as to be effective and useful for the users.
- The increasing availability of Internet connections in all the possible locations will stimulate an explosion of cooperative, multi-user applications. This will stimulate more research in models and tools that are able to highlight important aspects in such a class of applications to help their designers and developers. Such tools should be able to incorporate the social rules that steer the behaviour of groups of users. The mechanisms that drive the cooperations among such users should be able to adapt dynamically to the needs of such groups and the specific devices they use to interact with each other (see Figure 9.1).
- Another effect of the increasing Internet diffusion is the enormous amount of data that can be accessed and so there is a consequent need for applications able to highlight semantic relationships in such information and help the users to find what is of interest for them. An example of an application area where people have to access a great amount of data represented in multimedia forms is the digital library area.
- A further consequence of this Internet diffusion will be the diffusion of remote usability evaluation (in addition to remote cooperative design) thus decreasing the need for central usability laboratories. Such a remote analysis of users' behaviours will further use multimedia technology.

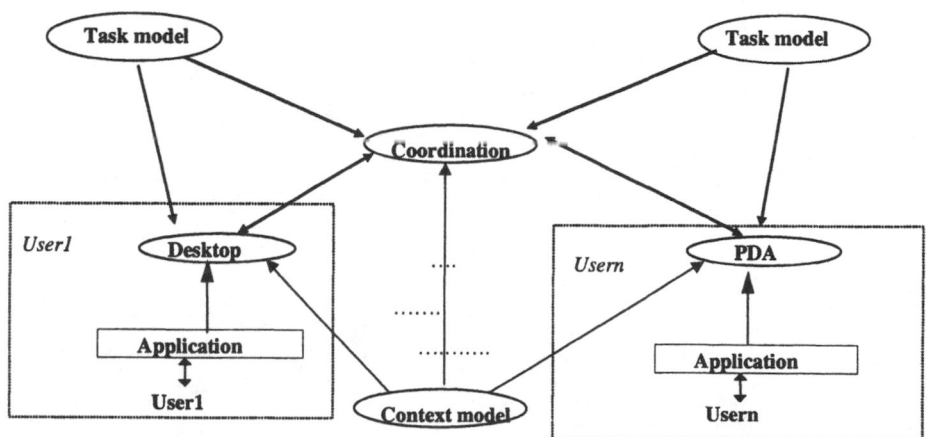

Figure 9.1: Model-Based Design of Adaptive Cooperative Applications

References

[A77] Alexander, C., *A Pattern Language*, Oxford University Press, 1977.

[ABPS98] Aloia, N., Bendini, T., Paternò, F., Santoro, C., "Design of Multimedia Semantic Presentation Templates: Options, Problems and Criteria of Use", *Proceedings AVI'98*, pp. 205-215, ACM Press, 1998.

[AD67] Annett, J., Duncan, K.D., "Task Analysis and Training Design", *Occupational Psychology*, 41, pp.211-221, 1967.

[AGJ98] Ait-Ameur Y., Girard P., Jambon F., "Using the B Formal Approach for Incremental Specification Design of Interactive Systems", *Proceedings EHCI'98*, pp. 91-110, Kluwer Academic Publisher, 1998.

[AH92] Appleby, S., Hall, A., "ASA User Interface Definition", Praxis document Reference S.P0204.43.3, August 1992.

[AM95] Alfred, C., Mellor, S., "Observations on the Role of Patterns in Object-Oriented Software Development", *Object Magazine*, May 1995.

[ASDR98] d'Ausbourg, B., Seguin, C., Durrieu, G., Rochè, P., "Helping the Automated Validation Process of User Interfaces Systems", *Proceedings ICSE'98*, pp. 219-228, 1998.

[AWM95] Abowd, G., Wang, H., Monk A., "A Formal Technique for Automated Dialogue Development", *Proceedings DIS'95*, pp. 219-226, ACM Press, 1995.

[B83] Buxton, W., "Lexical and Pragmatic Considerations of Input Structures", *Computer Graphics*, 17(1), pp.31-37, 1983.

[B91] Bass, L. et al.. "The Arch Model: Seeheim Revisited". CHI UIMS Developers' Workshop, New Orleans, 28-29 April, 1991.

[B92] Bowen, J.P., "X:Why Z?", *Computer Graphics Forum*, Vol.11, N.4, pp.221-234, 1992.

[BB95] Brun, P., Beaudouin-Lafon, M., "A Taxonomy and Evaluation of Formalisms for the Specification of Interactive Systems", *Proceedings HCI'95*, Cambridge University Press, 1995.

[BGW98] Brown, J., Graham, N., Wright, T., "The Vista Environment for the Coevolutionary Design of User Interfaces", *Proceedings CHI'98*, ACM Press, pp. 376-383, 1998.

[BHLV95] Bodart, F., Hennerbert, A., Leheureux, J., Vanderdonckt, J., "A Model-based Approach to Presentation: A Continuum from Task Analysis to Prototype", in F. Paternò (ed.), *Interactive Systems: Design, Specification, and Verification*, pp. 77-94, Springer Verlag, 1995.

[BM93] Benyon, D., Murray, D., "Adaptive Systems: from Intelligent Tutoring to Autonomous Agents", Knowledge-Based Systems, Vol6, N.4, pp. 197-219, 1993.

[BM95] Barnard, P. and May, J. "Interactions with Advanced Graphical Interfaces and the Deployment of Latent Human Knowledge", in F. Paterno' (ed.) *Interactive Systems: Design, Specification, Verification*, pp. 15-48, Springer Verlag, 1995.

[BMRSS96] Buschmann, F., Meunier, R., Rohnert, H., Sommerlad, P., Stal, M., *A System of Patterns: Pattern-Oriented Software Architecture*, John Wiley & Sons, 1996.

[BPS97] Breedvelt, I., Paterno', F., Severijns, C., "Reusable Structures in Task Models", *Proceedings DSV-IS'97*, pp. 251-265, Springer Verlag, 1999.

[BRJ99] Booch, G., Rumbaugh, J., Jacobson, I., *Unified Modeling Language Reference Manual*, Addison Wesley, 1999

[BS99] Bomsdorf, B., Szwillus, G., "Tool Support for Task-based User Interface Design", *Proceedings CHI'99*, Extended Abstracts, pp.169-170, 1999.

[BWSFK94] Byrne, M., Wood. S., Noi Sukaviriya, P., Foley, J., Kieras, D., "Automating Interface Evaluation", *Proceedings CHI'94*, pp. 232-237, ACM Press, 1994.

[C87] Coutaz, J., "PAC, an Object-Oriented Model for Dialog Design", *Proceedings Interact'87*, pp. 431-436, Elsevier Science Publisher, 1987.

[C91] Casner, S., "A Task-Analytic Approach to the Automated Design of Graphic Presentations", *ACM Trans. on Graphics*, 10, pp. 111-151, 1991.

[C94] Carr, D., "Specification of Interface Interaction Objects", *Proceedings CHI'94*, pp. 372-377, ACM Press, 1994.

[C95] Carroll, J. (Ed.), *Scenario-Based Design*, John Wiley and Sons & C., 1995.

[C97a] Casaday, G., "Notes on a Pattern Language for Interactive Usability", *Proceedings CHI97*, Late Breaking Results, 1997.

[C97b] Cockburn A., "Structuring Use Cases with Goals", Journal of Object-Oriented Programming, http://members.aol.com/acockburn, 1997.

[CCN97] Calvary, G., Coutaz, J., Nigay, L., "From Single-User Architectural Design to PAC*: a Generic Software Architecture Model for CSCW", *Proceedings CHI'97*, pp. 242-249, ACM Press, 1997.

[CI89] Clement, D., Incerpi, J.. "Specifying the Behaviour of Graphical Objects using Esterel", *Proceedings Tapsoft'89*, pp. 111-125, 1989.

[CM96] Comber, T., Maltby, J., "Investigation Layout Complexity", *Proceedings CADUI'96*, pp. 209-227, Presses Universitaires de Namur, 1996.

[CMN83] Card, S., Moran, T., Newell, A., *The Psychology of Human-Computer Interaction*, Lawrence Erlbaum, Hillsdale, 1983.

[CMP98] Chung-Man Tam, R., Maulsby, D., Puerta, A., "U-TEL: A Tool for Eliciting User Task Models from Domain Expert", *Proceedings IUI'98*, pp.77-80, ACM Press, 1998.

[CMS99] Card, S., Mackinlay, J., Shneiderman, B., (Eds.), *Readings in Information Visualization*, Morgan Kaufman, 1999.

[CP85].Cardelli L, Pike R.. "Squeak: a language for communicating with mice", *Proceedings SIGGRAPH'85*, Computer Graphics, 19, 3, pp. 215-224, ACM Press, 1995.

[D89] Diaper, D., *Task Analysis for Human-Computer Interaction*, Chichester: Ellis Horwood, 1989.

[D91] Dix, A., *Formal Methods for Interactive Systems*, Academic Press 1991.

[DD92] Duce D.A., Damnjanovic L.B., "Formal Specification in the Revision of GKS: An Illustrative Example". *Computer Graphics Forum*. Vol.11, N.1, pp.17-30, 1992.

[DDS98] De Carolis, B., de Rosis, F., Pizzutilo, S., "Formal description and evaluation of user-adapted interfaces", *International Journal of Human-Computer Studies*, 49, 1998.

[DFAB98] Dix, A., Finlay, E., Abowd, G., Beale, R., *Human-Computer Interaction*, Second Edition, Prentice Hall, 1998.

[DH95] D.Duke, M.Harrison, "Interactions and Task requirements", *Proceedings DSV-IS'95*, pp. 54-75, Springer Verlag, 1995.

[DHGL91] Duce, D., Hopgood, F., Gomez, R., Lee, J., (Eds.) *User Interface Management and Design*. Springer Verlag 1991.

[DHL90] Duce, D., ten Hagen, P.J.W., van Liere, R.. "An Approach to Hierarchical Input Devices", *Computer Graphics Forum*, Vol.9, N.1, pp. 15-26, 1990.

[DR94] Dumas, J.S. and Redish, J.C., *A Practical Guide to Usability Testing*, Ablex Publishing Corporation, 1994.

[ET97] Erickson, T., Thomas, J., "Putting it all together: pattern languages for interaction design." *Proceedings CHI97*, Extended Abstracts, 1997

[FHW98] Fields, R., Harrison, M., Wright, P., "THEA: Human Error Analysis for Requirements Definition", University of York, Department of Computer Science, Internal Report, 1998.

[FKKM91] Foley, J., Kim, W., Kovacevic, S., Murray, K., "UIDE – An Intelligent User Interface Design Environment", in *Architectures for Intelligent Interfaces: Element and Prototypes*, Sullivan J., Tyler S. (Eds.), Addison-Wesley, 1991.

[FP90] Faconti, G., Paternò, F.. "An Approach to the Formal Specification of the Components of an Interaction", *Proceedings Eurographics '90*, pp. 481-494, Elsevier, 1990.

[FPP95] Fuchs, L., Pankoke-Babatz, U., and Prinz,W., "Supporting Cooperative Awareness with Local Event Mechanisms: The Groupdesk System". In Marmolin H., Sundblad Y., and Schmidt K., (Eds.), *Proceedings. 4th European Conf. on CSCW*, pp. 247-262. Kluwer Academic Publishers, 1995.

[FR96] Fuller, Rodney, "Measuring User Motivation from Server Log Files", *Designing for the Web: Empirical Studies*, 1996.

[FS94] Foley, J., Sukaviriya, N., "History, Results, and Bibliography of the User Interface Design Environment (UIDE), an Early Model-based System for User Interface Design and Development", in F. Paterno' (ed.) *Interactive Systems: Design, Specification, Verification*, , pp. 3-14 Springer Verlag, 1994.

[FWC84] Foley, J., Wallace, V., Chan, P., "The Human Factor of Computer Graphics Interaction Techniques", *IEEE Computer Graphics & Applications*, 4(11), pp. 13-48, 1984.

[FWH95] Fields, R., Wright, P., Harrison, M., "A Task-centred Approach to Analysing Human Error Tolerance Requirements", *Proceedings Requirements Engineering '95*, pp. 18-26, 1995.

[GF92] Gieskens, D., Foley, J., "Controlling User Interface Objects through Pre- and Postconditions", *Proceedings CHI'92*, pp. 189-194, ACM Press, 1992.

[GHJV95] Gamma, E., Helm, R., Johnson, R., Vlissides, J., *Design Patterns: Elements of Reusable Object-Oriented Software*, Addison Wesley, 1995.

[GJA92] Gray, W., John, B., Atwood, M., "Project Ernestine: A Validation of GOMS for Prediction and Explanation of Real-World Task Performance", *Human-Computer Interaction*, 8, 3, pp. 207-209, 1992.

[GR83] Goldberg, M., Robson, D., *Smalltalk-80. The Language and Its Implementation*, Addison Wesley Publishing Company, 1983.

[GS98] Gray W., Salzman M., "Damaged Merchandise? A Review of Experiments that Compare Usability Evaluation Methods", *Human-Computer Interaction*, 13, 3, pp. 203-261, 1998.

[GYK97] Gray, W., Young, R., Kirschenbaum, S., Cognitive Architectures and Human-Computer Interaction, Special Issue of *Human-Computer Interaction*, 12, 4, 1997.

[H87] Harel, D., "Statecharts: A Visual Formalism for Complex Systems", *Science of Computer programming*, 8, 1987.

[H95] Hutchins, E., *Cognition in the Wild*, MIT Press, 1995.

[H99] Harel, A., "Automatic Operation Logging and Usability Evaluation", *Proceedings HCI International '99*, 1999.

[HT90] Harrison, M., Thimblebly, H. (Eds.), *Formal Methods in Human-Computer Interaction*, Cambridge University Press, 1990.

[HC98] Hartson, R., Castillo, J., "Remote Evaluation for Post-Deployment Usability Improvement", *Proceedings AVI'98*, pp. 22-29, ACM Press, 1998.

[HCKKN96] Hartson, R., Castillo, J., Kelso, J., Kamler, J., Neale, W., "The Network as an extension of the Usability Laboratory", *Proceedings CHI'96*, pp.228-235, ACM Press, 1996.

[HG92] Hartson R., Gray P., "Temporal Aspects of Tasks in the User Action Notation", *Human Computer Interaction*, Vol.7, pp.1-45, 1992.

[HH93] Hix, D. and Hartson, H.R., *Developing User Interfaces: Ensuring Usability Through Product and Process*. New York: John Wiley, 1993.

[HJKB99] Hudson, S., John, B., Knudsen, K., Byrne, M., "A Tool for Creating Predictive Performance Models from User Interface Demonstrations", *Proceedings UIST'99*, ACM Press, 1999.

[ISO88] ISO, "Information Processing Systems - Open Systems Interconnection - LOTOS - A Formal Description Based on Temporal Ordering of Observational Behaviour", ISO/IS 8807. ISO Central Secretariat, 1988.

[J91] Johnson, C., "Applying Temporal Logic to Support the Specification and Prototyping of Concurrent Multiuser Interfaces", *Proceedings HCI'91*, pp.145-156, Cambridge University Press, 1991.

[J92a] Johnson P., *Human-Computer Interaction. Psychology - task analysis and software engineering*, McGraw-Hill, 1992.

[J92b] Johnson J., "Selectors: Going Beyond User-Interface Widgets", *Proceedings CHI'92*, pp.273-279, ACM Press, 1992.

[J92c] Jacobson I. et al., *Object-Oriented Software Engineering – A Use Case Driven Approach*, Addison-Wesley, 1992.

[JJ91] Johnson, P. & Johnson, H., "Knowledge Analysis of Tasks: task Analysis and Specification for Human-Computer Systems", *in Engineering the Human-Computer Interface*, McGraw-Hill, 1991.

[JJWS88] Johnson, P., Johnson, H., Waddington, R., Shouls, A., "Task related Knowledge Structures: Analysis, Modelling, and applications", *Proceedings HCI'88*, Cambridge University Press, 1988.

[JK96] John, B., Kieras, D., "The GOMS Family of Analysis Techniques: Comparison and Contrast". *ACM Transactions on Computer-Human Interaction*, Vol.3, N.4, pp.320-351, 1996.

[JMWU91] Jeffries, R., Miller, J.R., Wharton, C. and Uyeda, K.M., "User Interface Evaluation in the Real World: A Comparison of Four Techniques". *Proceedings CHI'91*, pp. 119-124., ACM Press, 1991.

[JWZ93] Janssen, C., Weisbecker, A., Ziegler, J., "Generating User Interfaces from Data Models and Dialogue Net Specifications", *Proceedings INTERCHI'93*, pp.418-423, ACM Press, 1993.

[K92] Kletz, T., *HAZOP and HAZAN: Identifying and Assessing Process Industry Hazards*, Institution of Chemical Engineers, 1992.

[KD90] Karayana, K.T., Dharap, S., "Formal Specification of a Look Manager", *IEEE Transaction on Software Engineering*, 16, pp. 1089-1103, 1990.

[K96] Kieras D.E., "Guide to GOMS model usability evaluation using NGOMSL", in *The Handbook of Human-Computer Interaction*, 2nd edition, North Holland 1996.

[KA92] Kirwan, B. and Ainsworth, L.K., *A Guide to Task Analysis*, Taylor & Francis, 1992.

[KF93] Kim, W., Foley, J., "Providing High-Level Control and Expert Assistance in the User Interface Presentation Design", *Proceedings INTERCHI'93*, pp.430-437, ACM Press, 1993.

[KP88] Krasner, G. E., Pope, S. T., "A Cookbook for Using the Model-View-Control User Interface in Smalltalk-80", *JOOP*, August\September, pp 26-49, 1988.

[KSM97] Kieras, D., Scott, W., Meyer, D., "Predictive Engineering Models Based on the EPIC Architecture for a Multimodal Hugh-Performance Human-Computer Interaction Task", *ACM Transactions on Computer-Human Interaction*, 4, 3, pp.230-275, 1997.

[KWAH95] Kieras, D.E., Wood, S.D., Abotel, K. and Hornof, A, "GLEAN: A Computer-Based Tool for Rapid GOMS Model, Usability Evaluation of User Interface Designs". *Proceedings UIST'95*, pp. 91-100, ACM Press, 1995.

[L82] Lewis, C., "Using the Thinking Aloud Method in Cognitive Interface Design", *Research Report RC9265* IBM Thomas J.Watson Research Center, Yorktown Heights, 1982.

[L95] Lauridsen O., "Systemathic methods for user interface design" *Proceedings EHCI'95*, pp. 169-188, Chapman & Hall, 1995.

[LL94] Lim, K.Y. Long, J.B., *The MUSE Method for Usability Engineering*, Cambridge University Press, Cambridge, 1994.

[LPL98] Lu, S., Paris, C., Linden, K., "Towards the Automatic Construction of Task Models from Object-Oriented Diagrams", *Proceedings EHCI'98*, Kluwer, 1998.

[LP98] Lecerof, A., Paternò, F., "Automatic Support for Usability Evaluation", *IEEE Transactions on Software Engineering*, October, pp. 863-888, IEEE Press, 1998.

[LR93] Lewis, C. and Rieman, J., *Task-Centered User Interface Design: A Practical Introduction*, A shareware book published on the web by the authors: www2.umassd.edu/CoursePages/HCI/hcireadings/TextVersion/index.htm. Also available at ftp.cs.colorado.edu/pub/cs/distribs/clewis/HCI-Design-Book, 1993.

[M86] Mackinlay, J., "Automating the Design of Graphical Presentations of Relational Information", *ACM Transactions on Graphics*, 5, 2, April, pp.110-141, 1986.

[M90] Myers, B., "A New Input Model for Handling Input", *ACM Transactions on Information System*, July, 8, 3, , pp. 289-320, 1990.

[MBB94] Macleod, M., Bowden, R. and Bevan N. "The MUSiC Performance Measurement Method". In HCI '96, Tutorial 14, *Measuring Usability - MUSiC Methods*, (Bevan, N.). London: The British HCI Group, 1994.

[MC94] Monk, A., Curry, M., "Discount Dialogue Modelling with Action Simulator" *Proceedings HCI'94*, pp.327-338, Cambridge University Press, 1994.

[MCR90] Mackinlay, J., Card, S., Robertson, G., "A Semantic Analysis of the Design Space of Input Devices", *Human-Computer Interaction*, 5, pp.145-190, 1990.

[MPWJ96] Markopoulos, P., Pycock, J., Wilson, S., Johnson, P., "Adept – A Task Based Design Environment", *Proceedings CADUI'96*, Presses Universitaires de Namur, 1996.

[MR92] Myers, B., Rosson, M.B., "Survey on User Interface Programming", *Proceedings CHI'92*, pp. 195-202, ACM Press, 1992.

[MS97] Mahajan, R., Sheiderman, B., "Visual and Textual Consistency Checking Tools for Graphical User Interfaces", *IEEE Transaction on Software Engineering*, 23, 11, 1997.

[MSN94] Moriyon, R., Szekely, P., Neches, R., "Automatic Generation of Help from Interface Design Models", *Proceedings CHI'94*, pp.225-231, ACM Press, 1994.

[N88] Norman, D., *The Psychology of Everyday Things*, Basic Books, 1988.

[N93] Nielsen, J., *Usability Engineering*, Academic Press, 1993.

[NC91] Nigay, L., Coutaz, J., "Building User Interfaces: Organising Software Agents", *Proceedings Esprit '91*, pp. 707-719, 1991.

[O87] Olsen, D.R. (Ed.), ACM SIGGRAPH Workshop on Software Tools for User Interface Management, *Computer Graphics*, 21, 2,, pp.71-147, 1987.

[OD93] Olsen, D.R., Dempsey, E.P., "SYNGRAPH: A Graphical User Interface Generator", *Proceedings SIGGRAPH'83*, Computer Graphics, 17, 3, pp.43-50, 1983.

[P85] Pfaff, G.R. (Ed.), *User Interface Management Systems*, Springer-Verlag, 1985.

[P94] Paternò, F., "A Theory of User-Interaction Objects", *Journal of Visual Languages and Computing*, 5, 3., pp. 227-249, Academic Press, 1994.

[P95] Paternò, F. (Ed.), *Interactive Systems: Design, Specification, and Verification*, Springer Verlag, Focus on Computer Graphics Series, 1995.

[P97a] Paternò, F., Formal Reasoning about Dialogue Properties with Automatic Support, *Interacting with Computers*, 9, August, pp. 173-196, Elsevier, 1997.

[P97b] Puerta, A., A Model-Based Interface Development Environment, *IEEE Software*, pp. 40-47, July/August 1997.

[PB90] Palanque, P., Bastide, R., "Petri Nets with Objects for Specification, Design and Validation of User-driven Interfaces". *Proceedings INTERACT'90*, 1990.

[PB94] Palanque, P., Bastide, R.. "Petri Net based design of user-driven interfaces using the Interactive Cooperative Objects formalism". in F. Paternò (ed.) *Interactive Systems: Design, Specification, Verification*, pp. 383-400, Springer Verlag, 1994.

[PB95] Palanque, P., Bastide, R., "Verification of Interactive Behaviours", *Proceedings INTERACT'95*, pp. 191-196, Chapmann & Hall, 1995.

[PB99a] Paternò, F., Ballardin, G., "Model-Aided Remote Usability Evaluation", *Proceedings INTERACT'99*, pp. 434-442, IOS Press, 1999.

[PB99b] Paternò, F., Ballardin, G., "RemUSINE: a bridge between empirical and model-based evaluation when evaluators and users are distant", CNUCE Internal Report, 1999.

[PBD93] Palanque, P., Bastide, R., Dourte L., "Contextual Help for Free with Formal Dialogue Design", *Proceedings HCI'93 International*, pp. 615-620, 1993.

[PBD98] Paternò, F., Breedvelt-Schouten, I., deKonig, N., "Deriving Presentations from task Models", *Proceedings EHCI'98*, Kluwer Publisher, 1998.

[PCTM99] Puerta A., Cheng E., Tunhow O.., Min J., MOBILE: User-Centred Interface Building, *Proceedings ACM CHI'99*, pag.426-433, ACM Press, 1999.

[PE99] Puerta, A. and Eisenstein J.. Towards a General Computational Framework for Model-Based Interface Development Systems. in IUI99: International Conference on Intelligent User Interfaces. 1999. Los Angeles: ACM Press.

[PF92] Paternò, F., Faconti, G. "On the Use of LOTOS to Describe Graphical Interaction", *Proceedings HCI'92*, pp.155-173, Cambridge University Press, 1992.

[PG86] Payne, S., Green, T., "Task-Actions Grammars: A Model of the Mental Representation of Task Languages", *Human-Computer Interaction*, 2, pp.93-133, 1986.

[PL94] Paternò, F., Leonardi, A.. "A Semantics-based Approach to the Design and Implementation of Interaction Objects", *Computer Graphics Forum*, Blackwell Publisher, 13, 3, pp.195-204, 1994.

[PLRW92] Polson, P.G., Lewis, C., Rieman, J. and Wharton, C., "Cognitive Walkthroughs: A Method for Theory-based Evaluation of User Interfaces", *International Journal of Man-Machine Studies*, 36, pp. 741-773, 1992.

[PM97a] Paternò, F., Meniconi, S., "Patterns for Dialogue Representations", *Proceedings International Workshop on Representations in Interactive Software Development*, pp. 73-81, 1997.

[PM97b] Puerta, A. and Maulsby, D., "Management of Interface Design Knowledge with MOBI-D", *Proceedings IUI'97*, pp. 249-252, ACM Press, 1997.

[PM99a] Paternò, F., Mancini, C., "Designing Usable Hypermedia", *Empirical Software Engineering*, 4, 1, pp. 11-42, Kluwer, 1999.

[PM99b] Paternò, F., Mancini, C., "Developing Adaptable Hypermedia", *Proceedings IUI'99*, pp. 163-170, ACM Press, 1999.

[PM99c] Paternò, F., Mancini, C., "Developing Task Models from Informal Scenarios", *Proceedings CHI'99*, Late Breaking Results, pp. 228-229, ACM Press, 1999.

[PMA99] Paternò, F., Mancini, C., Alkemade, F., "Designing Web User Interfaces for Museum Applications to Support different Types of Users", *Proceedings Museums and the Web 1999*, pp.75-86, Archives & Museum Informatics, 1999.

[PMM97] Paternò, F., Mancini, C., Meniconi, S., "Engineering Task Models", *Proceedings IEEE Conference on Engineering of Complex Computer Systems*, pp.69-76, IEEE Computer Society Press, 1997.

[PP95] Pangoli, S., Paternò, F., "Automatic Generation of Task-oriented Help", *Proceedings UIST'95*, pp. 181-187, ACM Press, 1995.

[PP97] Palanque, P., Paternò, F., *Formal Methods in Human-Computer Interaction*, Springer Verlag, 1997.

[PRSBHC94] Preece J. (ed.), Rogers Y., Sharp H., Benyon D., Holland S. and Carey T. *Human-Computer Interaction*, Addison-Wesley, 1994.

[PSF99] Paternò, F., Santoro, C., Fields, B., "Analysing User Deviations in Interactive Safety-critical Applications", *Proceedings DSV-IS'99*, Springer Verlag, 1999

[PSL95] Paternò, F., Sciacchitano, S., Lowgren, J., "A User Interface Evaluation Mapping Physical User Actions to Task-driven Formal Specifications", *Proceedings DSV-IS'95*, pp. 35-53, Springer Verlag, 1995.

[PST98] Paternò, F., Santoro, C., Tahmassebi, S., "Formal Models for Cooperative Tasks: Concepts and an Application for En-Route Air Traffic Control", *Proceedings DSV-IS '98*, pp. 71-86, Springer Verlag, 1998.

[R90] Reason, J.T., *Human Error*, Cambridge University Press, 1990.

[R81] Reisner, P., "Formal Grammars and Human Factors Design of an Interactive Graphics System", *IEEE Transactions on Software Engineering*, 5, pp. 229-240, 1981.

[RG96] Roseman, M., Greenberg, S., "Building Real-Time Groupware with GroupKit, A Groupware Toolkit", *ACM Transaction on Computer-Human Interaction*, 3, 1, March, pp. 66-106, 1996.

[RKMG94] Roth, S., Kolojejchick, J., Mattis, J., Goldstein, J., "Interactive Graphic Design Using Automatic Presentation Knowledge". *Proceedings CHI'94*, pp. 112-117, ACM Press, 1994.

[RM90] Roth, S., Mattis, J., "Data Characterization for Intelligent Graphics Presentation", *Proceedings CHI'90*, pp. 193-200, ACM Press, 1990.

[RMC91] Robertson, G., Mackinlay, J., Card, S., "Cone Trees: Animated 3D Visualizations of Hierarchical Information", *Proceedings CHI'91*, pp. 189-195, ACM Press, 1991.

[S93] Sears, A. "Layout Appropriateness: A Metric for Evaluating User Interface Widget Layout", *IEEE Transactions on Software Engineering*, 17, 7, July, pp. 707-719, 1993.

[S95a] Sears, A., "AIDE: A Step Toward Metric-Based User Interface Development Tools", *Proceedings UIST'95*, pp. 101-110, ACM Press, 1995.

[S95b] Systa, K., "Adding User Interface to a Behavioural Specification", *Proceedings EHCI95*, pp. 227-244, Chapman & Hall, 1995.

[S97] Sutcliffe, A., "Task-related Information Analysis", *International Journal of Human-Computer Studies*, 47, pp. 223-257, 1997.

[S98] Shneiderman, B., *Designing the User Interface*. Third Edition, Addison Wesley, 1998.

[SDA99] Salber, D., Dey, A., Abowd, G., "The Context Toolkit: Aiding the Development of Context-Enabled Applications, *Proceedings CHI'99*, pp. 434-441, ACM Press, 1999.

[SE91] Siochi, A., Ehrich, R., "Computer Analysis of User Interfaces Based on Repetition in Transcripts of User Sessions", *ACM Transactions on Information Systems*, 9, 4, October, pp. 309-335, ACM Press, 1991.

[SE96] Schlungbaum, E., Elwert, T., "Automatic User Generation from Declarative Models", *Proceedings CADUI'96*, pp. 3-18, Presses Universitaires de Namur, 1996.

[SF90] Sukaviriya, P., Foley, J., "Coupling a UI Framework with Automatic Generation of Context-Sensitive Animated Help", *Proceedings UIST'90*, pp. 152-165, ACM Press, 1990.

[SF93] Sukaviriya, P., Foley, J., "Supporting Adapting User Interfaces in a Knowledge – Based User Interface Environment", *Proceedings of the Intelligent Interfaces Workshop*, pp.107-114, ACM Press, 1993.

[SF94] Sutcliffe, A., Faraday, P., "Designing Presentation in Multimedia Interfaces", *Proceedings CHI'94*, pp.92-98, ACM Press, 1994.

[SLN92] Szekely, P., Luo, P., Neches, R., "Facilitating the Exploration of Design Alternative: The HUMANOID Model of User Interface Design", *Proceedings CHI'92*, pp. 507-515, ACM Press, 1992.

[SLN93] Szekely, P., Luo, P., Neches, R., "Beyond Interface Builders: Model-Based Interface Tools". *Proceedings INTERCHI'93*, pp. 383-390, ACM Press, 1993.

[SM86] Smith, S.L., Mosier, J.N., "Design Guidelines for the User Interface Software", *Technical Report ESD-TR-86-278*, Massachusetts, 1986.

[SMSG94] Sukaviriya, P., Muthukumarasamy, J., Spaans, A., de Graaf, H.J., "Automatic Generation of Textual, Audio, and Animated Help in UIDE", *Proceedings AVI'94*, pp.44-52, ACM Press, 1994.

[SP89] Scapin, D., Pierret-Golbreich, C., "Towards a Method for Task Description: MAD", *Proceedings Work with Display Unit*, Elsevier, 1989.

[SSCMS95] Szekely, P., Sukaviriy, P., Castells, P., Muthukumarasamy, J., Salcher, E., "Declarative Interface Models for User Interface Construction Tools: the Mastermind Project", *Proceedings EHCI'95*, pp.120-150, Chapman & Hall, 1995

[T90] Tauber, M., "ETAG: Extended Task Action Grammar - A language for the Description of the User's Task Language", *Proceedings INTERACT'90*, pp.163-174, Elsevier, 1990.

[TC99] Thevenin D., Coutaz J., "Plasticity of User Interfaces: Framework and Research Agenda", *Proceedings INTERACT'99*, pp. 110-117, IOS Press, 1999.

[TMP98] Tam, R.C.-M., Maulsby, D., and Puerta, A., "U-TEL: A Tool for Eliciting User Task Models from Domain Experts", *Proceedings IUI'98*, ACM Press, 1998

[VG94] Vanderdonckt, J., Gillo, X., "Visual Techniques for Traditional and Multimedia Layouts", *Proceedings AVI'94*, pp. 95-104, ACM Press, 1994.

[VLB96] van der Veer, G., Lenting, B., Bergevoet, B., "GTA: Groupware Task Analysis - Modelling Complexity", *Acta Psychologica*, 91, pp. 297-322, 1996.

[WJKCM93] Wilson, S., Johnson, P., Kelly, C., Cunningham, J. and Markopoulos, P., "Beyond Hacking: A Model-based Approach to User Interface Design". *Proceedings HCI'93*. Cambridge University Press, 1993.

[WRLP94] Wharton, C., Rieman, J., Lewis, C. and Polson, P. "The Cognitive Walkthrough: A Practitioner's Guide". In *Usability Inspection Methods*, Nielsen J. and Mack R.L. (eds.), John Wiley & Sons, 1994.

[WVE98] van Welie M., van der Veer G.C., Eliëns A., "An Ontology for Task World Models", *Proceedings DSV-IS'98*, pp.57-70, Springer Verlag, 1998.

[WZ91] Wing, J., Zaremski A., "A Formal Specification of a Visual Language Editor". *Proceedings of Sixth International Workshop on Software Specification and Design*, 1991.

Subject Index